CHRIST ACROSS THE DISCIPLINES

Christ across the Disciplines

Past, Present, Future

Edited by

Roger Lundin

WILLIAM B. EERDMANS PUBLISHING COMPANY

GRAND RAPIDS, MICHIGAN / CAMBRIDGE, U.K.

Published 2013 by
Wm. B. Eerdmans Publishing Co.
2140 Oak Industrial Drive N.E., Grand Rapids, Michigan 49505 /
P.O. Box 163, Cambridge CB3 9PU U.K.
www.eerdmans.com

Printed in the United States of America

19 18 17 16 15 14 13   7 6 5 4 3 2 1

Library of Congress Cataloging-in-Publication Data

Christ across the disciplines: past, present, future / edited by Roger Lundin.
    pages   cm
Includes bibliographical references and index.
ISBN 978-0-8028-6947-0 (pbk.: alk. paper)
1. Jesus Christ.   2. Christianity.   I. Lundin, Roger.

BT203.C46   2013
261.5 — dc23

                                          2013019866

Contents

Contents

Acknowledgments

I wish to begin by thanking Wheaton College's Provost, Stan Jones, without whose encouragement and unstinting support *Christ across the Disciplines* would never have come into being. It was Stan who had the idea for a yearlong lecture series to celebrate Wheaton's sesquicentennial and highlight the college's commitment to the faith and learning enterprise. He was also eager to have those lectures become a book that would map the challenges and opportunities facing contemporary Christian scholars.

I want to thank as well several other individuals who helped me at key points. My friend and colleague Tim Larsen provided vital assistance as we conceptualized the lecture series and assembled a diverse roster of outstanding scholars for it. Joy Trieglaff coordinated myriad details involving schedules, travel, and housing over the course of the year, and she did so with breathtaking efficiency and unfailing graciousness. In the preparation of the manuscript, two student assistants, Aubrey Penney and Benjamin Holland, gave me critical help in checking sources, standardizing the format, and building the index.

At Eerdmans Jon Pott provided, as always, a perfect blend of wry commentary and generous support for a project he believed in, and Jenny Hoffman once again proved herself to be an editor with a sharp eye and a seemingly endless supply of patience.

Finally, I wish to remember Arthur Holmes and give thanks to God for his remarkable life and vision. As I explain in my introduction, through his teaching, writing, and leadership, Art played a central role in the creation of the contemporary faith and learning project. For several generations of students, colleagues, and readers, he served as a model of intellectual clarity and Christian charity, and we miss him dearly.

Contributors

STEPHEN M. BARR
Professor of Physics
Bartol Research Institute
University of Delaware

KATHERINE CLAY BASSARD
Professor of English
Virginia Commonwealth University

DAVID W. BEBBINGTON
Professor of History
University of Stirling

JEREMY S. BEGBIE
Thomas A. Langford Research Professor of Theology
Duke University

DAVID N. LIVINGSTONE
Professor of Geography and Intellectual History
Queen's University, Belfast

ROGER LUNDIN
Arthur F. Holmes Professor of Faith and Learning
Wheaton College

Contributors

JOHN SCHMALZBAUER
Associate Professor and Blanche Gorman Strong Chair
   in Protestant Studies
Missouri State University

SUJIT SIVASUNDARAM
University Lecturer in World and Imperial History since 1500
Cambridge University

ELEONORE STUMP
Robert J. Henle Professor of Philosophy
St. Louis University

JOHN WEBSTER
Professor of Divinity
University of St. Andrews

Introduction

ROGER LUNDIN

Almost four decades ago, a professor of philosophy at a Midwestern liberal arts college published a slim volume on Christian higher education. It was, he explained years later, a book he wrote out of frustration "at narrower views of education and Christian service" he had encountered early in his teaching career. His goal was to promote an alternative view of education as the "integration of faith and learning that brings Christian beliefs and attitudes into all of life and all the arts and sciences."

This book, *The Idea of a Christian College*, became a classic of its kind, and its author, Arthur Holmes, went on to exercise a powerful influence on the academic practices of several generations of Christian professors. A key to the outsized importance of Holmes's book had to do with the forcefulness of its argument and the clarity of its expression. *The Idea of a Christian College* is a model of crisp, clear prose pressed into the service of a wise and deeply learned intellect. In the evangelical Protestant world of that time — 1975 — perhaps only Arthur Holmes could have produced such a work.

Strong historical forces and cultural dynamics coursed their way through *The Idea of a Christian College* and its arguments for the integration of faith and learning. Holmes wrote the book while teaching at his alma mater, Wheaton College. When he enrolled at Wheaton as a freshman in the fall of 1947, the college and the fundamentalist tradition it represented were gradually taking the form of what would eventually become modern evangelicalism. By the time Holmes set out to write about faith and learning in the early 1970s, the evangelical movement had expanded rapidly, and its colleges were energized

1

to engage the academic disciplines in ways that fundamentalism had rarely sought to do.

This meant that those colleges and their professors had to think hard about how they could bring their clear and sometimes pointed Christian beliefs into dialogue with a wide array of scientific discoveries, theoretical developments, and cultural changes. From the civil rights movement of the 1960s, Holmes appropriated the language of integration, as he championed "an education that cultivates the creative and active integration of faith and learning, of faith and culture." He distinguished the "integration" approach from two other models, which he labeled "interaction" and "indoctrination." In the former, faith and learning "sit side by side in real contact" and "engage in dialog on a variety of particulars," but they remain distinctly separate and do not merge together. "Indoctrination," on the other hand, merely transmits "prepackaged answers" that can hardly satisfy restless minds and the questions they confront.[1]

With the seeds having been planted by Holmes and others, the integration model took root at countless evangelical colleges in the 1970s and 1980s. A number of schools added seminars to train incoming faculty in the practice of integrating faith and learning, and many established tenure and promotion requirements that included faith and learning components. Although the term had little resonance outside the world of Christian higher education, the *integration of faith and learning* stood as a hallmark of a distinctively Christian approach to teaching and scholarship alike.

Yet the ground began to shift and new approaches began to spring up in the final decade of the twentieth century, as the influence of the Anabaptist tradition grew markedly within the world of evangelical higher education. The changes were owing in part to the interest that evangelical scholars and activists had developed in John Howard Yoder and Stanley Hauerwas, whose vision of culture and Christian thought differed sharply from the Reformed slant built into the language of integration. In terms established by H. Richard Niebuhr's *Christ and Culture* — a work to which Yoder took powerful exception — the integration model rested upon the view of Christ as the "transformer of culture." Yoder called instead for an education model that

1. Arthur F. Holmes, *The Idea of a Christian College*, rev. ed. (1975; Grand Rapids: Eerdmans, 1987), pp. 6, 45-46.

would take the radical nature of Jesus' commands seriously and seek to instantiate the counter-cultural values of Christ within institutions as well as minds.[2]

In the past decade, the Anabaptist critique of the integration model has been supplemented by models from many different theological corners of the Christian world, and in certain respects, *Christ across the Disciplines* is a product of this broadened search for viable faith and learning models.[3] Yet, there is also a significant difference between this volume and a number of other recent forays into the field, and it has to do with the stance the authors assume.

To describe the approach to faith and learning taken by the authors in this book, we might begin by acknowledging the remarkable diversity evident among them. They are, to start, a theologically diverse group, with representatives from the Catholic and Anglo-Catholic traditions as well as from several Protestant denominations; some are emerging scholars of great promise, while others are established figures of long-standing importance within their fields; they have ethnically diverse backgrounds and represent an international, three-continent range of nations and cultures. As a result, whether they are developing possibilities or confronting challenges to Christian thought, the authors in this book do so as representatives of vibrant Christian traditions rather than as members of a cohort seeking to supplant what they take to be a shopworn faith and learning model.

Which is another way of saying that these authors and their essays seek to do what Arthur Holmes did almost half a century ago. They strive to cultivate the life of the mind for the sake of the Body of Christ, the church universal, which has been seeking, however imperfectly, for

---

2. See Glen H. Stassen, D. M. Yeager, and John Howard Yoder, *Authentic Transformation: A New Vision of Christ and Culture* (Nashville: Abingdon, 1996).

3. See Douglas Jacobsen and Rhonda Hustedt Jacobsen, eds., *Scholarship and Christian Faith: Enlarging the Conversation* (New York: Oxford University Press, 2004); Todd C. Ream, Jerry Pattengale, and David L. Riggs, eds., *Beyond Integration: Inter/Disciplinary Possibilities for the Future of Christian Higher Education* (Abilene, TX: Abilene Christian University Press, 2012). A recent volume in the discipline of history gives a good idea of the search for new faith and learning models: John Fea, Jay Green, and Eric Miller, eds., *Confessing History: Explorations in Christian Faith and the Historian's Vocation* (Notre Dame, IN: University of Notre Dame Press, 2010). For a contemporary examination of faith and learning that attempts to recapture a sense of its importance for the classroom, see David I. Smith and James K. A. Smith, eds., *Teaching and Christian Practices: Reshaping Faith and Learning* (Grand Rapids: Eerdmans, 2011).

two thousand years to love and serve God with all that the human heart, soul, mind, and strength can offer.

Historical Background

David Bebbington's essay, "The Discipline of History and the Perspective of Faith since 1900," opens our exploration of faith and learning, and it is the first of three chapters that situate our present intellectual moment within a rich and complex historical context. Bebbington frames his discussion of the question of history by beginning with the story of an English museum that seeks to narrate the modern history of its region. In its exhibits, the complex political and economic history of modernity is "powerfully illustrated," but "what of religious history?" The answer is that in Newcastle-upon-Tyne's Discovery Museum, there is virtually nothing on that subject from the past five hundred years, save for one lonely picture of a building in which John Wesley once lived.

To Bebbington, such an egregious "oversight matters," because visitors, particularly children, are likely to leave the museum assuming that religion "became insignificant during the whole modern epoch." And when they reach such a conclusion, he notes, the children are merely echoing the judgments that many academic historians have reached and promoted over the past century. Bebbington observes that, for many of the historians who dominated British intellectual life in the decades after the Second World War, religion deserved to be treated as a "triviality," because it was clear — to them at least — that "economics and politics . . . controlled the fate of humanity."

Things began to change, however, when two significant developments altered the disciplinary dynamics, and historians slowly began to take religion seriously. The first had to do with the emergence of a cadre of North American historians whose "excellent scholarship . . . insisted that history ought to be written in a Christian manner." At the center of this cohort were George Marsden, Mark Noll, and Nathan Hatch, and the group grew to include a "large body of people practicing the discipline, professing the Christian faith, and wanting to relate the two." Their influence extended across North America and overseas, as a new generation of historians felt emboldened to treat religion as a dynamic variable in the play and writing of history.

The opening of history to religious viewpoints was also hastened by what Bebbington calls "the postmodern turn." This "major cultural wave sweeping over Western civilization" enabled many historians to move beyond the Enlightenment and Romantic dichotomies — between science and reason on one side and emotion and intuition on the other — that had long hindered the development of Christian historiography. Bebbington welcomes the postmodern opening, which he believes has made it possible for "ideas and religion" to move from the periphery "to the center of the discipline" of history. The challenge for Christian historians, he believes, "is to come to terms with the postmodern phenomenon. Their wisest course will be a discriminating approach that combines sympathy with criticism." If Christian historians can manage to strike a balance on this front, "they will be able to write history that appeals to the twenty-first century," even as it faithfully bears witness "to all the dimensions of biblical revelation."

While David Bebbington focuses primarily on the theory of history as elaborated and practiced in the twentieth-century academy, John Schmalzbauer trains his sights on the history and influence of evangelicalism in American culture since World War II. In considering what resources are especially important for contemporary Christian scholars, he chooses to draw upon "the *internal* resources of the evangelical tradition" rather than upon "new theologies, liturgies, and literatures." In particular, Schmalzbauer is intrigued by the tension between the provincial passion of the fundamentalist pioneers and the intellectual daring of their academically inclined evangelical heirs. "Many evangelical scholars have turned their backs on fundamentalism," he writes, and they find it difficult to be at ease either in the church or in the academy. "Caught between a conservative subculture and the wider academy, they have searched for an intellectual home."

Schmalzbauer focuses upon the "creative tensions in evangelical intellectual life" by means of a series of short case studies of scholars such as Edward John Carnell and Paul Holmer, both of whom emerged from a rigid fundamentalist past into a fluid and uncertain evangelical present. Such scholars bridged "multiple worlds" and were subject to "social, cultural, and theological tensions" that proved to be painful and, in some cases, destructive. Nevertheless, over time such tensions gave rise to "a renaissance in evangelical intellectual life" that blended the "fertile source" of fundamentalist belief with the "uneasy conscience" that such belief fostered in many of its most intelligent adherents.

The first generation of evangelicals was hindered by attitudes of wariness and hostility that had long marked fundamentalism's engagement with the intellectual life; but, according to Schmalzbauer, the second generation faced an even greater obstacle, that being the alliance of mainstream evangelicalism with the moralizing politics of Jerry Falwell's Moral Majority and the libertarian economics of Ayn Rand's individualism. Schmalzbauer is a sociologist by training and trade, and in matters political and intellectual alike he would prefer American evangelicals to join their faith to their learning in the space that opens up somewhere between the evangelical subculture on the right and the "academy that leans to the left."

David N. Livingstone's "Science and Religion: Place, Politics, and Poetics" is the third historically situated essay in the group that forms the opening section of *Christ across the Disciplines*. Like Schmalzbauer, Livingstone deals extensively with the political dimensions of Christian thought. Yet his interests have to do not with the generational tensions of fundamentalism but with the tensions generated by what he calls the advocates of "the science-religion culture wars."

The assumption that there is an inherent conflict between science and religion is held by many religious thinkers and scientists alike, and to challenge it Livingstone offers a three-part strategy for "thinking about the historical relations between science and religion." That strategy challenges us to ask pointed questions about *place, politics*, and *poetics* when we think of the modern history of science and religion. By *place* he means the physical and social locations in which debates about science and religion "take place." In considering *politics*, Livingstone has in mind the role "political atmospherics" play in these discussions, which are carried on in lecture halls and lecture chambers as well as on the printed page and the smartphone's electronic screen. And for him *poetics* calls "attention to questions of rhetoric and idiom in the conduct of debates." By tending to place, politics, and poetics, he suggests, we can get a better "handle on the encounters between science and faith" and their implications for the Christian life of the mind.

Livingstone considers the idea of a perpetual war between science and religion to be a "mythology" that serves the interests of partisans on both sides. To challenge the idea, he offers a richly detailed and compelling account of four *places* — Toronto, Columbia (South Carolina), Edinburgh, and Belfast — where Darwinian theory came into contact and conflict with the Christian church in the final decades of the nineteenth century. In those different times and places, he finds a stunning variety among the Christian responses made to Darwin. That is why debates about "science and faith" must always "be located — physically, politically, and culturally." And in like manner, that which is true for the participant "in science-religion debates has self-referential implications for those in the academy with their own religious convictions. For we, too, are located; and, if history is anything to go by, we are all too apt to mistake the particular for the transcendental, cultural forms for theological principles, contingency for necessity." To remain vital and viable, Christian traditions need to engage in "constant, critical dialogue" within their own ranks and with the larger academic community, scientific and otherwise, outside their walls.

Theological and Philosophical Foundations

With the appearance of John Webster's "On the Theology of the Intellectual Life," *Christ across the Disciplines* takes a distinct theological turn. The common ground of history is ironizing narrative, a form in which strengths and weaknesses, insights and folly, noble deeds and crass actions are weighed in the balance by an observer whose stance is one of critical — and sometimes sympathetic — detachment. As we move from history to theology, however, and beyond that to the humanities and the sciences more generally, the chapters in *Christ across the Disciplines* become more confessional and apologetic in tone, as they set out to sketch specifically Christian responses to modern intellectual practices and thought.

Before we can develop a theology of the intellectual life, John Webster argues, we must first define the task of theology: "The object of Christian theological inquiry is God and all things in relation to God." Theology takes as its subject the nature of God himself and "the eternal, perfect, and eternally blessed life of God the Holy Trinity in his inner works." At the same time, theological inquiry involves the study of God's "economy," or those "outer works" in which we come to know God as the "creator, reconciler, and perfecter of creatures." This twofold charter makes theological inquiry "comprehensive in scope," but even though "theology is about everything," it is so only in the sense that is "about everything *in relation to God*" (emphasis added).

For Webster, we develop an account of the nature of created things — including the human intellect — by seeking to understand them, first, in terms of *principles,* "those realities and powers by virtue of which other things exist and can be known," and then by viewing them in the light cast by "the history of fellowship between God and creatures." That history is the story of God's gracious creation, reconciliation, and consummation of all things. Its scope, which encompasses the gospel of Christ, "is universal. 'In him all things in heaven and on earth were created . . . all things have been created through him and for him. He himself is before all things . . . he is the beginning, . . . so that he might come to have the first place in everything' (Col. 1:16-18)."

Webster reflects upon the intellect both as God created it in its ideal state and as it exists in its fallen and frustrated forms. According to him, the doctrine of creation teaches us that we fulfill our nature when our emotions and desires are directed, through the governing power of the intellect, to their right and proper ends. Yet we must also confront the reality of sin, which involves the "betrayal of our created nature and refusal to live out the vocation that [our created] nature entails." The hold of sin upon us is powerful, and only through the work of the reconciling "Word made flesh" can our intellects assume a new nature and resume their work of pursuing the ends for which God has made us.

At the heart of John Webster's theology of faith and learning lies a vision of "the gift of thought." The workings of the human mind are created realities best understood "by reference to God's loving work of origination, preservation, reconciliation, and perfection." Because we can experience such love and charity only to the degree that we respond to the grace of God, "Christians cannot escape a measure of estrangement from their neighbors who do not make the Christian confession." In turn, these neighbors may at times look upon the Christian life of the mind with disdain or hostility. When we face opposition or outright dismissal, Webster says we should do so with tranquil confidence, as well as with modesty and charity, for "calm exposition of first principles serves the gospel best. The truth will establish itself; we must simply let it run on its own path."

As John Webster does, Eleonore Stump also champions a quiet but bold confidence as the approach Christian scholars ought to take when they face the twofold "contemporary challenge" of academic culture. That challenge is external, in that it involves a hostility to Christianity that can be found in many regions of the academy, and it is internal as well, in that it frequently stems from deep divisions within Christianity itself.

According to Stump, the external challenge is rooted in the Enlightenment belief in learning as a universal and generically human enterprise. When learning is seen in these terms, science emerges as the preeminent scholarly enterprise, for it deliberately disregards human particularities — of race or gender, class or religion — and insists that truth is available equally and openly to all through the exercise of reason and the pursuit of method. Within the tradition of Enlightenment modernism, passion and commitment have no place in the scholarly enterprise, and scientific detachment becomes the standard.

In recent decades, such modernist assumptions have come under attack from those whom Stump terms the "postmodernists," who reject the very idea of a generically human, and unbiased, scholarship. Instead, they assume all human endeavors, including the scientific enterprise, to be riddled with biases, self-interested actions, and the quest for power and domination.

Stump understands why the postmodern view seems plausible, especially given the mixed record of the Enlightenment tradition and its ostensible commitment to scholarly objectivity and neutrality. Yet, in the end, she concludes that the postmodernist position is untenable, because it fails to provide any conceivable basis for criticism or change. On postmodern grounds, individuals who find themselves under the sway of one particularity have no grounds for judging someone who acts on the basis of different, highly particular premises. Without such a basis, "it is hard to see how postmodernism can do much except support the status quo" in matters of justice or the pursuit of truth.

As an external challenge, "postmodernism" concerns Stump, but so do those internal conflicts that impede the Christian community's witness to the faith. In particular, she believes the distinction between *believers* and *heretics* has had a pernicious effect on Christian thought. "It is a wretched mistake," she writes, "to judge a person's character or his standing with God" on the basis of having judged that person to hold heretical beliefs. Stump grants that it is crucial to distinguish between orthodox and heretical beliefs, but she also insists that "we ought to value love of truth above success in finding it" and "distinguish between rejecting beliefs and rejecting the persons who hold them." Christianity is, after all, a part of "one universal truth" that holds for all people, and it can thereby be "integrated with any other academic pursuit of truth." She holds that this integration will develop most effectively in a pluralistic environment, one in which truth and orthodoxy are coveted even as adversaries and heretics are protected. "Even in the academy, for the integration of faith and learning, it is crucial for Christians to love and protect those they take to be their enemies."

With an Eye to the Future

Representing as they do the powerful traditions of Reformed Protestantism and Roman Catholicism, the essays by John Webster and Eleonore Stump provide a useful frame for the historical narratives that come before them and for the prospective chapters that follow upon them. I am using the word *prospective* here in its original, sixteenth-century sense of "looking forward, having foresight." In the final four chapters — which cover science and religion, theology and the arts, literature and race, and the global future — we come upon a series of disciplinary perspectives on the current challenges and future prospects that engage Christian scholars.

Stephen M. Barr's essay "Modern Physics and Ancient Faith" plays a transitional role, in that it simultaneously looks back to first principles and forward to present challenges. Barr begins by asking what has become a perennial question of contemporary thought: "Is there a conflict between religion and science?" His answer is a qualified "No." Such a conflict is not inevitable, if by *religion* one means *biblical religion* as it has been understood, embraced, and practiced in the mainstream history of Roman Catholicism, Protestantism, and Judaism, and if by *science* one means the inductive practices of astronomers, physicists, biologists, and chemists as they have been developed and refined over the course of centuries.

Although there may not be a perennial conflict between science and religion, there is one "between religion and scientific materialism," which Barr defines as the philosophical theory "that the ultimate reality is matter, and everything that exists and everything that happens can therefore be explained by the laws of physics and blind chance." For scientific materialists, religion serves as a necessary enemy; it is essential to the materialist view of the world "that there be a conflict between science and religion."

There are, Barr says, three elements at the heart of the dispute between Christianity and materialism. The first has to do with the supposed long history of religious opposition to science, with the seventeenth-century trial of Galileo serving as the centerpiece of the historical claim of an irresolvable conflict. This historical argument has often been linked to the claim that science and religion are inherently incompatible, because the former is grounded in reason, while the latter must lean on dogma and mystery for support. In turn, the distinction between reason and superstition has been enlisted in the cause of materialism's assertion that the discoveries of science over the past four centuries have given us a far clearer picture of the world than religion has ever been able to offer.

Barr gives a clear and nuanced account of scientific materialism's narrative of the history of cosmology, physics, and mathematics over the past four centuries. The materialist narrative begins with the displacement of the Earth from the center of the universe in the Copernican revolution. That was followed several centuries later by the overturning of the proofs of God that depended on the argument from design. In turn, the overthrow of design went hand in hand with what biologist Stephen Jay Gould called the "dethronement of man," which resulted from the banishment of teleology by modern physics. Rather than standing at the apex of creation, human beings — or so the argument goes — are but one of an infinite array of byproducts of the vast mechanistic process that has produced the world as we know it.

Barr takes the materialist arguments seriously and believes that Christian scholars ought not to dismiss them lightly. Yet through an extended discussion of scientific developments in the past century, he mounts a spirited critique of the materialist premise and concludes that, at the start of the twenty-first century, "we who are Christians or Jews look around and find ourselves in very familiar surroundings." That is, we discover ourselves to be living in a universe that had a beginning and is governed by laws whose grandeur and sublimity "bespeak design." Furthermore, it appears those laws were built into the structure of the cosmos from its very beginning. We have come to realize, once again, "that the deepest discoveries of modern physics and mathematics give hints, if not proof, that the human mind has something about it that lies beyond the power of either physics or mathematics to describe."

With Jeremy S. Begbie's essay, we move from the sciences to the arts. More than anyone else in the past several decades, Begbie has led the way in establishing the field of "theology and the arts." That field is burgeoning, yet he has a fundamental concern about its current state — namely, that among many practitioners there is a "distinct unease or awkwardness about Protestantism, and especially of the Reformed variety." To address that unease, he seeks to add a distinctively Reformed Protestant voice to what has become almost exclusively a Roman Catholic and Anglo-Catholic chorus. There is, Begbie says, a "curious freshness" to elements of the Reformed tradition, and his chapter explores that freshness, as he considers the themes of beauty, sacrament, and language.

On the theme of beauty, Begbie argues that Reformed Christianity makes a distinctive contribution with its tripartite emphases upon the goodness of creation, the transforming power of the cross, and the promise of eschatological deliverance. In like manner, he stresses the vital importance of the doctrine of creation for an understanding of art and sacrament. Having failed to discover "a sufficiently robust and theologically compelling case for extending the language of sacramentality to the practices and products of the arts," Begbie turns instead to a " 'covenant ontology' . . . grounded in the Father's love for the Son in the Spirit" to examine the relationship of art and sacrament.

When we speak of art and sacrament, so much depends "on holding to what has been uniquely *enacted and achieved* in Christ." The same holds true for language. In Begbie's words, the theorist of the arts must "struggle . . . to hold at one and the same time that the church is called" to be faithful to "the discourse God has graciously appropriated" *and* that the non-verbal arts also "mediate dimensions of the very realities" of which language speaks. This is to say that the arts "do their own kind of work in their own kind of way, articulating depths of the Word of the gospel and our experience of it that are otherwise unheard or unfelt."

Begbie closes with a reflective paragraph that goes to the heart of the question concerning faith and learning. He says that in his teaching in Great Britain and America over the years, he has met countless students who seem to be on a quest to find the one theologian who will answer their every question and resolve their every quandary. Or they think there must be one tradition that will resolve every contradiction and relieve them of the onerous burden of feeling that they "need to read everything" ever written on their theological topic. Begbie says it would be "foolish in the extreme" to think Reformed Christianity could or should serve as such a totalizing force in the conversation about theology and the arts. "My claim . . . is more modest," he says, and it is that in a conversation that has been informed deeply by Catholic and Anglo-Catholic understandings, the Reformed tradition has "considerably more to offer than is often supposed, especially if we are seeking to delve more deeply into the plotlines and harmonies of a scripturally rooted and vibrant trinitarian faith."

Katherine Clay Bassard also grounds her reflections on faith and learning in a particular context, in this case "the rapidly changing discourse . . . about race" in America during the era of Barack Obama. To understand the way in which President Obama has become "a symbolic representation of the hopes and fears in America around the nexus of race and religion," she undertakes a discussion of three African American novels published within the past decade. Her purpose is to enlist these novels as part of an effort to articulate how Christian scholars should and must "lead in developing a discourse of reconciliation and redemption."

To explain the vital relevance of the doctrine of redemption for Christian scholarship, Bassard describes it as involving "a *reinvestment* of history" to account for present and future change. So understood, redemption seeks not to rewrite the facts of history but to reinvest them "with new meanings and significance." She takes her cue from St. Paul's eagerness to take his history of "confidence in the flesh" — his status as one "circumcised on the eighth day, a member of the people of Israel, of the tribe of Benjamin, a Hebrew born of Hebrews" — and bring it into the new life he experienced in Jesus Christ. According to Bassard, "a redemptive view of race" confronts the facts of slavery but seeks to "reinvest race and slavery with significance within a larger narrative of freedom and . . . hope and possibility."

With the aid of novels by Edward Jones, James McBride, and Toni Morrison, Bassard explores the means by which a theology of redemption enables a reader "to hold two narratives in view simultaneously, privileging the one (and the One) that offers us 'hope and a future.'" The novels she discusses are "neo-slave narratives," which is to say they adopt the conventions and assume the first-person voice of the myriad accounts published by former slaves in the decades before the Civil War. In many respects, these narratives resemble classic Christian stories of redemption, in that they "frame the discussion of the past in order to define [the] future." When analyzed skillfully and sympathetically by Christian readers, such stories redeem the past and proclaim a prophetic word of hope for the future.

That future is the subject of Sujit Sivasundaram's concerns in this volume's final chapter. In his essay, he ambitiously proposes to provide a Christian analysis of the concepts of race, culture, and nation. These are, he points out, concepts that have a deep indebtedness to the Christian tradition. Christianity may not serve as their sole point of origin, but it unquestionably "played a critical part in their dispersal across the world."

In the nineteenth century, at the height of imperial expansion and the peak of the missionary movement, Christian discussions of race, culture, and nation sought to encompass both unity and diversity within their concerns. Christians stressed the "oneness of humanity," even as they, in their roles as missionaries and agents of the empire, also "charted differences in appearance, language, heritage, [and] political tradition." That balance between "commonality" and "difference" was lost over time, however, and Sivasundaram asks what it might mean for Christian scholars across the disciplines "to return to the study of the world," equipped with a more nuanced understanding of the productive tension between "global symmetries and local circumstances."

To ground our thinking about Christian scholarship in the future, Sivasundaram focuses his attention on three case studies from the nineteenth-century history of Christian engagement with global cultures. On *race*, he details the career of James Cowles Prichard, the Anglican founder of the science of ethnology; his subject for the study of *culture* is John Williams, "Britain's first missionary hero"; and to delve into *nation*, he tells the story of Pandita Ramabai Saraswati, who championed the rights of women in India, became one of the trailblazing women scholars of the subcontinent, and still serves as a model of what Sivasundaram calls "trans-national scholarship."

Here in the early years of the twenty-first century, according to Sivasundaram, Christians have largely forgotten the central role they played in the emergence of global understanding. He believes it to be essential for Christian scholars to retrieve this history, as they seek to "re-engage the status of the globe." The challenge is a difficult one, because it requires balancing localized attachments to our ethnic, cultural, and national heritages with a call to think beyond the particular and to negotiate the complexities of global commerce and culture. The importance of maintaining this balance is greater than ever at a time when the center of gravity for Christianity is shifting dramatically away from its longstanding European base. If scholars manage to strike a balance between respect for difference and commitment to unity, "global Christianity may continue to be cohesive," as the church abides in the promise that there will one day be a great multitude "from every nation, from all tribes and peoples and languages, standing before the throne and before the Lamb" (Rev. 7:9).

Sivasundaram follows that citation with the brief observation that the Book of "Revelation does not suggest that differences are obliterated. There are still worshipers from different nations, tribes, peoples, and languages." In like manner, *Christ across the Disciplines* suggests that, decades after Arthur Holmes first articulated his vision for the integration of faith and learning, that work continues to thrive, as scholars from different nations, peoples, and languages continue to bring the gospel of Jesus Christ to bear upon the desires of our hearts, the longings of our souls, and the life of our minds.

CHAPTER 1

The Discipline of History and the Perspective of Faith since 1900

David W. Bebbington

In the city of Newcastle-upon-Tyne in the northeast of England stands the excellent Discovery Museum. Recently established in a former warehouse, the museum sets out to explain the history of the region. It attracts a large number of tourists and caters specifically to schoolchildren, offering an abundance of hands-on activities. The displays reveal much about local industry, especially the shipbuilding yards that once dominated the Tyne. There is a great deal about processes of manufacture, marketing successes, and conditions of employment. The economic history of the city and its vicinity is powerfully illustrated. What of religious history? It is properly covered for the Middle Ages, with illustrations of parish churches and their art. After that, however, it stops. The only exception is a picture of a building where John Wesley stayed in the city. There is, however, no explanation of the identity of Wesley, the founder of Methodism. There is not even a mention of Methodism itself, despite the fact that Newcastle was one of its three main centers in England. Nor is there any coverage of the chapel life that shaped the cultural achievements of the city during the nineteenth century. There is a virtual blank about religion over the past five hundred years. This oversight matters. Visitors, including children, will go away supposing that religion, though a potent force in the Middle Ages, became insignificant during the whole modern epoch. Christianity will not seem an option in the modern world. Of course the museum forms only one element in the experience of those who pass through its doors. Representatives of churches may call on homes with invitations to carol services, and schools may teach more about recent religious developments. Nevertheless the museum helps create worldviews by its contents and by its omissions. It reflects the historical scholarship of the twentieth century, the subject of this essay. That history, through such agencies as the Newcastle Discovery Museum, is shaping assumptions about the Christian faith.

How the practice of history reflects and molds our worldviews was the theme of a book called *Patterns in History*, which I published in 1979. Like the series of lectures forming the present volume, it tried to explore the relationship of the Christian faith to an academic discipline, in that case history. It discussed the worldviews embodied in historical works over the centuries. It compared a Christian perspective on history with other understandings — the ancient cyclical view, the idea of progress associated with the Enlightenment, the German historicist approach, and Marxist historical theory.[1] Each of these schools of thought has generated its own way of writing history. Historians do not come to their evidence with blank minds, analyzing data with the detachment of computers. Rather, historians are shaped by their fundamental beliefs. Thus Edward Gibbon, the author of one of the greatest monuments of eighteenth-century historiography, *The History of the Decline and Fall of the Roman Empire* (1776-88), argued that Rome was a victim, as he trenchantly put it, of "the triumph of barbarism and religion."[2] As a believer in progress of the age of Enlightenment, Gibbon saw these twin forces as the enemies of all he revered. Gibbon stood for civilization and rationalism, the opposites, as he supposed, of barbarism and religion. Accordingly, he held that they must have been the factors that sapped the Rome he admired so fervently. Such underlying presuppositions as these down the centuries were the theme of *Patterns in History*. The book, however, treated the twentieth century rather cursorily and necessarily omitted its last thirty years because they were still to come when the book was written. This essay is designed to bring the story up-to-date. How has the practice of history developed during the twentieth century? What is the situation in the early twenty-first century? How should an exponent of a Christian worldview contribute to contemporary historiography?

1. David Bebbington, *Patterns in History* (Leicester, Eng.: Inter-Varsity, 1979).
2. Edward Gibbon, *The History of the Decline and Fall of the Roman Empire*, ed. J. B. Bury, vol. 7 (London: Methuen, 1900), p. 308.

David W. Bebbington

Art or Science? Modern Views of History

The first third of the twentieth century was dominated by the issue of science versus literature. Which was the better way to describe history? Perhaps the subject ought to be seen as a rigorous mode of inquiry like the natural sciences; or, on the other hand, perhaps it should be appreciated as an art form designed to educate and entertain. In 1902 there was a firm statement on the subject. J. B. Bury, in his inaugural lecture as Regius Professor of History at Cambridge, declared: "History is a science, no less and no more."[3] As an undergraduate, Bury had specialized in classical philology, and his approach to history reveals the meticulous concern for accuracy of that discipline. He called for historians to be scrupulous in their handling of evidence, as painstaking as the natural scientists whose prestige was in the ascendant. Historians, like scientists, could aspire to establishing laws of cause and effect. Bury took the opportunity to berate literary historians such as Thomas Babington Macaulay, the celebrated author of the immensely popular *History of England from the Accession of James II* in the mid-nineteenth century. Macaulay's rhetorical techniques, according to Bury, should be banished from history. This assault on the reputation of Macaulay, however, provoked another Cambridge historian, G. M. Trevelyan, into a reply. Trevelyan was Macaulay's great-nephew: the "M" in his name stood for "Macaulay." He rose to the defense of his relation, together with his literary approach to the subject, in an essay of the following year. History, argued Trevelyan, is like poetry in being an art form, available for people to enjoy. He pointed out that the ancient Greeks treated the subject in that way, with Clio, one of the Muses, as its patron.[4] Symbolically, Trevelyan was to succeed Bury as Regius Professor at Cambridge in 1927. The two men stood for contrasting ideals of the discipline: history as science and history as literature.

In the United States the standing of science was even higher than in Britain. Any academic pursuit at the opening of the twentieth century had to justify itself as "scientific." History was becoming professionalized. The first Ph.D. program in the discipline, following a German

3. J. B. Bury, "The Science of History," in *Selected Essays of J. B. Bury*, ed. Harold Temperley (Cambridge: Cambridge University Press, 1930), p. 4.
4. G. M. Trevelyan, "Clio, a Muse," in *Clio, a Muse, and Other Essays* (London: Longmans, Green, 1930).

model, had been introduced at Johns Hopkins University in 1872. From then on the practitioners of the subject became increasingly concerned to establish their credentials as men (or occasionally women) of science. A crucial text was Frederick Jackson Turner's *The Significance of the Frontier in American History* (1893). Turner argued that the process of settling the frontier shaped the whole of the American experience, creating a new and distinctive society.[5] America was, as it were, a laboratory for examining the evolution of a civilization. Turner, with others of his generation, constituted a group of Progressive historians who dominated the emerging profession. They shared the belief that the immigrants who formed America must be studied in their new setting. Traditional political history was therefore not enough. It must be supplemented by economic, social, and psychological techniques, all working to scientific standards.[6] The members of this generation established the ideal of objectivity. Historians, they held, must aim for total detachment from the events they are analyzing.[7] Empiricism, the method of science, was the sole avenue to truth. History, if properly pursued, would be established as fully scientific.

In Britain, by contrast, the literary ideal was more deeply entrenched. Herbert Butterfield, a historian who entered Cambridge in 1919 and who was to go on to become Regius Professor there in 1963, showed the persistent strength of that approach. Trained as a diplomatic historian, Butterfield believed in the value of technical historical skills that could be called scientific. Yet he also contended that the past was a subject for art. His first publication, *The Historical Novel* (1923), argued that historical fiction could capture the reality of the past more effectively than ordinary historical practice. He tried in his next book, *The Peace Tactics of Napoleon* (1929), to reproduce the narrative style of Macaulay. Trevelyan was for a while Butterfield's mentor, confirming his belief that history was at its best a literary achievement. There was a constant and creative tension in Butterfield's own mind between the notion that historical research had to be conducted scientifically and the

5. Frederick Jackson Turner, *The Significance of the Frontier in American History* (New York: Henry Holt, 1920).

6. Georg G. Iggers, *Historiography in the Twentieth Century: From Scientific Objectivity to the Postmodern Challenge* (Middletown, CT: Wesleyan University Press, 1997), p. 42.

7. Peter Novick, *That Noble Dream: The "Objectivity Question" and the American Historical Profession* (Cambridge: Cambridge University Press, 1988).

hope that history could be seen as a form of literature.[8] His stance bore witness to the power of both tendencies in interwar Britain.

Butterfield, however, has importance for our central theme for another reason. He was the most prominent spokesman for a Christian standpoint in historiography during the twentieth century. His *Christianity and History* (1949) became a bestseller. In his mature thought, Butterfield expounded not a duality between science and literature but a threefold view of historical events. In the first place, the biographical way of looking at events meant recognizing that human beings freely made moral decisions. Second, the "historical" way was "the scientific examination of the deep forces and tendencies in history," revealing how they can be reduced to laws.[9] And third, there was providence. Unless events were to be treated as the products of chance, Butterfield argued, they must be understood as governed by divine command. Thus the First World War was simultaneously the outcome of decisions of the statesmen of 1914 (the biographical level), the result of forces and tendencies operating over the fifty years before 1914 (the historical level), and the judgment of God on the evils of Western civilization (the providential level). Here was an exposition of a Christian perspective on the past that remains worthy of attention today. Butterfield was a rare example of a historian of stature who in the middle years of the twentieth century attempted to relate his faith to his discipline.

It was the scientific trend in history, however, that carried increasing weight in that period. In the United States economic analysis gathered pace in historical studies. In 1913 Charles Beard published *An Economic Interpretation of the Constitution*, contending that the founding fathers had been divided by different property-based interests. Throughout a long career, Beard continued to probe economic issues with similar sophistication. Other historians of the next generation emphasized conflict far less than Beard, but were often still preoccupied with economics. In the wake of the Second World War, America seemed classless and (un-American individuals apart) free of ideological divisions, a model for all modernizing societies. Walt Rostow's *Stages of Economic Growth* (1960) generalized about the laws of development in

---

8. C. T. McIntire, *Herbert Butterfield: Historian as Dissenter* (New Haven, CT: Yale University Press, 2004), pp. 53-54.

9. Herbert Butterfield, *Writings on Christianity and History*, ed. C. T. McIntire (New York: Oxford University Press, 1979), p. 10.

a strongly scientific manner. Four years later, Robert Fogel's *Railroads and American Economic Growth* assessed the impact of the railroads by counter-factual analysis, asking how the economy of the United States would have differed had they not existed. The issue was determined by hard economic data alone. Such historiography operated within the model of classical political economy going back to Adam Smith and David Ricardo, assuming the existence of economic laws.[10] Here was an apparently objective type of analysis. Scientific models enjoyed great prestige in the historical profession. They seemed to provide a foundation for an essentially conservative analysis of the past that vindicated free-market capitalism. History in the United States down to the 1960s had become predominantly scientific and, at least in terms of prestige, principally economic.

In Europe there was a greater emphasis on the analysis of society. Yet once more there was a typically scientific preoccupation with causes, laws, and generalization. In France the journal *Annales*, founded in 1929, encouraged the study of social structures and social change by a variety of methods. The ultimate aim of some in this school was to create what was called a "science of man."[11] In Britain a leading historian in the interwar period was R. H. Tawney, a Christian socialist deeply committed both to understanding attitudes in the past and to influencing policy in the present. Despite his socialism, Tawney was utterly opposed to Marxism. Tawney, unlike Marxists, believed that religious ideas shaped history, as he showed in his *Religion and the Rise of Capitalism* (1926). But in the years after the Second World War it was Marxists claiming to write truly scientific history who took the lead in British historiography. From 1947 to 1956 a Communist Party Historians' Group flourished, including such luminaries as Christopher Hill and E. P. Thompson. Both were from Methodist homes, but both turned their backs on their Christian inheritance. Hill's *Economic Problems of the Church* (1956) scrutinized religious texts, but used them as a quarry in order to support a Marxist view that the seventeenth-century Puritans represented a rising middle class driven by economic interests. Thompson's *The Making of the English Working Class* (1963) concentrated on the emergence of class struggle, a favorite Marxist theme, and described Methodist chapels

---

10. Iggers, *Historiography in the Twentieth Century*, p. 45.
11. Iggers, *Historiography in the Twentieth Century*, p. 55.

as "traps for the human psyche."[12] Both works were deeply researched and attractively written, but in each case religion was reinterpreted in other categories. Partly in its place, class became the central theme of British historical writing, whether about the early modern or about the later modern period. To a quite remarkable degree, Marxism set the agenda. The prevailing "scientific" models in British historiography came from the left.

There was nevertheless resistance, both to the Marxist challenge and to the broader rise of history claiming scientific status. At Oxford, Hugh Trevor-Roper, later Regius Professor there, attacked the notion that there had been a "rise of the gentry" in the early seventeenth century. His immediate target was Tawney, but he was equally hostile to the Marxist understanding of the seventeenth century as class struggle. Trevor-Roper, however, was not advocating an understanding of the period that gave weight to the religious movements of the time as agents of change. On the contrary, he explicitly rejected the view that what he called "theological niceties" were capable of bringing about "a redistribution of political power."[13] For Trevor-Roper and other more conservative historians, what counted in history was brute power. In Cambridge, Geoffrey Elton purveyed a similar perspective. In his *Practice of History* (1967) he attacked all attempts to assimilate the discipline to the social sciences. History, he insisted, was autonomous, having different foci of attention. It was not concerned, as were the social sciences, with the structures of society, but with events, with change, and with the particular. Unlike the scientific model, history was not about generalizing in order to create laws. What counted in the past was the individual's exercise of power. Although an uncle of Elton had been a distinguished Lutheran pastor, the historian showed no sympathy for the belief that religion had provided powerful motivation for historical agents. The one thing we know about the English Civil War, Elton remarked in one of his undergraduate lectures in 1969, is that it was not caused by religion.[14] The normal perspective of those with conservative inclinations was to reject not only Marxism and social science but also the importance of religion as a factor in the past.

---

12. E. P. Thompson, *The Making of the English Working Class* (Harmondsworth, Middlesex: Penguin, 1968), p. 404.

13. Adam Sisman, *Hugh Trevor-Roper: The Biography* (London: Weidenfeld & Nicolson, 2010), p. 72.

14. The writer heard the remark at the lecture.

The developments reviewed so far brought about the situation that prevailed when the present writer was an undergraduate at Cambridge between 1969 and 1971. The period around those years has rightly been hailed as a golden age for Cambridge history.[15] Yet there were problems for a young believer studying the discipline. There was a conspiracy of opposites. On the left there were Marxists and Marxist fellow travelers, probably far more of the latter than of the former. In the heady days of student revolt, it was typical that Peter Laslett, one of the lecturers in the History Faculty, should pin up a notice saying that he had canceled a lecture in solidarity with the students. Christopher Hill and E. P. Thompson were greatly respected. Ideas and religion in the past, by contrast, were treated as unimportant or as fit subjects for reinterpretation. On the right there were the conservative opponents of Marxism. Sometimes they were admirers of American economic analysis in history. Others, with Elton at their head, deplored the rise of the social sciences. For some explicitly, and for most implicitly, ideas and religion could be treated as trivialities. According to both the left and the right, economics and politics, in differing degrees, controlled the fate of humanity. This undergraduate crept off to the Divinity School in quest of mental stimulus and was grateful to find it there.

There was, however, one dimension of mainstream history that dealt with ideas. This intellectual oasis was the history of political thought. Lectures were given by the young Quentin Skinner, just launching a revamping of the sub-discipline. Ideas, he argued, must be studied not just in isolated thinkers, the great theorists of the past. Rather, ideas can be understood only as they were discussed in debate between different thinkers. Although this approach was exciting, it was not integrated into the rest of the curriculum. Political thought was a separate object of inquiry, restricted to specific papers in the examinations. Furthermore, political thought was limited to politics conceived in a narrow fashion. As practiced by Skinner, religion was minimized or even extinguished as a factor in the past.[16] So in around 1970 the outlook for studying religion, especially theology, within history seemed

15. David Cannadine, "British History — Past, Present — and Future?" *Past and Present* 116 (1987): 169-91.

16. John Coffey, "Quentin Skinner and the Religious Dimension of Early Modern Political Thought," in *Seeing Things Their Way: Intellectual History and the Return of Religion*, ed. Alister Chapman, John Coffey, and Brad S. Gregory (Notre Dame, IN: University of Notre Dame Press, 2009), pp. 46-74.

unpromising. Religion, particularly in its intellectual aspect, seemed marginal in all the best historical works.

Making Space for Faith:
History and Christianity in the Modern Academy

Help was at hand from two sources. One had a Christian origin; the other arose from the evolution of the discipline. The Christian source was the rise of an evangelical school of historians in America.[17] An early text was *A Christian View of History?* (1975), edited by George Marsden and Frank Roberts. George Marsden himself contributed an essay arguing that history should be studied not neutrally but from a Christian perspective. In 1977 a group of Christian historians in the United States started to meet regularly in order to coordinate their thinking and action. The initiator was Mark Noll, soon to become a professor of history at Wheaton College. Others were drawn in, with Nathan Hatch, Harry Stout, and Joel Carpenter among them. They produced excellent scholarship such as Marsden's *Fundamentalism and American Culture* (1980). Building on the analysis of Dutch Reformed scholars stemming from Abraham Kuyper, they insisted that history ought to be written in a Christian manner. Others launched a Conference on Faith and History, which published a periodical called *Fides et Historia.* It reinforced the quest for a distinctively Christian voice within the chorus of historical scholarship. In Britain there were faint echoes of this flurry of evangelical activity within the discipline. The InterVarsity Fellowship set up a small historians' study group, which encouraged thinking along similar lines. Equivalent groups arose elsewhere in the world — in Australia and the Netherlands, for example — and for a while in the 1990s they were bound together in an international association. Yet the fulcrum of the global movement remained Wheaton College, in the Institute for the Study of American Evangelicals. Its 1992 conference on transatlantic evangelicalism was a high-water mark, bringing together many international participants. Being drawn into these circles was a hugely rewarding experience for many people, including the present writer. There emerged a body of people practicing the discipline, professing the Christian faith, and wanting to relate the two.

17. Maxie B. Burch, *The Evangelical Historians: The Historiography of George Marsden, Nathan Hatch, and Mark Noll* (Lanham, MD: University Press of America, 1996).

The other source of help for the Christian historian in the late twentieth century came from the development of historical scholarship itself. There were, of course, many significant shifts in the period. A central one was the rise of women's history in the 1960s and 1970s, followed by the usually more sophisticated gender history. Here was a major alteration in content. The single-minded stress on class that was the legacy of the Marxist paradigm now had to be tempered by attention to the difference — or similarity — between the sexes. But there was an even greater transformation in the whole way of doing history. This change arose from the impact of postmodernism on the discipline, and it calls for more sustained exploration. First we will investigate what the slippery phenomenon labeled "postmodernism" actually is. Then we will consider the influence it has exerted over the practice of history, before addressing, in a final section, the question of how the Christian historian ought to approach it.

The Postmodern Turn

Postmodernism ought to be recognized as an expression of a major cultural wave sweeping over Western civilization.[18] Previous cultural waves on a similar scale have included the Enlightenment and Romanticism. The Enlightenment was a phenomenon of the eighteenth century emphasizing reason, deploring superstition, and admiring scientific inquiry. Its votaries included not just Edward Gibbon but also Adam Smith, with his analysis of capitalism in *The Wealth of Nations* (1776). Such writers were introducing the modern. In the nineteenth century Romanticism was a variation on the modern, stressing will, emotion, and intuition. Its exponents showed a greater sensitivity to the past, as in Sir Walter Scott's novel *Waverley* (1815), but they believed in incorporating the past in the present. Gothic architecture, for example, was not imitated slavishly from the Middle Ages but was adapted for practical use in the buildings of the Victorian era. Modernity still prevailed. Each of these profound cultural movements began among writers, think-

---

18. The following analysis is based on David Bebbington, "Evangelical Christianity and the Enlightenment," "Evangelical Christianity and Romanticism," and "Evangelical Christianity and Modernism," *Crux* 25, no. 4 (1988): 29-36; 26, no. 1 (1990): 9-15; and 26, no. 2 (1990): 2-9.

ers, and artists and slowly filtered out over time to sway the masses. The legacy of both the Enlightenment and Romanticism continued to be felt powerfully in the twentieth century and still does much to mold the presuppositions of the early twenty-first century. Postmodernism, however, should be seen as a cultural wave beginning in the twentieth century and gradually superseding the ways of thinking associated with its predecessors. It spread slowly during the century from another creative elite to affect broad ways of thinking, including the various academic disciplines.

"Postmodernism" clearly indicates "after the modern," but which type of the modern is meant? A contrast needs to be drawn between modernity and modernism. Modernity, according to sociologists, was what replaced traditional society. It was associated with the Enlightenment, capitalism, and industrialism from the eighteenth century onwards. Postmodernism is what has come after this modernity. It aspires to replace the inheritance of the Enlightenment, representing a reaction against the application of reason and science to society. The concept of reason, according to postmodernists, is dubious because it denies the complexity of the human psyche. The enterprise of science is dangerous because, among other crimes, it damages the environment. Modernism, by contrast, is a label for the literary and artistic movement that turned against Romanticism in the early twentieth century. It rejected the sentiment of the Victorians and the idealization of the rural in favor of a stern facing up to the ills of urban/industrial society. In Germany it was associated with Expressivism, as in the architecture of the Bauhaus school. In Britain its pacemaker was the Bloomsbury Group and its quintessence was the fiction of Virginia Woolf. Postmodernism is not "after modernism" in this sense. There is indeed a great deal of continuity between literary and artistic modernism at the opening of the twentieth century and postmodernism at its end, for the same intellectual influences, supremely Nietzsche and Freud, molded them both. Rather, postmodernism should be located as the characteristic novel cultural movement of its century, slowly supplanting the inheritance from previous generations of Western civilization.

The impact has been particularly striking in philosophy. There had previously been a preoccupation in the discipline with the theory of knowledge. Since Immanuel Kant in the late eighteenth century, philosophers had persistently engaged with the question of how we know what we know. Postmodernism, however, changed the terms of the debate. The alteration is evident, for instance, in the American philosopher Richard Rorty's *Philosophy and the Mirror of Nature* (1979). There is no mirror of nature, according to Rorty, in the human mind. We cannot know the world as it really is by establishing ground rules for what knowledge is. We have to be content with a pragmatic view of knowledge: we think we know enough to get by. This approach constitutes a dismissal of foundationalism, the supposition that we can discover firm foundations for knowing. On this view we have to surrender that illusory goal, and must resign ourselves to our perception being fragmentary. The implications for history are clear. Historians cannot be confident about their knowledge of the past. The effect is to undermine the whole drift of twentieth-century historical scholarship toward a scientific model. The precise methods of science, however thorough, do not generate authentic knowledge. Such thinking as this has led to a reconsideration of historical method at a basic level.

Another dimension of postmodernism that is crucial in its implications for history is its rejection of "metanarrative." Postmodernism characteristically denies that there can be any overarching scheme of meaning in the world. In the words of Jean-François Lyotard, a leading French theorist, the postmodern can be defined as "incredulity toward metanarratives."[19] Broad schemes of historical interpretation have to be abandoned. There can be no toying with the idea of progress or the dialectic of class. Equally there can be no acceptance of a Christian vista on the past. All patterns in history have to be discarded. Hence the historian cannot understand particular happenings as pieces in a larger jigsaw. There is no meaning inherent in events. Thus, for example, the Magna Carta in 1215 was not a stage in the achievement of constitutional liberty. Any such significance is artificially imposed by the historian. Historical judgments, according to postmodernists, are much more arbitrary than used to be supposed.

The impact of postmodernism on the discipline of history came in the last thirty years of the twentieth century. The first major practitioner in English was Hayden White, who in 1973 published his *Metahistory*, a study of the historical imagination in nineteenth-century Europe. The case was that written history is not the result of the patient sifting of evidence. Rather, it is the result of the historian's artistry: "the historian

---

19. Jean-François Lyotard, *The Postmodern Condition: A Report on Knowledge* (1979), in *The Postmodern History Reader*, ed. Keith Jenkins (London: Routledge, 1997), p. 36.

performs an essentially *poetic* act."[20] Any writer of history uses rhetorical forms, "tropes," and produces works of the imagination. Here was a shift back from science to literature as the ideal for historical practice, a shift far more drastic than anything Trevelyan had envisaged. White studied the texts of nineteenth-century historiography, paying attention to the precise wording in a way characteristic of those swayed by postmodernism. This change of gear into a postmodern idiom was often called "the linguistic turn." Whereas historians had previously studied events, they now investigated language. The classic instance in Britain was Gareth Stedman Jones's *Languages of Class* (1983). Stedman Jones examined the Chartists, a mid-nineteenth-century working-class pressure group. They had usually been seen as protestors against capitalism, a socioeconomic movement. Stedman Jones, however, scrutinized what Chartists said, finding that they sought political goals. He therefore showed that they were at heart a constitutional movement. Other historians have likewise concentrated on "discourse," a key word in the postmodernist vocabulary. History entered a revolutionary phase that is not yet over. Postmodernism has challenged historical conventions.

The result has been a flurry of writing, both for and against postmodernism. Where should the Christian stand? What should be the response of the believing historian? As Christian historians look to the future, how far should they adopt a postmodern perspective? There is, in the first place, a case for embracing postmodernism. It was set out years ago in the writings of Paul Tillich, who long taught theology at Union Theological Seminary and the University of Chicago Divinity School. There has been, according to Tillich, a pattern in the evolution of recent Western civilization. The Enlightenment acted as a type of thesis to which Romanticism posed the antithesis, with Existentialism operating as the synthesis. The commitment of Existentialism to authentic living made this force, alongside the Freudian impulse, one of "the providential allies of Christian theology."[21] For Tillich "Existentialism" was a broad term covering the cultural self-expression of the twentieth century. He was deploying the word to characterize what has come to be called postmodernism (a word not yet in vogue in Tillich's day).

---

20. Hayden White, *Metahistory: The Historical Imagination in Nineteenth-Century Europe* (Baltimore: Johns Hopkins University Press, 1973), p. x.

21. Paul Tillich, *A History of Christian Thought: From Its Judaic and Hellenistic Origins to Existentialism*, ed. Carl E. Braaten (New York: Simon & Schuster, 1968), p. 541.

Consequently, the theologian was baptizing postmodernism as an inherently Christian form of culture. There are, however, problems with this analysis. It talks of God, but does not contemplate his transcendence. God, Tillich would have us believe, is an expression of human depth psychology, and no more. This representation is not the Bible's living God, who created the world and human beings from the outside. So Tillich's approach, however fascinating, does not square with the evidence of revelation. Postmodernism cannot be seen as a fresh body of Christian perceptions. Much about postmodernism, in fact, appears alien to the Christian faith. Its rejection of metanarrative in particular does not tally with the Christian valuation of the providential schema of Scripture. The believer possesses a vision of the historical process that postmodernists characteristically deny. The simple acceptance of postmodernism does not seem an option for the Christian historian.

Another possibility would be the outright dismissal of postmodernism. That path has attractions. The whole approach seems burdened with obscure jargon and impenetrable metaphysics. Practitioners, for instance, constantly use the term "privilege," urging that one position ought not to be "privileged" over another. The decision makers, however, writes Lyotard, attempt to manage these clouds of sociality according to input-output matrices, following a logic that implies that their elements are commensurable and that the whole is determinable.[22] Such obscurities make it tempting to dismiss the whole phenomenon as a passing fad. That course of action, however, would not be a wise policy. Postmodernism has made its mark on history, and it is virtually impossible to avoid debate with its protagonists. More important, the postmodern idiom molds contemporary culture more broadly. Since postmodernism represents a major cultural wave, it will no more go away than the Enlightenment could vanish in the eighteenth century. The postmodern cast of mind will continue to influence history, like everything else, as the twenty-first century advances. Christian historians must not refuse to address their contemporaries, entering a cultural ghetto. Total rejection of postmodernism is no more an option than wholesale acceptance.

What is required, therefore, is evaluation. The postmodern style must be sifted to separate the wheat from the chaff. Like any cultural phenomenon, it will be found to contain much of both. Postmodern-

---

22. Lyotard in Jenkins, ed., *Postmodern History Reader*, p. 37.

ism will emerge as ambiguous, neither entirely hostile to Christian values nor in complete alliance with them. A preliminary — and far from exhaustive — analysis can be attempted here. We can scrutinize three aspects of postmodern claims, those relating to method, texts, and evidence.

In the first place, there are questions of method. The rise of postmodernism has reactivated debate about the techniques of history. Literature on historiography has poured from the press over the last twenty years. That in itself is surely a good thing, inviting Christians to reflect on what gives quality to history. It is much harder than it was forty years ago to regard theory with a jaundiced eye. Then, according to Geoffrey Elton, authors were to pursue their study of the past without troubling about debates surrounding method. Theoretical engagement, he wrote, only hinders the practice of history.[23] That stance is now wholly impossible. Postmodernism, by undermining the foundations of traditional historical writing, compels self-criticism. Historians are required to question their assumptions about how to undertake their craft. For the Christian, that is a virtue, a form of humility. The postmodernist stirring of the waters over theoretical issues is to be welcomed.

On the other hand, some postmodernist articulations of historical method seem mistaken. The conclusions of Keith Jenkins, a popular proponent of postmodern theory as applied to history, are a case in point. History, claims Jenkins, now appears to be just one more foundationless, positioned expression in a world of foundationless, positioned expressions.[24] On such a reading, historiography is reduced to absolute subjectivity. The writers of history expound nothing but their personal prejudices. There is no order in historiography because there is no order in the universe. But Christians profess a different understanding of the world. In Christ, they read in Colossians 1, all things hold together. Christ is the foundation of the intelligible structure of the universe. Hence there is order in the past; Christians need to look for it.

Second, there are issues surrounding texts. The concentration on discourse among postmodernists has generated real benefits. There has been close attention to texts, probing their phrasing with a view to deconstructing them and so revealing contradictions. Such close critical read-

---

23. G. R. Elton, *The Practice of History* (Sydney: Sydney University Press, 1967), p. vii.

24. Jenkins, ed., *Postmodern History Reader*, p. 6.

ing is an asset to the discipline. Thus in Dror Wahrman's postmodernist analysis of the emergence of class in late-eighteenth-century and early-nineteenth-century Britain there is careful scrutiny of how the term was used in political debate. There was no simple arrival of "class" as a term of analysis in that period, but rather the employment of the word was strongly contested.[25] Such precise interrogation of texts yields benefits to understanding of wider questions. This aspect of postmodernist practice reflects a high estimate of the importance of words that Christians share. For them, the *logos* is of supreme significance: God spoke his word to communicate with the world. The Almighty sets a high value on words, revealing himself through the Scriptures. Here is common ground between the postmodernist enterprise and Christian conviction.

Yet a common postmodernist assumption about texts is unwelcome. It is frequently asserted by those of postmodernist opinions that what an author wishes to convey cannot be inferred from a written document. According to Jacques Derrida, the most celebrated French philosopher of this school, there is nothing outside the text.[26] A written text, that is to say, becomes independent of its author. The intention of the writer cannot be discovered from what was put down in the document. Hence any source is multivocal. A text can legitimately be read as stating the obvious; equally, however, it can be interpreted as ironically stating the opposite, as when, during an intense rainstorm, we may remark what a fine day it is. No single understanding of a text is preferable to another. But this viewpoint is uncongenial to Christian believers. They know that God, who has purposes, made human beings in his image. Human beings, we conclude, also have purposes, not least when they write. The documents they compose have an intended meaning. It may be difficult to recover the intention of the author, but unraveling what a writer meant to convey is a valued skill among historians. Consequently, historians of Christian conviction will admire the postmodernist fascination with texts, but will wish to defend the concept of intention against postmodernist critiques.

Third, there are also questions around evidence. At least since the professionalization of the discipline, historians have normally believed

---

25. Dror Wahrman, *Imagining the Middle Class: The Political Representation of Class in Britain, c. 1780-1840* (Cambridge: Cambridge University Press, 1995).

26. Jacques Derrida, *Of Grammatology*, trans. G. Spivak (Baltimore: Johns Hopkins University Press, 1976), p. 158.

that their analyses ought to be based on evidence. In the age of scientific history, handbooks were written on how to interpret evidence in order to reach the correct conclusions. Probably the most celebrated example of the genre was French, the *Introduction aux études historiques* (1898) by Charles-Victor Langlois. Postmodernism, however, has shown that there is a problem here. A stern critic of postmodernism in history, Arthur Marwick, contended that documents should be interpreted not arbitrarily, as he claimed was the manner of his opponents, but according to professional standards.[27] Hayden White, however, made a telling reply from a postmodernist standpoint, pointing out that rules of evidence, as formulated by authorities such as Langlois, changed over time. There is no single logic of inquiry, independent of shifting fashions, for the historical process itself has shaped the development of the discipline.[28] That case should elicit a warm response from Christian historians. They uphold a historical faith. Divine providence guides the world, shaping all developments, including those in historiography. Hence standards for the interpretation of evidence alter over the years. In this area there is likely to be sympathy for the postmodernist claim.

Yet a stronger postmodernist tenet in this field will be challenged by the Christian. This is the contention, often put forward by postmodern theorists, that there is no difference between valid and invalid accounts of the past. There is no boundary, in this view, between a work of history and a novel. Histories, according to Hayden White, are "verbal fictions."[29] Simon Schama wrote *Dead Certainties (Unwarranted Speculations)* (1991) in order to vindicate this case. It includes an account of the murder of a Harvard professor in the mid-nineteenth century, suggesting that we cannot separate truth from fiction in the testimony given to the court. The book straddles the divide between history and fiction, suggesting the conclusion that certainties about the past are dead.[30]

27. Arthur Marwick, "Two Approaches to Historical Study: The Metaphysical (including 'Postmodernism') and the Historical," *Journal of Contemporary History* 30 (1995): 5-35.

28. Hayden White, "Response to Arthur Marwick," *Journal of Contemporary History* 30 (1995): 233-46.

29. Hayden White, "The Historical Text as Literary Artifact," in *The Tropics of Discourse: Essays in Cultural Criticism* (Baltimore: Johns Hopkins University Press, 1978), p. 82.

30. Simon Schama, *Dead Certainties (Unwarranted Speculations)* (London: Granta Books, 1991).

That standpoint, however, neglects the disciplinary power of evidence. There are indications in the sources that some events actually happened. The Holocaust, the destruction of millions of Jews in Nazi-ruled Europe, is a case in point. Refusal to accept the verdict of the evidence on this subject is a crime in several countries. Even Hayden White has been forced, against the implications of his theory of history, to concede that the Holocaust did take place.[31] Christians will wish to affirm that evidence enables us to describe the past beyond reasonable doubt. Their faith is concerned with truth, and so there will be an enduring Christian insistence that truth about the past matters. The boundary between history and fiction does exist and ought to be respected. Christians may share the postmodernist suspicion about absolute rules for interpreting evidence, but they will urge that evidence needs to be deployed in order to discover the reality of the past.

Thus, with an eye to the future, the Christian historian will be well advised to take a selective approach to postmodern influence over the discipline. Neither wholesale acceptance nor outright rejection is the right course. Rather, Christians will want to engage with postmodernism, deciding which features are welcome and which are not. Their stance will be exactly what marked the most fruitful Christian responses to the Enlightenment and to Romanticism: an attitude of discrimination.

The Newcastle Discovery Museum, with its gap where modern Christianity should be, is a product of the historiography of a past generation. Its largely exclusive preoccupation with economic history is a symptom of the history prevailing in the 1960s. The approach of historians at that time, whether right-wing or left-wing in inclination, carried much of the prestige of science. The story of historiography down to the 1960s is of the increasing assimilation of history into the scientific model. Opponents of this trend, the traditionalists who objected to the treatment of history as a social science, were no better disposed toward emphasizing religion or ideas. The rise of social-science history, furthermore, was associated with an ideal of objectivity that ruled out of court any Christian perspective on the past. Few Christians resisted the exclusion of faith from history, though Herbert Butterfield was an honorable exception. In the decades since the 1970s, however, the situation has been transformed. Evangelical historians have shown that good his-

---

31. Richard J. Evans, *In Defence of History* (London: Granta, 1997), p. 125.

tory can be written from a Christian perspective. At the same time, the tsunami of postmodernism has swept over the holiday beaches of history. Theory has become fashionable. Science is no longer the model for the best historiography. Ideas and religion have returned to the center of the discipline. The challenge for Christian historians is to come to terms with the postmodern phenomenon. Their wisest course will be a discriminating approach that combines sympathy with criticism. Then they will be able to write history that appeals to the twenty-first century but remains faithful to all the dimensions of biblical revelation.

CHAPTER 2

The Blessings of an Uneasy Conscience: Creative Tensions in Evangelical Intellectual Life

JOHN SCHMALZBAUER

As I consider what resources from the Christian tradition are particularly important to the scholar of today, rather than focusing on new theologies, liturgies, and literatures, I'd like to turn my attention to the *internal* resources of the evangelical tradition. In taking this approach, I realize I may come up dry. As Mark Noll tells us in *The Scandal of the Evangelical Mind*, "at this stage in our existence, evangelicals do not have a lot to offer in intellectual terms as such. We have frittered away a century or more, and we have much catching up to do. We need a lot of help, which may come from other Christian traditions."[1]

And yet much of the energy in evangelical intellectual life comes from its own history and conflicts. At the risk of being parochial, I will examine the tradition of post-war evangelicalism as a resource for Christian scholarship. Following Alasdair MacIntyre, I define tradition as "an historically extended, socially embodied argument" spanning multiple generations. More than a set of static ideas, evangelicalism is an ongoing argument about its own deepest commitments.[2]

In thinking about this multigenerational argument, I was transported back to a public lecture at Wheaton College more than two decades ago. I remember the chapel service in which theologian Carl F. H. Henry spoke on "Coming Home and Saying Good-Bye." Having read

1. Mark Noll, *The Scandal of the Evangelical Mind* (Grand Rapids: Eerdmans, 1995), p. 250.

2. Alasdair MacIntyre, *After Virtue: A Study in Moral Theory* (Notre Dame, IN: University of Notre Dame Press, 1984), p. 222.

Henry's critique of fundamentalism's uneasy conscience, I had viewed him as an intellectual hero. In the aftermath of the Great Depression and World War II, he questioned evangelicalism's divorce from social engagement. As a young evangelical, I was thrilled to see this septuagenarian alumnus take the stage of Edman Chapel.[3] Although Henry was to live another decade, he was already the grandfather of evangelical theology. As such he was often the target of criticism.

Much of the drama of evangelical thought has revolved around the difficulty of transmitting a religious tradition across multiple generations. In *Growing Pains: Learning to Love My Father's Faith*, Columbia University historian Randall Balmer focuses on the "generational problem in religion: How do you pass the faith from one generation to the next?" Balmer's book is one of several recent memoirs that constitute what might be called an evangelical autobiographical moment. Written by Christian scholars and public intellectuals, they are preoccupied with a related question: What should be transmitted and what should be left behind?[4]

In pondering this question, I am reminded of yet another public lecture, also on the topic of cultural transmission. In 1937 historian Marcus Hansen addressed the "problem of the third generation immigrant" on the campus of Augustana College. Speaking to an audience of Swedish Americans, he noted that the children of the immigrants were "subjected to the criticism and taunts of the native Americans and to the criticism and taunts of their elders as well." Faced with such cross pressures, the second generation often jettisoned the heritage of the Old World. The third generation was a different matter. In the words of Hansen's famous law, "What the son wishes to forget the grandson wishes to remember."[5]

---

3. Carl F. H. Henry, "Coming Home and Saying Good-Bye," *Wheaton Alumni*, June/July 1990, pp. 12-14.

4. Randall Balmer, *Growing Pains: Learning to Love My Father's Faith* (Grand Rapids: Brazos, 2001), p. 36. See also Jon Sweeney, *Born Again and Again: Surprising Gifts of a Fundamentalist Childhood* (Brewster, MA: Paraclete, 2005); Frank Schaeffer, *Crazy for God: How I Grew Up as One of the Elect, Helped Found the Religious Right, and Lived to Take All (or Almost All) of It Back* (Cambridge, MA: Da Capo, 2008); Lauren Winner, *Girl Meets God: A Memoir* (New York: Random House, 2003). The notion of an autobiographical moment is borrowed from the African American literary theorist Houston Baker as quoted in Robert Boynton, "The New Intellectuals," *Atlantic Monthly*, March 1995, www.robertboynton.com/articleDisplay.php?article_id=23. Baker wrote of an African American autobiographical moment.

5. Peter Kivisto and Dag Blanck, *American Immigrants and Their Generations: Studies*

Though Hansen was talking about ethnicity, many of the same dynamics can be found in evangelical intellectual life. Historian George Marsden proposes an "extended analogy" between fundamentalists and immigrants. Like Hansen's immigrants, fundamentalists created "their own equivalent of the urban ghetto . . . building a subculture with institutions, mores, and social connections that would eventually provide acceptable alternatives to the dominant cultural ethos." Like Hansen's second generation, many evangelical scholars have turned their backs on fundamentalism. Caught between a conservative subculture and the wider academy, they have searched for an intellectual home.[6]

One of Carl Henry's colleagues at Fuller Theological Seminary, Edward J. Carnell, struggled mightily with this search. In *The Making and Unmaking of an Evangelical Mind*, Rudolph Nelson chronicles the pain and anguish of Carnell's marginality. During his years as president of Fuller Seminary, Carnell absorbed the taunts and criticism of evangelicalism's right flank. Rejecting fundamentalism as "orthodoxy gone cultic," he called himself a "post-fundamentalist." Despite this effort to forget, Carnell never escaped what Nelson calls the "stigmata of fundamentalism." Though his work improved the image of evangelicalism, he never achieved the academic recognition that he craved. After a lifetime grappling with the contradictions in his background, he succumbed to an overdose of sleeping pills in 1967.[7]

Most evangelical scholars have had a happier relationship with their religious backgrounds. Consistent with Hansen's Law, some have tried to remember. Oozing with nostalgia, Richard Mouw's book *The Smell of Sawdust: What Evangelicals Can Learn from Their Fundamentalist Heritage* epitomizes this approach. Like Carnell before him, Mouw served as president of Fuller Seminary. Unlike his mid-century predecessor,

---

and *Commentaries on the Hansen Thesis After Fifty Years* (Urbana: University of Illinois Press, 1990), pp. 192, 49.

6. George Marsden, *Fundamentalism and American Culture* (New York: Oxford University Press, 1981), p. 204. This paragraph draws on John Schmalzbauer, "Reading Herberg from Wheaton: *Protestant, Catholic, Jew* and American Evangelicalism," *U.S. Catholic Historian* 23, no. 1 (2005): 25-39.

7. This paragraph draws heavily on the account in Rudolph Nelson, *The Making and Unmaking of an Evangelical Mind: The Case of Edward Carnell* (New York: Cambridge University Press, 1987). Carnell called fundamentalism "orthodoxy gone cultic" in *The Case for Orthodox Theology* (Philadelphia: Westminster, 1959), pp. 113, 124. See also Edward J. Carnell, "Post-Fundamentalist Faith," *Christian Century*, 26 August 1959, p. 8.

he recounts fond memories of revival songs and passionate sermons. Praising fundamentalism's willingness to fight for the truth, he wishes for a little more tension in evangelical public discourse.[8]

Tension is precisely the quality that makes evangelicalism a rich tradition to employ in thinking about culture. As sociologist Christian Smith argues, the evangelical subculture "flourishes on difference, engagement, tension, conflict, and threat." Smith was talking about differences with outsiders, but this tension can also be internal, running through organizations and individuals. Sometimes it is rooted in theological disagreements, such as the conflict between fundamentalists and evangelicals. At other times it is rooted in social class. Sociologist Michael Lindsay explores this tension in *Faith in the Halls of Power*, discussing the gap between cosmopolitan and populist evangelicals. This gap can be seen in the ways evangelicals approach such disparate topics as nationalism, economics, and the merits of gospel music. A final tension concerns the relationship between Christianity and America. While some have collapsed the distance between the biblical narrative and the American story, others have rejected the idolatry of Christian nationalism.[9]

Most of these tensions are related to generational shifts in American evangelicalism, dividing parents from children and professors from students. Following Hansen's lead, this essay will focus on three generations of evangelical scholars: the post-war generation of Carl Henry and Edward Carnell, the sixties generation of Richard Mouw and Mark Noll, and my own generation of post-sixties evangelicals. In each generation, I will explore how Christian scholars have negotiated the tensions between the evangelical subculture and the wider academic world, as well as the tensions within evangelicalism. In focusing on tension, I am highlighting what James Davison Hunter calls the double marginality of evangelical scholars. Hunter portrays such marginalization as an impediment to Christian intellectual life. While marginality certainly has a down side, it can also be a potent resource. As Robert Wuthnow noted in a lecture at Wheaton, evangelicals enjoy "certain gains associ-

8. Richard Mouw, *The Smell of Sawdust: What Evangelicals Can Learn from Their Fundamentalist Heritage* (Grand Rapids: Zondervan, 2000).

9. Christian Smith, *American Evangelicalism: Embattled and Thriving* (Chicago: University of Chicago Press, 1998), p. 153; Michael Lindsay, *Faith in the Halls of Power: How Evangelicals Joined the American Elite* (New York: Oxford University Press, 2007), p. 219.

ated with disadvantage and denial, particularly the freedom that comes with exclusion, the creativity that comes with marginality." According to sociologist Georg Simmel, marginality allows for a "unity of nearness and remoteness."[10]

A unity of nearness and remoteness is especially important in the contemporary American political context. Amid the polarizations of American politics and culture, we need people who can move between worlds. In the 1980s and 1990s, evangelical higher education played a modest role in bridging the nation's cultural divide, distancing itself from both the right and the left. In light of today's conflicts, there is an even greater need for a healing word. To negotiate these tensions, we must learn from those who have gone before.[11]

In selecting which evangelical scholars to discuss in this chapter, I have admittedly been shaped by my own background. As Timothy Larsen notes, in both Britain and the United States there is a "readily identifiable network" of leaders in American and British evangelicalism. For example, the *Encyclopedia of Evangelicalism* was written almost exclusively by Randall Balmer and includes entries on his father, Sunday school teacher, and alma mater. In the words of a perceptive reviewer, it reads "like a family album."[12]

In my case, the family album is more than a metaphor. Before her death in 2001, my grandmother, Evelyn Viken, was a loyal supporter of Jerry Falwell, Pat Robertson, and Billy Graham. During the holidays, she proudly displayed the Christmas cards they sent her next to those from family and friends. In my grandmother's photo album, pictures of Jerry and Macel Falwell, Pat and Dede Robertson, and Billy and Ruth Graham appeared alongside snapshots of my sister and me. In a strange way, their stories were family stories. Though these photo albums did

10. James Davison Hunter, *To Change the World: The Irony, Tragedy, and Possibility of Christianity in the Late Modern World* (New York: Oxford University Press, 2010), p. 86; Robert Wuthnow, "Living the Question: Evangelical Christianity and Critical Thought," *CrossCurrents*, Summer 1990, www.crosscurrents.org/wuthnow.htm; Georg Simmel, "The Stranger," in *The Sociology of Georg Simmel*, ed. Kurt H. Wolff (New York: Free Press, 1950), p. 402.

11. Robert Wuthnow discussed this bridging role in *The Struggle for America's Soul: Evangelicals, Liberals, and Secularism* (Grand Rapids: Eerdmans, 1989), p. 168.

12. Timothy Larsen, ed., *The Biographical Dictionary of Evangelicals* (Leicester, Eng.: Inter-Varsity, 2003), p. 1; Randall Balmer, *Encyclopedia of Evangelicalism* (Waco, TX: Baylor University Press, 2004); Elesha Coffman, "All in the Family," *Christianity Today*, January 2003, p. 67.

not feature any scholars, her library did contain a book by Carl Henry. Like the genealogies of Scripture, my account of the lineage of evangelical scholarship is also family history. I will begin this genealogy in the 1940s, when my grandmother's contemporaries helped remake the evangelical mind.[13]

Post-War Evangelical Scholarship: "Harvard Fundamentalists"

How can we sing the songs of Zion in a strange land? More than a snippet of psalmody, this question haunted fundamentalists in the 1930s and 1940s. Humiliated by their defeat in the Scopes trial and exiled from the mainstream denominations, they had wandered in the wilderness. Reflecting their immigrant status, they sang songs like, "I am a stranger here, within a foreign land; My Home is far away upon a golden strand." As George Marsden writes, such lyrics summed up the experience of "finding themselves in a culture that was turning from God."[14]

This turning could be seen in the modernist denial of key Christian doctrines, as well as the liberalization of Protestant colleges and universities. Evangelical writer Paul Hutchens captured this sense of alienation in *The Voice*, a 1937 novel. Published by Eerdmans, it tells the story of a fundamentalist at a modernist college. In the words of the protagonist, "I knew all along that this school was modernistic, but I wanted the degree and the name of Carroway College on my diploma, I compromised." Early in the novel, Hutchens takes note of the student's "inferiority complex," adding that the college president's "big bushy eyebrows, the heavy graying sideburns that dropped low in front of his ears, the scholarly bearing and the deep, authoritative voice — the whole dynamic personality — seemed to defy any disagreeing opinions."[15]

Though conservative Protestants could be found in every social class, they were seriously underrepresented in the college-educated professions. Reading the biographies of key post-war evangelicals, one is struck by their humble origins. With few exceptions, they came from

13. This paragraph draws on "The Uneasy Conscience of a Fundamentalist Grandson," unpublished paper delivered at the opening of the Evangelical Mind Conference, Boston University, December 2007.

14. Marsden, *Fundamentalism and American Culture*, p. 205.

15. Paul Hutchens, *The Voice* (Grand Rapids: Eerdmans, 1937), pp. 42, 40.

the lower rungs of the social ladder. Harold John Ockenga's dad was employed by the Chicago Rapid Transit Company. George Eldon Ladd grew up in a working-class home. So did Francis Schaeffer. The son of a German pastry chef, Carl Henry's father abandoned the name Heinrich after the United States entered World War I. Had his parents not succumbed to assimilationist pressures, the evangelical theologian would have been known as Carl Ferdinand Howard Heinrich. As Henry later wrote, this name "had an uncomfortably Prussian ring."[16]

Discomfort was a leitmotif in the story of theologian Edward J. Carnell. Raised in the English working class, Carnell's immigrant father harbored a lifetime of class resentment. A Baptist pastor who attended Moody Bible Institute, Herbert Carnell never overcame his proletarian upbringing. A measure of this inferiority was passed on from father to son. Having worked his way through Wheaton College as a dishwasher, Edward Carnell felt out of place at Harvard Divinity School. Despite this sense of marginality, he was not alone, for Carnell was part of a cohort of "Harvard fundamentalists." Sometimes ill-prepared for the rigors of modern graduate education, they were the beneficiaries of an institution that needed students. At least one of Carnell's peers had been denied admission to other graduate programs. Shortly after applying to the philosophy department at Boston University, George Eldon Ladd received a letter urging him to "brush up on spelling." Even after being admitted to Harvard, some failed to impress their teachers. Carnell's Harvard file includes a letter from Professor Elton Trueblood complaining of "narrow dogmatism" and "some emotional disturbance."[17]

For some post-war evangelical scholars, the goal of developing an intellectually respectable faith was psychologically taxing and profes-

16. John Schmalzbauer, *People of Faith: Religious Conviction in American Journalism in Higher Education* (Ithaca, NY: Cornell University Press, 2003), pp. 21, 22; Garth M. Rosell, *The Surprising Work of God: Harold John Ockenga, Billy Graham, and the Rebirth of Evangelicalism* (Grand Rapids: Baker Academic, 2008), p. 39; John D'Elia, *A Place at the Table: George Eldon Ladd and the Rehabilitation of Evangelical Scholarship in America* (New York: Oxford University Press, 2008); Frank Schaeffer, *Crazy for God*, p. 19; Carl F. H. Henry, *Confessions of a Theologian: An Autobiography* (Waco, TX: Word, 1986), p. 16.

17. Nelson, *Making and Unmaking of an Evangelical Mind*, p. 18. This paragraph draws heavily on Nelson's biography of Carnell, where he uses the term "Harvard fundamentalists." See also Nelson, "Fundamentalism at Harvard: The Case of Edward John Carnell," *Quarterly Review* 2, no. 2 (1982): 79-98. The quotation about Ladd is found in D'Elia, *Place at the Table*, p. 13. The quotation from Trueblood is from Nelson, *Making and Unmaking of an Evangelical Mind*, p. 60.

sionally humiliating. Struggling to address the world outside evangelicalism, Carnell's colleague George Ladd suffered crushing emotional pain, descending into alcoholism and depression. In his biography of Ladd, John D'Elia recounts the wounds left by a scathing review and a frustrated career. Carnell's books of apologetics also met with mixed reviews and weak sales. Besides a lackluster academic reputation, he had to contend with persistent doubts about the Christian faith.[18]

Beyond these personal struggles, the unfulfilled mission of the new evangelicalism was to transform American intellectual life. This ambitious agenda was laid out in such works as Carl Henry's *Remaking the Modern Mind*. It did not work out that way. Though the Harvard fundamentalists improved the public image of evangelical Christianity, they did not remake the modern mind. Despite valiant efforts to construct a coherent apologetics, they did not reshape the philosophy of religion. Such disciplinary success would have to wait until the 1970s and 1980s.[19]

Yet if the Harvard fundamentalists failed to transform modern thought, they succeeded in remaking fundamentalism. As an act of theological rebranding, evangelicalism succeeded in distancing itself from a movement that was veering perilously close to theological heresy and cultural irrelevance.[20] No text had a greater impact than Carl Henry's 1947 manifesto, *The Uneasy Conscience of Modern Fundamentalism*.

On one level, it was a call for social engagement, criticizing the "evaporation of fundamentalist humanitarianism." Condemning "the evils of racial hatred" and the "wrongs of current labor-management relations," Henry urged fundamentalists to take a stand. On another level, it was a bold reaffirmation of the kingdom of God. Describing his

18. D'Elia, *Place at the Table*; Nelson, *Making and Unmaking of an Evangelical Mind*.

19. Carl F. H. Henry, *Remaking the Modern Mind* (Grand Rapids: Eerdmans, 1948). My account of this period draws on Joel Carpenter, *Revive Us Again: The Reawakening of American Fundamentalism* (New York: Oxford University Press, 1999); George Marsden, *Reforming Fundamentalism: Fuller Seminary and the New Evangelicalism* (Grand Rapids: Eerdmans, 1987). For a discussion of the late-twentieth-century influence of conservative Protestants in the philosophy of religion, see Quentin Smith, "The Metaphilosophy of Naturalism," *Philo* 4, no. 2 (2001), www.philoonline.org/library/smith_4_2.htm.

20. D. G. Hart discusses the rebranding of fundamentalism in *Deconstructing Evangelicalism: Conservative Protestantism in the Age of Billy Graham* (Grand Rapids: Baker Academic, 2004), p. 23. According to Hart, "They wanted to reform conservative Protestantism and smooth its rougher edges. In so doing, they opted for a new label — *evangelical* instead of fundamentalist."

own tradition, Henry wrote, "recent Fundamentalism increasingly reflects a marked hesitancy about kingdom preaching." Insisting that "the kingdom is here, and that it is not here," he rejected both liberal optimism and fundamentalist pessimism. Criticizing dispensationalism for its "despair over the present social order," Henry called for a new eschatology.[21]

Far too often fundamentalist prophecy beliefs led to a conspiratorial view of American culture and politics. Such speculation reached fever pitch during Franklin Roosevelt's New Deal, when prophecy buffs from Los Angeles to the Missouri Ozarks identified the National Recovery Administration's Blue Eagle with the mark of the beast. Though most evangelicals voted for FDR, some saw his policies as a prelude to socialism. A minority joined the ranks of the Roosevelt haters. In Kansas, the Reverend Gerald Winrod promoted bizarre conspiracy theories through his newspaper and preaching tours. Maintaining ties with a wide network of fundamentalist leaders, he was given an honorary degree from the Bible Institute of Los Angeles in 1935 for his work in "Christian Journalism" and "Biblical Scholarship." Two years earlier, Winrod had begun promoting the *Protocols of the Elders of Zion*, an infamous anti-Semitic forgery. Portraying the New Deal as a Jewish plot, he argued that President Roosevelt was descended from the tribe of Dan, adding that "it is now generally known that he comes from Dutch Jewish stock." Others, including the Reverend Gerald L. K. Smith, produced tracts on Roosevelt's "Jewish family tree."[22]

---

21. Carl F. H. Henry, *The Uneasy Conscience of Modern Fundamentalism* (Grand Rapids: Eerdmans, 1947), pp. 1, 39, 43, 48, 17.

22. On evangelical voting patterns, see Lyman Kellstedt, John Green, Corwin Smidt, and James Guth, "Faith Transformed: Religion and American Politics from FDR to George W. Bush," in *Religion and American Politics: From the Colonial Period to the Present*, ed. Mark A. Noll and Luke E. Harlow (New York: Oxford University Press, 2007), pp. 269-95. This paragraph draws on Paul Boyer, *When Time Shall Be No More: Prophecy Belief in Modern American Culture* (Cambridge, MA: Harvard University Press, 1992); Timothy Weber, "Dispensationalism's Dark Side," in Weber, *On the Road to Armageddon: How Evangelicals Became Israel's Best Friend* (Grand Rapids: Baker Academic, 2004), pp. 129-53. On the NRA Eagle in the Ozarks, see Vance Randolph, *Ozark Magic and Folklore* (New York: Columbia University Press, 1947), p. 338; Boyer, *When Time Shall Be No More*, p. 107. On Winrod, see Leo Ribuffo, *The Old Christian Right: The Protestant Far Right from the Great Depression to the Cold War* (Philadelphia: Temple University Press, 1983), pp. 80-127; Weber, *On the Road to Armageddon*, pp. 133-46; James C. Juhnke, *A People of Two Kingdoms: The Political Acculturation of the Kansas Mennonites* (Newton, KS: Faith and

My hometown of Minneapolis did not escape the taint of fundamentalist anti-Semitism. Once an advocate of civic reform, the Reverend William Bell Riley openly promoted the *Protocols*, calling nonpracticing Jews the "most vicious atheists and the most intolerable communists I have met." Echoing Winrod, he said, "The present Roosevelt regime is a Jewish controlled regime." Like Winrod, he never apologized for such views. During the 1930s, members of the paramilitary Silver Shirts were rumored to attend Riley's church. Responding to such allegations, Riley preached on the topic, "Why Shiver at the Sight of a Shirt?" calling them defenders of the Constitution. He was also an admirer of Father Charles Coughlin, the Detroit demagogue who railed against Jewish bankers. Founder of the World's Christian Fundamentals Association, Riley once had close ties to Wheaton College, and during a 1947 bedside meeting, he designated Billy Graham as his heir, telling him, "Billy, you are the man to succeed me." In 1948 Graham assumed the leadership of Riley's Northwestern Schools.[23]

Many fundamentalist leaders opposed the spread of anti-Semitism. Writing in the *Sunday School Times*, Wheaton President J. Oliver Buswell expressed "regret at the prevalence of race prejudice recently manifesting itself among some of our Fundamentalist brethren," adding, "I do not feel that any race can be blamed for the spread of the evil propaganda of Communism." Despite Buswell's words, anti-Semitic beliefs were far too common in conservative circles. In 1921 Moody Bible Institute President James Gray called the *Protocols* "a clinching argument for

---

Life, 1975). The Winrod quotation comes from Robert C. Fuller, *Naming the Antichrist: The History of an American Obsession* (New York: Oxford University Press, 1995), p. 141. The Smith tract is mentioned in Kurt Schuparra, *Triumph of the Right: The Rise of the California Conservative Movement, 1945-1966* (Armonk, NY: M. E. Sharpe, 1998), p. 17. For a discussion of Smith's extensive ties to southern California fundamentalists, see Darren Dochuk, *From Bible Belt to Sunbelt: Plain-Folk Religion, Grassroots Politics, and the Rise of Evangelical Conservatism* (New York: Norton, 2011). On the "Roosevelt family tree" booklets, see Arnold Forster and Benjamin Epstein, *Cross-Currents* (New York: Doubleday, 1956), p. 29.

23. Minneapolis was not unique in its prejudice. Darren Dochuk notes that Los Angeles was a "hotbed for anti-Semitism" in *From Bible Belt to Sunbelt*, p. 85. The first Riley quote is from Carpenter, *Revive Us Again*, p. 99. The others are from William Vance Trollinger, *God's Empire: William Bell Riley and Midwestern Fundamentalism* (Madison: University of Wisconsin Press, 1990), pp. 73, 76, 77, 152. This paragraph draws heavily on Trollinger's account. See also William Bell Riley, *The Philosophies of Father Coughlin: Four Sermons by W. B. Riley, DD* (Grand Rapids: Zondervan, 1935).

premillennialism." In the 1930s, notorious anti-Semite Elizabeth Dilling spoke over the airwaves of Moody radio. According to Dilling, Pastor Harry Ironside "introduced me as the only woman he had ever asked to occupy his pulpit in the Moody Church."[24]

I call attention to this sad chapter in the history of American fundamentalism because of my own family history. In the 1920s, my Norwegian great-grandfather attended Moody Church. As a young housewife in the post-war era, his daughter, my grandmother, attended a Bible study led by William Bell Riley's widow. Earlier in her life, Grandma was a member of evangelist Luke Rader's River-Lake Gospel Tabernacle. According to historian Hyman Berman, "It was the worst place, barring none in the Twin Cities, as far as anti-Semitic vitriol." Somehow my grandmother left the orbit of these anti-Semitic figures, joining the more moderate Swedish Covenant Church. Somehow she became a strong supporter of the state of Israel.[25]

As her grandson, I am grateful that fundamentalism changed. As a scholar, I know that Carl Henry helped tame its destructive impulses. Though he never mentioned it, anti-Semitism was another reason for fundamentalism's uneasy conscience. Though many dispensationalists repudiated the excesses of this period, Henry's manifesto did even more to resist its dark side. So did the scholarship of George Eldon Ladd. In his thirty years at Fuller, Ladd published several critiques of dispensationalism. By modeling rigorous biblical scholarship, he helped discourage wild eschatological speculation. By getting the biblical narra-

---

24. Buswell's *Sunday School Times* article is quoted in Keith Leroy Brooks, *The Jews and the Passion for Palestine in Light of Prophecy* (Grand Rapids: Zondervan, 1937), p. 46. Gray is quoted in Weber, *On the Road to Armageddon*, p. 132. The reference to Ironside is from Elizabeth Dilling, *The Plot Against Christianity* (Omaha, NE: The Elizabeth Dilling Foundation, 1964), http://www.come-and-hear.com/dilling/whois.html. For more on Dilling, see Glen Jeansonne, *Women of the Far Right: The Mother's Movement and World War II* (Chicago: University of Chicago Press, 1997), pp. 10-28. Dilling was a student of Moody Bible Institute instructor Iris McCord, who became her close friend.

25. Hyman Berman is quoted in Maura Lerner, "Razing Old Lake Street Tabernacle Stirs Up Memories of a Darker Era," *Star Tribune*, 15 September 2002, B11. This paragraph draws on "The Uneasy Conscience of a Fundamentalist Grandson," unpublished paper delivered at the opening of the Evangelical Mind Conference, Boston University, December 2007. In that paper I discussed my disappointment with my grandmother, as well as my relief that she rejected these unsavory figures. I also praised the Evangelical Covenant Church's 2005 "Resolution on Anti-Semitism," available at http://www.covchurch.org/resolutions/2000-anti-semitism.

tive straight, he helped guard against a conspiratorial view of American history.[26]

Like Henry and Ladd, many evangelical intellectuals hailed from Baptist and Reformed backgrounds. Yet scholars from Wesleyan and pietist traditions occasionally had more impact on their disciplines. This was true at the University of Minnesota, where two young evangelicals made their mark in the humanities.

Across town from an ailing William Bell Riley, Paul Holmer taught philosophy from 1946 to 1960. As an undergraduate at Minnesota he had studied with David Swenson, a pioneering Kierkegaard scholar and one of Riley's chief antagonists. Like Swenson, he was a son of the Swedish Covenant Church. In 1961 Holmer joined the faculty of Yale Divinity School, influencing a whole generation of American theologians, including Stanley Hauerwas and William Willimon. According to Hauerwas, he was a "Swedish pietist disguised as a philosopher." In the 1970s, Holmer spoke of "suffering the angularity of trying to be evangelical and an intellectual," noting that "what I have been rather slowly and painstakingly getting clear for myself by fighting my way through philosophical and theological thickets turns out to be not altogether different from what my parents, with their evangelical ardor for my very soul, told me when I was too young to accept or desist."[27]

26. On dispensationalist critiques of anti-Semitism, see Weber, *On the Road to Armageddon*, pp. 129-53. On Ladd's critique of dispensationalism, see D'Elia, *Place at the Table*, pp. 61-90.

27. See Philip J. Anderson, "David F. Swenson, Evolution, and Public Education in Minnesota," in *Swedes in the Twin Cities: Immigrant Life and Minnesota's Urban Frontier*, ed. Philip J. Anderson and Dag Blanck (St. Paul: Minnesota Historical Society, 2001), pp. 309-10. During the 1920s, Swenson tangled with Riley over the evolution issue. In 1923 Riley held an anti-evolution rally at the Swedish Tabernacle in Minneapolis, Swenson's childhood congregation. Bruce Carlson, "Tribute to Paul Holmer," *Pietisten*, Fall 2004, www.pietisten.org/fall04/paulholmer.html; Mark Horst, "Disciplined by Theology: A Profile of Paul Holmer," *Christian Century*, 12 October 1988, pp. 891-95, www.religion -online.org/showarticle.asp?title=58; William Willimon, "Teaching Moments," *Christian Century*, 22 February 2005, www.christiancentury.org/article/2005-02/teaching -moments-1; "Theologist Paul L. Holmer: An Authority on Kierkegaard," *Yale Bulletin and Calendar*, 17 September 2004, www.yale.edu/opa/arc-ybc/v33.n3/story24.html; Stanley Hauerwas, *Hannah's Child: A Theologian's Memoir* (Grand Rapids: Eerdmans, 2010), pp. 53, 60. The quotation is from Paul Holmer, "Contemporary Evangelical Faith: An Assessment and Critique," in *The Evangelicals: What They Believe, Who They Are, Where They Are Changing*, ed. David Wells and John Woodbridge (Grand Rapids: Baker, 1977), p. 89.

Like Holmer, the Nazarene historian Timothy Smith spent his early career at Minnesota, joining the faculty in 1961. Earning a doctorate at Harvard, he wrote his first book on "the evangelical origins of social Christianity." Published in 1957, *Revivalism and Social Reform* questioned received views of evangelicalism. In the preface, he thanked his parents, "holiness preachers and friends of reform — at whose knees I learned to appreciate both Christian faith and social compassion." Like Carl Henry, Smith challenged the uneasy conscience of evangelicalism. Yet his Nazarene background led him to recover a very different branch of the evangelical family tree.[28]

In a similar way, Holmer's Swedish pietism led him to appreciate a side of the evangelical subculture that those with more refined tastes looked down upon or ignored. Henry criticized the "tendency to replace great church music by a barn-dance variety of semi-religious choruses," echoing J. Gresham Machen's complaint about "the blowing of enormous horns or other weird instruments" at an Indiana Bible conference. The son of a Baltimore lawyer, Machen reflected the highbrow tastes of the Southern upper class. By contrast, Paul Holmer was raised with the music of working-class Swedes. Recalling his childhood in Minneapolis, he wrote that Christian faith there "was still at home with nasal tenors, string bands, informal expression and those strong hands and backs." In 1975 he credited evangelicalism's "rich and folkish hymnody" for preserving the gospel story. As a young man, Holmer played piano for evangelist Mordecai Ham and maestro Dimitri Metropolis. Straddling the worlds of fundamentalism and high culture, he was not a snob.[29]

28. Timothy L. Smith, *Revivalism and Social Reform: American Protestantism on the Eve of the Civil War* (New York: Abingdon, 1957), pp. 148, 10; "Obituary: Historian Smith, 72, Dies," *Christianity Today*, 7 April 1997, http://www.christianitytoday.com /ct/1997/april7/1997-04-07-obituary-historian-smith-72-dies.html; "Timothy Smith and the Recovery of the Nazarene Vision," *Holiness Today*, March 1999, www.nazarene .org/ministries/administration/archives/ourarchives/researchers/smith/display.aspx.

29. Henry, *The Uneasy Conscience of Modern Fundamentalism*, p. 5. Machen is quoted in Marsden, *Fundamentalism and American Culture*, p. 138. Marsden discusses Machen's roots in the Southern aristocracy. Holmer is quoted in Glen Wiberg, *This Side of the River: A Centennial Story, Salem Covenant Church, 1888-1988* (Salem Covenant Church, 1995), p. 63; Holmer, "Contemporary Evangelical Faith," p. 100. For a sampling of Swedish-American folk hymnody, see Wiberg, *Singing the Story: Sightings in Christian Music* (Seattle and Minneapolis: Pietisten, 2011). On Holmer, Ham, and Metropolis, see Richard John Neuhaus, "While We're At It," *First Things*, November 2004, www .firstthings.com/print.php?type=article&year=2009&month=02&title_link=episcopal

Holmer provides an example of one of evangelicalism's greatest strengths — and weakness — which involves its capacity to adapt to the American vernacular. From the "Jazz Age Evangelism" of the 1920s to the Youth for Christ choruses of the 1940s, it has preached and sung in the language of ordinary people. It is no accident that early rock and roll was produced by country boys raised in Baptist and Pentecostal churches. As the folkish sounds of Sun Records drifted slowly northward, barn dance music became the soundtrack of American culture. As the fusion of gospel, country, and blues, the music of Elvis Presley, Jerry Lee Lewis, and Johnny Cash was an expression of evangelicalism's conflicted soul.[30]

The Harvard fundamentalists were no strangers to such conflict. Bridging multiple worlds, they experienced social, cultural, and theological tensions. Living in the space between religion and academia was often painful. So was the tension between fundamentalism and evangelicalism. Yet out of these tensions came a renaissance in evangelical intellectual life. Forgetting the conspiratorial rhetoric of fundamentalism, a new generation of scholars acknowledged the fundamentals but sought to reform and rearticulate them. In retrospect, fundamentalism's uneasy conscience was a fertile source of intellectual creativity.

Evangelical Scholars and "Christian America": From Nixonland to the New Christian Right

As evangelicalism entered the 1950s, its tension with American culture appeared to lessen. Nowhere was this more apparent than in the success of Billy Graham. As historian Grant Wacker notes, "When Gra-

---

-straight-talk — 39. Sadly, Mordecai Ham was an outspoken anti-Semite. It is impossible to know whether Holmer knew about this side of the Baptist evangelist.

30. See the 2005 Billy Graham Center Archive's online exhibit, "Jazz Age Evangelism," at http://www.wheaton.edu/bgc/archives/exhibits/cgt/rader02intro.html; Thomas Bergler, "'I Found My Thrill': The Youth for Christ Movement and American Congregational Singing, 1940-1970," in *Wonderful Words of Life: Hymns in American Protestant History and Theology,* ed. Richard J. Mouw and Mark A. Noll (Grand Rapids: Eerdmans, 2004), pp. 123-49; Rodney Clapp, *Johnny Cash and the Great American Contradiction: Christianity and the Battle for the Soul of a Nation* (Louisville: Westminster John Knox, 1989); James Goff, "Conflicted by the Spirit: The Religious Life of Elvis Presley," *Assemblies of God Heritage,* 2008.

ham spoke, middle America heard itself." This was certainly true of my grandmother and her children. They heard Graham in 1950, the summer following his triumphant Los Angeles campaign. My mother and her little brother spent their days swimming in Lake Minnetonka and their evenings under Graham's tent. Unbeknownst to my family, a young Tim LaHaye parked cars there that summer. Far from everyone's minds was the topic of partisan politics. For them and for millions of Americans, the fifties were a time of relative consensus.[31]

Despite the illusion of unity, deep fissures remained below the surface. On the far right, the John Birch Society looked for subversion in high places, accusing President Eisenhower of being "a dedicated, conscious agent of the Communist conspiracy."[32] To their credit, the editors of the new evangelical magazine, *Christianity Today,* rejected such extremism and condemned the red-baiting of Carl McIntire and Billy James Hargis. McIntire returned the favor, criticizing editor Carl Henry's "soft hand in dealing with Communism." Closely associated with Billy Graham and the new evangelicalism, the magazine struck a more irenic tone as the Eisenhower era drew to a close.[33]

Sun Oil founder J. Howard Pew was the primary backer of *Christianity Today.* He was also a board member for *American Opinion,* the official magazine of the John Birch Society. A friend of Birch Society founder Robert Welch (the inventor of the Junior Mint), Pew was an outspoken critic of "New Dealism, Socialism, and Communism." In the 1950s,

31. The quote is from Grant Wacker, "Charles Atlas with a Halo: America's Billy Graham," *Christian Century,* 1 April 1992, pp. 336-41. A version of this family story appeared in John Schmalzbauer, "Route 66 Evangelicals," *Evangelical Studies Bulletin,* Summer 2011. The Billy Graham Evangelistic Association chronology at the Billy Graham Center Archives indicates that Graham was at the Youth for Christ Mound Camp in July of 1950. This chronology is available at www.wheaton.edu/bgc/archives /bgeachro/bgeachro02.htm. Tim LaHaye's parking attendant duties are mentioned in Doris Greig's section of *Billy Graham: A Tribute from Friends,* ed. Vernon McLellan (New York: Warner Books, 2002), p. 80.

32. John Birch Society founder Robert Welch is quoted in Alan F. Westin, "The John Birch Society: 'Radical Right' and 'Extreme Left' in the Political Context of Post World War II," in *The Radical Right,* ed. Daniel Bell (New Brunswick, NJ: Transaction, 2002), p. 244. For an account of those years at *Christianity Today,* see Henry, *Confessions of a Theologian: An Autobiography.*

33. Robert Booth Fowler, *A New Engagement: Evangelical Political Thought, 1966-1976* (Grand Rapids: Eerdmans, 1982), pp. 11, 12. The McIntire quote is from Martin Marty, *Modern American Religion: Under God Indivisible, 1941-1960* (Chicago: University of Chicago Press, 1996), p. 367.

he joined the Mont Pelerin Society, a group that included economists Ludwig von Mises and Friedrich von Hayek. Worried that the churches were promoting socialism, Pew funded *Christian Economics*, a libertarian magazine mailed to 175,000 clergy. Co-founded by Quaker Howard Kershner and the Reverend Norman Vincent Peale, it was the official publication of the Christian Freedom Foundation. Some of its contributors were atheists or agnostics, including Mises and Hayek.[34] Eager for Pew's support, some writers sprinkled their speech with pious references. Commenting on such behavior, Catholic conservative Russell Kirk noted that "[Frank] Chodorov, an atheist, now tosses in an occasional condescending reference to God, in the hopes of pleasing Mr. J. Howard Pew." A spiritual seeker, Chodorov embraced "a vaguely deistic religion without a deity." Affirming the "God-idea," he wrote a column for *Faith and Freedom*, the voice of Spiritual Mobilization, another Pew-funded project. Equally heterodox, Spiritual Mobilization director James Ingebretsen acknowledged that "fighting the forces that wanted to abolish the free enterprise system was my mission, not promoting Christ." Later Ingebretsen experimented with Eastern religions and LSD. Reflecting these eclectic interests, *Faith and Freedom* mixed Christian libertarianism with the spiritual avant-garde. An expression of post-war religious pluralism, such initiatives helped introduce American Protestants to free-market thought.[35]

34. The Pew quote comes from Allan J. Lichtman, *White Protestant Nation: The Rise of the American Conservative Movement* (New York: Atlantic Monthly, 2008), p. 75. See also Michael C. Jensen, "The Pews of Philadelphia," *New York Times*, 10 October 1971, F1; Benjamin R. Epstein and Arnold Foster, *Report on the John Birch Society: 1966* (New York: Random House, 1966), p. 91. This paragraph draws heavily on Kim Phillips-Fein, *Invisible Hands: The Businessmen's Crusade Against the New Deal* (New York: Norton, 2009). For contrasting views of Pew's support for Christian libertarianism, see Lee Haddigan, "The Importance of Christian Thought for the American Libertarian Movement: Christian Libertarianism, 1950-1971," *Libertarian Papers* 2, no. 14 (2010): 1-31, available at http://libertarianpapers.org/2010/14-haddigan-christian-libertarianism/; Chip Berlet, "Von Mises Rises from the Scrap Heap of History," *Z Magazine*, May 2009, http://www.zcommunications.org/von-mises-rises-from-the-scrap-heap-of-history-by-chip-berlet.

35. Kirk is quoted in Lichtman, *White Protestant Nation*, p. 206. Darren Dochuk describes several initiatives introducing evangelicals to Austrian economics in *From Bible Belt to Sunbelt*. The "vaguely deistic" quotation is from George H. Nash, *Reappraising the Right: The Past and Future of American Conservatism* (Wilmington, DE: ISI Books, 2009), p. 91. Ingebretsen is quoted in Phillips-Fein, *Invisible Hands*, p. 75. See Ingebretsen, *Apprentice to the Dawn: A Spiritual Memoir* (Los Angeles: Philosophical Research Society,

A conservative Presbyterian, Pew lent his support to the Billy Graham Evangelistic Association, the National Association of Evangelicals, Fuller Seminary, and Gordon College. A critical player in the revitalization of evangelical intellectual life, *Christianity Today* was part of a wider strategy to influence American culture. Thus, it was no small matter when the editor of *Eternity* told Pew, "Carl Henry is a socialist." He was wrong. As *Christianity Today* chairman L. Nelson Bell explained to his fellow board members, "Carl takes the position that Capitalism and Labor *both* must come under the scrutiny of God and his holy laws."[36] If anything, the magazine leaned to the right. While disapproving of racial segregation, *Christianity Today* did not promote the civil rights movement. As Henry wrote in *Confessions of a Theologian*, if liberal Protestants took a "Johnny come lately" approach to racial discrimination, "evangelical engagement was admittedly 'Johnny come later.'" Though associate editor Frank E. Gaebelein reported on the march in Selma, his accounts were never published. This inattention to civil rights reflected the conviction that changed hearts, not changed laws, would lead to racial harmony.[37] Showing its appreciation for the post-war conservative movement, *Christianity Today* commemorated the tenth anniversary of William F. Buckley's *National Review*. Though Henry lasted a dozen years as editor-in-chief, he was too moderate for Pew. Under Henry's successor Harold Lindsell, the magazine published a critique of Social Security and "glowing reviews of striking libertarian work," including Robert Nozick's *Anarchy, State, and Utopia*. An analysis of *Christianity Today*'s early years (1956-76) revealed a "metaphysic with an atomistic worldview," emphasizing "personal morality over social

---

2003). For the influence of some of these figures on evangelical libertarians and Christian Reconstructionists, see Michael McVicar, "The Libertarian Theocrats: The Long, Strange History of R. J. Rushdoony and Christian Reconstructionism," *The Public Eye*, Fall 2007, http://www.publiceye.org/magazine/v22n3/libertarian.html. For an engaging account of Spiritual Mobilization and Pew's involvement, see Brian Doherty, *Radicals for Capitalism: A Freewheeling History of the Modern American Libertarian Movement* (New York: Public Affairs, 2007).

36. Waldemar A. Nielsen, *The Big Foundations* (New York: Columbia University Press, 1972); Mary Sennholz, *Faith and Freedom: The Journal of a Great American, J. Howard Pew* (Grove City, PA: Grove City College, 1975). On the *Eternity* accusation, see Henry, *Confessions of a Theologian: An Autobiography*, p. 162.

37. Henry, *Confessions of a Theologian*, p. 158; Peter Heltzel, *Jesus and Justice: Evangelicals, Race, and American Politics* (New Haven, CT: Yale University Press, 2009), p. 83.

ethics, individual transformation as the key to social change, laissez-faire economics, and a politics extolling freedom of the individual and a limited state."[38]

Like the editors of *Christianity Today*, many evangelicals were unsettled by the upheavals of the 1960s. Searching for law and order, some turned to Richard Nixon. In *Nixonland*, journalist Rick Perlstein chronicles the "rise of a president and the fracturing of America." According to Perlstein, millions of Americans perceived a "pitched battle between the forces of darkness and the forces of light. The only thing was: Americans disagreed radically over which side was which." Casting his lot with Nixon, Harold Lindsell made it clear whom he was voting for in 1968. So did Billy Graham, stopping just short of an endorsement.[39]

Though establishment evangelicals resided in Nixonland, a younger generation searched for a new political home. For some, that meant voting for South Dakota Senator George McGovern, who paid a visit to Wheaton College in October 1972. The leadership of Evangelicals for McGovern included Ronald Sider, Robert Webber, Richard Pierard, Lewis Smedes, Stephen Monsma, and Anthony Campolo. According to Mark Noll, it was the first major evangelical group to endorse a presidential candidate. It provided the nucleus for the 1973 Chicago Declaration of Evangelical Social Concern.[40]

38. On *Christianity Today*'s view of Buckley's magazine and Nozick's libertarianism, see Fowler, *A New Engagement*, pp. 34, 27. Marsden discusses Henry's exit from *Christianity Today* in *Fundamentalism and American Culture*, p. 241. This content analysis of *Christianity Today* can be found in Dennis Hollinger, *Individualism and Social Ethics: An Evangelical Syncretism* (Lanham, MD: University Press of America, 1983), p. 44. These quotes from Hollinger's book are taken from Christian Smith, *American Evangelicalism: Embattled and Thriving* (Chicago: University of Chicago Press, 1998), p. 189.

39. Rick Perlstein, *Nixonland: The Rise of a President and the Fracturing of America* (New York: Simon and Schuster, 2008), p. xii; Fowler, *A New Engagement*, p. 33. In 1926 Nixon responded to an altar call by Paul Rader, the brother of the man who preached to my grandmother at the River-Lake Gospel Tabernacle in Minneapolis. See Conrad Black, *Richard Nixon: A Life in Full* (New York: Public Affairs, 2008). On Graham's involvement in the 1960 presidential race, see Shaun Casey, *The Making of a Catholic President: Kennedy vs. Nixon, 1960* (New York: Oxford University Press, 2009).

40. McGovern spoke in Edman Chapel. His text was Micah 6:8. On McGovern's visit to Wheaton College, see Theodore H. White, *The Making of the President 1972* (New York: HarperCollins, 2009), p. 338. For a discussion of "Establishment Evangelicals," see Richard Quebedeaux, *The Young Evangelicals: Revolution in Orthodoxy* (New York: Harper & Row, 1974), p. 3. See also Fowler, *A New Engagement*, and David Swartz, "Left Behind: The Evangelical Left and the Limits of Evangelical Politics, 1965-1988" (unpub-

Historian Donald Dayton was part of this restless cohort. Like the Evangelicals for McGovern, Dayton recognized the rhetorical signifi-cance of Wheaton. In *Discovering an Evangelical Heritage,* he began with a chapter on abolitionist Jonathan Blanchard, noting that "if there is a single symbol of modern Evangelicalism, it is Wheaton College." Comparing the radicalism of Wheaton's founder with the quietism of his successors, he condemned evangelicals for abandoning their roots. Later Dayton criticized Wheaton President V. Raymond Edman for ig-noring the radicalism of Charles Finney. In *Finney Lives On,* Edman had deleted resistance to social reform from Finney's list of twenty-four ob-stacles to revival. A work of history and a tract for the times, Dayton's book first appeared as a series of magazine articles in Jim Wallis's *Post-American,* the forerunner to *Sojourners.* At times, Dayton seemed to re-make evangelicalism in the image of the American left. Searching for a usable past, he did not mention Jonathan Blanchard's crusade against freemasonry.[41]

Consistent with evangelicalism's development as a historically em-bodied argument, Dayton framed his critique in generational language. Acknowledging the autobiographical roots of his project, he wrote that "this book is a product of the author's struggle to reconcile the seem-ingly irreconcilable in his own experience: the Evangelical heritage in which he was reared and values bequeathed to him by the student movements of the sixties." A second-generation academic, he was stra-tegically located in evangelicalism's master-pupil chains. Though a Wesleyan educator, Dayton's father studied with Carl Henry at North-ern Baptist Seminary, internalizing the "Reformed Scholasticism" of post-war evangelicalism. Despite deep roots in the Wesleyan Church, the younger Dayton first encountered John Wesley at Yale in a course with Paul Holmer, the Swedish pietist. Rejecting neo-evangelicalism's Calvinist influence, Dayton reclaimed the theological heritage of his forebears. He was not alone. Active in the Evangelical Women's Caucus, Lucille Sider Dayton was an advocate for gender equality. In "Women in the Holiness Movement," the Daytons located the origins of feminism

---

lished doctoral dissertation, University of Notre Dame, 2008). On Evangelicals for Mc-Govern, see Mark Noll, "Jesus and Jefferson," *New Republic,* 9 June 2011, p. 35.

41. Donald Dayton, *Discovering an Evangelical Heritage* (New York: Harper & Row, 1976), p. 7. Not surprisingly, my grandmother owned a copy of V. Raymond Edman's *Finney Lives On: The Man, His Revival Method and His Message* (New York: Revell, 1951).

in their own tradition. Their coauthor was Nancy Hardesty, the "founding mother of the Biblical feminist movement."[42]

In the early 1970s, evangelicalism seemed to be moving left. At the *Reformed Journal*, a cohort of young Calvinists called for greater political engagement. In *Political Evangelism*, then Calvin College professor Richard Mouw offered an intellectual rationale for this involvement, noting that his "training within the environs of 'conservative-evangelical' Christianity did not provide me with a theological framework adequate to deal with the concerns over social injustice, racism, and militarism that were so much a part of the years I spent doing graduate study at secular universities." In *Politics and the Biblical Drama*, he located political action within the story of creation, fall, redemption, and coming kingdom, anticipating the narrative theology of the 1990s. In a more vivid dramatization of the kingdom, black evangelical Tom Skinner electrified InterVarsity's 1970 Urbana conference, proclaiming that "the liberator has come." According to one account, "the gathering of more than 11,000 college students leaped to its feet, exploding in applause and cheers."[43]

Despite this exuberance, the political rebirth of evangelicalism took a very different path. By November 1980 the rise of the New Christian

---

42. The notion of master-pupil chains comes from Randall Collins, *The Sociology of Philosophies: A Global Theory of Intellectual Change* (Cambridge, MA: Harvard University Press, 1998), p. 7. This concept is used by Michael Lindsay in *Faith in the Halls of Power*, p. 274. Dayton, *Rediscovering an Evangelical Heritage*, p. 1; "Are Charismatic-Inclined Pietists the True Evangelicals? And Have the Reformed Tried to Hijack Their Movement?" Interview with Donald Dayton, *Modern Reformation*, March/April 2010, pp. 40-49, www.modernreformation.org/default.php?page=articledisplay&var1=ArtRead &var2=400&var3=main. See Pamela Cochran, *Evangelical Feminism: A History* (New York: New York University Press, 2005), p. 44; Nancy Hardesty, Lucille Sider, and Donald W. Dayton, "Women in the Holiness Movement: Feminism in the Evangelical Tradition," in *Women of Spirit: Female Leadership in Jewish and Christian Traditions*, ed. Rosemary Ruether and Eleanor McLaughlin (New York: Simon & Schuster, 1979), pp. 226-54. See also Julie Ingersoll, "Nancy Hardesty, Founding Mother of the Biblical Feminist Movement (1941-2011)," *Religion Dispatches*, 13 April 2011, http://www .religiondispatches.org/dispatches/julieingersoll/4498/nancy_hardesty,_founding _mother_of_biblical_feminist_movement_%281941-2011%29_/.

43. Swartz, "Left Behind"; Fowler, *A New Engagement*; Richard Mouw, *Political Evangelism* (Grand Rapids: Eerdmans, 1973), p. 7; Mouw, *Politics and the Biblical Drama* (Grand Rapids: Eerdmans, 1976); Edward Gilbreath, "A Prophet Out of Harlem," *Christianity Today*, 16 September 1996, www.ctlibrary.com/ct/1996/september16/6ta036 .html.

Right had thrown the balance of evangelical public opinion behind Ronald Reagan. Dismayed with Jimmy Carter's positions on the family and school prayer, evangelicals largely abandoned him for the Gipper. Since the late seventies, the religious right has been identified with the issues of abortion and homosexuality. On abortion in particular, one book published in 1979, C. Everett Koop and Francis Schaeffer's *Whatever Happened to the Human Race?*, galvanized evangelical thought.[44]

Although the fight against abortion came to dominate the New Christian Right, there were other issues on the table. For starters, the persistence of high inflation and anemic growth under Carter led many to embrace Reagan's supply-side economics. Though the economy was never their main focus, Jerry Falwell and Pat Robertson celebrated the free market. In *Listen, America!* (1980) Falwell quoted Milton Friedman's critique of the "overgoverned society." Robertson concurred, noting that "the struggles and strivings and aspirations of a society" take place in the marketplace. According to Robertson, the government "should only interfere with that market to keep certain individuals from harming others."[45]

These positions had deep roots in mid-century evangelicalism. In *From Bible Belt to Sunbelt*, Darren Dochuk notes that free-market thought developed a strong following among college-educated evangelicals, who devoured "classic treatises by Friedrich von Hayek and Russell Kirk, or recent hits like Ayn Rand's *Atlas Shrugged*." Evangelical educators affirmed the promise of American capitalism. While Harding College's George Benson promoted conservative economics, Pepperdine University played host to Buckley and Friedman. Similar attitudes could be found in the Wheaton president's office, where

44. My account of the rightward turn of public evangelicalism draws on Swartz, "Left Behind"; Robert Wuthnow, *The Restructuring of American Religion* (Princeton, NJ: Princeton University Press, 1989); William Martin, *With God on Their Side: The Rise of the Religious Right in America* (New York: Random House, 2005); C. Everett Koop and Francis Schaeffer, *Whatever Happened to the Human Race?* (Old Tappan, NJ: Revell, 1979).

45. Michael Lienesch, *Redeeming America: Piety and Politics in the New Christian Right* (Chapel Hill: University of North Carolina Press, 1993), p. 121; Jerry Falwell, *Listen, America!* (New York: Doubleday, 1980), p. 80; Milton and Rose Friedman, *Free to Choose: A Personal Statement* (New York: Harcourt Brace Jovanovich, 1979); Pat Robertson, *The Collected Works of Pat Robertson* (New York: Inspirational, 1994), p. 29. This quotation originally appeared in Robertson's *The New Millennium: 10 Trends That Will Impact You and Your Family* (Lightning Source, 1990).

V. Raymond Edman wrote that "the Scriptures teach capitalism and not Communism."[46]

Though evangelical scholars could be found across the political spectrum, many embraced libertarian and conservative economics. In the 1980s, several published critiques of the evangelical left. A response to Ron Sider's *Rich Christians in an Age of Hunger* (1978), David Chilton's *Productive Christians in an Age of Guilt Manipulators* (1981) made heavy use of Hayek and Mises. In *Is Capitalism Christian?* (1985), Franky Schaeffer reprinted Richard John Neuhaus's scathing review of Nicholas Wolterstorff's *Until Justice and Peace Embrace* (1983). Sometimes these critiques were justified. In the fifth edition of *Rich Christians* (2005), Sider acknowledged his economic naïveté, noting that "first-rate economists have provided extensive advice over the course of the several editions." In *Idols for Destruction* (1983), Herbert Schlossberg made a similar point, arguing that "Sider has not bothered to learn anything about the economic processes on which he expresses such strong positions." Articulating a different conception of the welfare state, Schlossberg likened government redistribution to theft, drawing on the nineteenth-century French philosopher Frédéric Bastiat.[47]

In 1990 Sider and Schlossberg came together for a conference on religion and the economy. An opportunity for frank conversation, it produced the Oxford Declaration on Christian Faith and Economics, a statement issued by over one hundred scholars and practitioners. Although he had been initially skeptical, Wheaton economist Peter J. Hill concluded, "the final document did not represent just empty rhetoric."

---

46. Dochuk, *From Bible Belt to Sunbelt*, p. 187. This paragraph draws heavily on Dochuk's account. The Edman quotation is from Earle Cairns, *V. Raymond Edman: In the Presence of the King* (Chicago: Moody, 1972), p. 204. It originally appeared in Edman, "Spiritual Clinic," *Christian Life*, June 1957, p. 104.

47. Craig Gay, *With Liberty and Justice for Whom? The Recent Evangelical Debate Over Capitalism* (Grand Rapids: Eerdmans, 1991); John E. Anderson, "Economics and the Evangelical Mind," *Bulletin of the Association of Christian Economists*, Fall 1996, pp. 5-24; David Chilton, *Productive Christians in an Age of Guilt Manipulators* (Tyler, TX: Institute for Christian Economics, 1981); Richard John Neuhaus, "The Goal Is Not to Describe: A Review of Nicholas Wolterstorff's *Until Justice and Peace Embrace*," in *Is Capitalism Christian?* ed. Franky Schaeffer (Westchester, IL: Crossway, 1985), pp. 449-56. Herbert Schlossberg is discussed in Lienesch, *Redeeming America*, p. 120. See Schlossberg, *Idols for Destruction: The Conflict of Christian Faith and American Culture* (Nashville: Thomas Nelson, 1983); Ronald Sider, *Rich Christians in an Age of Hunger*, 5th ed. (Nashville: Thomas Nelson, 2005).

To Hill, it was "interesting to see some members from the left agree that inflation and protectionism were truly significant problems" and conservatives and libertarians agree that "the culture of capitalism can be decidedly non-Christian and that there can be undue concentrations of wealth and power under markets."[48] Despite these concessions, deep divisions remained between left and right.

Like their counterparts in academia, ordinary evangelicals have adopted a wide range of economic positions. Although surveys have documented a shift to the right, this is a relatively recent development. From the populism of William Jennings Bryan to the Huey Long–style movements of California fundamentalists, conservative Protestants have always included an egalitarian tradition. Such views persisted well into the 1990s. Analyzing General Social Survey data from the late 1980s, economist Laurence Iannaccone noted that most "rank and file evangelical-fundamentalists are not economic conservatives." Likewise, a 1992 survey found that evangelicals supported "tough environmental regulations, comprehensive health insurance, and efforts to ease poverty and hunger." In spite of these commitments, white evangelical Protestants voted overwhelmingly for Ronald Reagan and George H. W. Bush, drawn to their positions on abortion and family values. In "It's the Culture, Stupid! 1992 and Our Political Future," political scientists Lyman Kellstedt, John Green, James Guth, and Corwin Smidt argued that the "conventional wisdom on the role of economic factors in elections is overstated." Surveys of Protestant clergy from the same period revealed that Baptist and Pentecostal ministers rarely addressed economic issues. While a regular theme in mainline Protestant preaching, they were missing from evangelical sermons.[49]

48. Herbert Schlossberg, Vinay Samuel, and Ronald J. Sider, eds., *Christianity and Economics in the Post–Cold War Era* (Grand Rapids: Eerdmans, 1994). Peter J. Hill's comments can be found in the chapter entitled "Information, Values, and Government Action," pp. 100-101.

49. On the contemporary overlap of the Tea Party movement and Christian conservatives, see Robert Jones and Daniel Cox, *Religion and the Tea Party in the 2010 Election* (Washington, DC, 2010), http://www.publicreligion.org/objects/uploads/fck/file /AVS%202010%20Report%20FINAL.pdf. See also "Survey: Plurality of Americans Believe Capitalism at Odds with Christian Values," http://www.publicreligion.org/research /published/?id=554. On the Huey Long–style "Ham and Eggs" movement in southern California, see Dochuk, *From Bible Belt to Sunbelt*; Laurence R. Iannaccone, "Heirs to the Protestant Ethic? The Economics of American Fundamentalists," in *Fundamentalisms and the State: Remaking Polities, Economies, and Militance* (Chicago: University of Chicago

Economic issues were also missing from the early histories of the religious right. In most accounts, the movement began with a skirmish over education. In 1974, Kanawha County, West Virginia, parents fought over the content of public school textbooks. While some of the offending works contained overt sexual material, others were perceived as anti-American. In the words of a local pastor, "These books challenged the sacredness of everything we believed about America. I'm sure that America's wrong at times, but we believe it's the best thing we've come across in this world."[50] With the rise of Jerry Falwell and the Moral Majority came a new emphasis on America's sacred past. While Falwell led "I Love America" rallies on the steps of forty-four state capitols, evangelicals imagined a new history of America. In *The Light and the Glory*, Peter Marshall and David Manuel described "God's plan for America." Drawing on a long tradition of American civil religion, they depicted the colonists as God's chosen people and the United States as a new Promised Land. According to the authors, "In the virgin wilderness of America, God was making His most significant attempt since ancient Israel to create a new Israel of people living in obedience to the laws of God." Like many evangelical leaders, they exaggerated the Christian beliefs of the founding fathers.[51]

Press, 1996), p. 342; Lyman Kellstedt, John Green, James Guth, and Corwin Smidt, "American Evangelicals: Left and Right," *ESA Advocate*, April 1993, pp. 1-4. On the dominance of moral over economic issues in evangelical voting, see Lyman Kellstedt, John Green, James Guth, and Corwin Smidt, "It's the Culture, Stupid! 1992 and Our Political Future," *First Things*, April 1994, pp. 28-33; James Guth, John Green, Corwin Smidt, Lyman Kellstedt, and Margaret Poloma, *The Bully Pulpit: The Politics of Protestant Clergy* (Lawrence: University Press of Kansas, 1997), p. 83. I develop some of the themes from this paragraph in John Schmalzbauer, "It's the Economy *and* the Culture, Stupid!" 18 January 2008, *The Immanent Frame*; accessed 30 May 2011, http://blogs.ssrc.org/tif/2008/01/18 /it%e2%80%99s-the-economy-and-the-culture-stupid/.

50. Martin, *With God on Their Side*, p. 123. William Martin includes only a handful of references to religion and free enterprise. Although the evangelical discovery of neo-classical economics gets a little more attention in Daniel K. Williams's *God's Own Party: The Making of the New Christian Right* (New York: Oxford University Press, 2010), it is not a major theme. By contrast, Michael Lienesch devotes an entire chapter to economics in *Redeeming America*, pp. 94-138. Citing Paul Weyrich, Randall Balmer dates the birth of the religious right to a 1975 effort to preserve the tax-exempt status of Bob Jones University. See Balmer, *Thy Kingdom Come, An Evangelical's Lament: How the Religious Right Distorts the Faith and Threatens America* (New York: Basic, 2006), pp. 13-15.

51. Peter Marshall and David Manuel, *The Light and the Glory* (Grand Rapids: Revell, 1977), pp. 25, 23.

Taking issue with this populist historiography, a trio of evangelical historians rejected the revisionism of *The Light and the Glory*. In *The Search for Christian America*, Mark Noll, Nathan Hatch, and George Marsden argued that "a careful study of the facts of history shows that early America does not deserve to be considered uniquely, distinctly or even predominately Christian, if we mean by the word 'Christian' a state of society reflecting the ideals presented in Scripture." Noting the influence of deism on the founding fathers and the absence of theological reasoning in the founding documents, they wrote that "there is no lost golden age to which American Christians may return."[52]

In some way, this struggle to define America's past was a reflection of class differences within the evangelical subculture. Commenting on the West Virginia textbook battle, Calvin Trillin wrote that working-class evangelicals felt "that they and their religious beliefs were being mocked by those who were educated and powerful," adding "they were right, of course." Boasting earned doctorates from Yale, Vanderbilt, and Washington Universities, Marsden, Noll, and Hatch were separated from the populist right by a substantial gap in education. Part of an "emerging evangelical intelligentsia," they were caught between their religious subculture and the guild of professional historians. By contrast, the New Christian Right was being led by a cadre of Southern televangelists, most of whom lacked advanced education.[53]

At the same time, there were indications that the battle over American history was being waged *within* the evangelical intelligentsia itself. One of the chief theoreticians for the Christian right was apologist Francis Schaeffer. A pupil of J. Gresham Machen, Schaeffer shared a direct theological bloodline with George Marsden, whose father had studied with the Presbyterian controversialist. Like many evangelical scholars, Schaeffer and his son Franky had been profoundly influenced by the 1960s, welcoming Led Zeppelin's Jimmy Page to their Swiss compound.

52. Mark Noll, Nathan Hatch, and George Marsden, *The Search for Christian America* (Colorado Springs, CO: Helmers and Howard, 1989), p. 17. It was originally published by Crossway Books in 1983. On the rising influence of Southern televangelists during the 1970s and 1980s, see Wuthnow, *The Restructuring of American Religion*, pp. 194-97.

53. Calvin Trillin is quoted in Sam Tanenhaus, "God and Politics, Together Again," *New York Times*, 4 September 2010, http://www.nytimes.com/2010/09/05/weekinreview /05tanenhaus.html?pagewanted=2. See the Emerging Evangelical Intelligentsia Project at Boston University. Noll and Marsden spoke at the project's 2007 conference, described at http://www.bu.edu/cura/calendar/eeip/.

As Franky later recalled, "we Schaeffers had *become* these hippies." In *How Should We Then Live?* his father engaged the popular culture of the times, including Federico Fellini's *Juliet of the Spirits* and Bob Dylan's *Blonde on Blonde*. In *A Christian Manifesto*, he argued that Dylan and the Scottish theologian Samuel Rutherford "would have understood each other," clinching his argument with a quote from *Slow Train Coming*.[54]

While introducing American evangelicals to a new style of cultural criticism, Schaeffer often got things dead wrong. Hip references to Bob Dylan aside, his claim that Samuel Rutherford strongly influenced the founding fathers had little basis in fact. In a 1982 interview with *Newsweek*, Mark Noll criticized Schaeffer's approach to history, telling Kenneth Woodward, "The danger is that people will take him for a scholar, which he is not. Evangelical historians are especially bothered by his simplified myth of America's Christian past." Despite their shared theological DNA, Schaeffer and the evangelical historians became embroiled in a passionate debate over American history, recently chronicled by Barry Hankins. Conducted through private correspondence and Schaeffer's subsequent books, it underscored a continuing theme in evangelical intellectual life: the tension between credentialed scholars and popular experts. In *The Anointed: Evangelical Truth in a Secular Age*, Randall Stephens and Karl Giberson note that "charismatic and media-savvy creationists, historians, psychologists, and biblical exegetes continue to receive more funding and airtime than their more qualified counterparts." Not surprisingly, Schaeffer's works sold much better than *The Search for Christian America*. In *Bad News for Modern Man*, Franky Schaeffer lashed out at the Christian academy, noting that "we find many evangelical historians such as George Marsden and Ronald Wells of Calvin College joining the revisionist throng and downplaying America's Judeo-Christian heritage."[55]

---

54. The next two paragraphs draw extensively on Barry Hankins, *Francis Schaeffer and the Shaping of Evangelical America* (Grand Rapids: Eerdmans, 2008). Frank Schaeffer, *Crazy for God*, p. 216. See also Preston Shires, *Hippies of the Religious Right* (Waco, TX: Baylor University Press, 2007); Francis Schaeffer, *How Should We Then Live? The Rise and Decline of Western Thought and Culture* (Old Tappan, NJ: Revell, 1976); Francis Schaeffer, *A Christian Manifesto* (Westchester, IL: Crossway, 1981), p. 105. For an account of Marsden's father and J. Gresham Machen, see Schmalzbauer, *People of Faith*, p. 94. See also Barry Hankins, "The Mark of a Schaefferite: The Lasting Influence of Francis Schaeffer," available at http://www.qideas.org/blog/the-mark-of-a-schaefferite.aspx.

55. Hankins, *Francis Schaeffer*, pp. 211-19. The Noll quote appears in Kenneth

This was a false accusation. Strong believers in biblical authority, the evangelical historians wanted to preserve the integrity of the Christian faith. In their view, the myth of Christian America risked conflating the biblical narrative with the story of the United States. While acknowledging America's "flight from morality and godliness," they urged evangelicals to resist the temptation to romanticize the past. Such myth making was not just bad history. It was bad theology. In *A History of Christianity in the United States and Canada,* Noll argued that the end of "Christian America" could be viewed as both "a blessing as well as a tragedy." By freeing themselves "from the burden of American messianism," he wrote, "churches may find it possible to concentrate more on the Source of Life than on the American Way of Life."[56]

Yet, by questioning the myth of Christian America, Noll and Marsden put themselves in a difficult spot. When the Schaeffers accused Wheaton and Calvin of selling out to secularism, it hit close to home. The fact that Noll went to church with their editor at Crossway Books led to tensions in local congregational life. To be sure, both historians were acquainted with theological conflict. In the 1930s, Marsden's father followed J. Gresham Machen out of Princeton Seminary into the tiny Orthodox Presbyterian Church. Along the same lines, Mark Noll has lived within shouting distance of fundamentalism. As he told me in a 1994 interview, "I have been close enough to some of the fundamentalist Bible wars to really feel fried." Perhaps Noll was feeling fried when he wrote *The Scandal of the Evangelical Mind,* published in the following year. Billed as "an epistle from a wounded lover," it was dedicated to the faculty and trustees of Wheaton College, "where we together fight the fights and inflict, sometimes on each other, the wounds that are the subject of this book." Noll's heartfelt plea echoed the passionate polem-

---

Woodward, "The Guru of Fundamentalism," *Newsweek,* 1 November 1982, p. 88. According to Hankins, Noll later regretted this statement. The quotation from Karl Giberson and Randall Stephens comes from the Harvard University Press description of their book *The Anointed: Evangelical Truth in a Secular Age* (Cambridge, MA: Harvard University Press, 2011). See http://www.hup.harvard.edu/catalog.php?isbn=9780674048188. The Schaeffer quote is from Franky Schaeffer, *Bad News for Modern Man* (Wheaton, IL: Crossway, 1984).

56. Noll, Hatch, and Marsden, *Search for Christian America,* p. 14; Mark Noll, *A History of Christianity in the United States and Canada* (Grand Rapids: Eerdmans, 1992), p. 552.

ics of Carl Henry and Edward J. Carnell. Like their post-war critiques, his analysis was a response to evangelicalism's right flank.[57]

Ironically, the current renaissance of evangelical intellectual life owes much of its vitality to the Moral Majority and the Christian Coalition. By putting religion and politics back on the national agenda, these populist movements fostered a curiosity about the history and culture of evangelicalism. While distancing themselves from the religious right, evangelical scholars were able to capitalize on its prominence. Published in 1980, Marsden's *Fundamentalism and American Culture* coincided with the electoral triumph of Ronald Reagan and the Moral Majority. Suddenly, it became fashionable to study religious conservatives. Sponsored by the University of Chicago, the multivolume Fundamentalism Project was funded by the MacArthur Foundation. Wondering why a progressive foundation would pour millions of dollars into the study of fundamentalism, sociologist Peter Berger concluded that it "was a matter of knowing one's enemies."[58]

For evangelical scholars, it was a matter of knowing one's relatives. Few organizations contributed more to this effort than did the Institute for the Study of American Evangelicals (ISAE) at Wheaton College. Beginning with the Bible in American Culture conference in 1979, ISAE inaugurated a thirty-year tradition of academic excellence. Foundation support from the Pew Charitable Trusts and the Lilly Endowment played a key role in facilitating the rise of the "new evangelical historiography." In ways that no one could anticipate, J. Howard Pew (who died in 1971) continued to shape the development of evangelical intellectual life. An early backer of conservative causes, his foundation now bankrolled the critical study of the New Christian Right. I was an undergraduate during the golden age of the ISAE. During the late eighties, the college was blessed with the presence of Edith Blumhofer, Joel Carpenter, Larry Eskridge, Daryl Hart, Lyman Kellstedt, Roger Lundin, James Mathisen, and Mark Noll. Together with their colleagues in other institutions, these scholars helped revitalize the study of religion and American culture. By 1991 historian Jon Butler could describe the

---

57. For a discussion of the tensions in Noll's congregation, see Hankins, *Francis Schaeffer*, p. 221. On Marsden and Machen, see Schmalzbauer, *People of Faith*, p. 94. The quote about Wheaton is from Mark Noll, *Scandal of the Evangelical Mind*, p. ix.

58. Marsden, *Fundamentalism and American Culture*; Peter Berger, "The Desecularization of the World: A Global Overview," in *The Desecularization of the World: Resurgent Religion and World Politics*, ed. Peter Berger (Grand Rapids: Eerdmans, 1999), p. 2.

"evangelical paradigm" as "the *single* most powerful explanatory device adopted by academic historians to account for the distinctive features of American society, culture, and identity." Around the same time, my mentor Lyman Kellstedt helped political scientists rediscover the religious factor in American elections.[59]

To be sure, Wheaton's faculty was not afraid to criticize the evangelical subculture. In *The Scandal of the Evangelical Mind,* Noll offered a withering critique of the "intellectual disaster of fundamentalism." Yet that was not his last word. During a three-year project on the history of American hymnody, Wheaton celebrated what Noll called "evangelicalism at its best," sounding the depths of love divine. In *Her Heart Can See: The Life and Hymns of Fanny J. Crosby,* Edith Blumhofer told the story of America's most prolific hymn writer, giving serious attention to a woman often ignored by academic historians. Grounded in extensive archival research, Blumhofer's study was also enriched by childhood memories. In a moving piece on her family's congregation in Brooklyn, she recalled singing Crosby's "All the Way My Savior Leads Me" prior to her great-uncle's departure for Europe. Along the same lines, Richard Mouw offered "an evangelical testimony about the importance of hymns" in the introduction to *Wonderful Words of Life.* Like Paul Holmer's memories of Swedish string bands, this project was an act of remembrance. Such *anamnesis* could be seen at an author-meets-critics session on Joel Carpenter's *Revive Us Again,* a history of mid-century fundamentalism. One of the reviewers commented on the frequent appearance of gospel lyrics in Carpenter's account. At that point the panel nearly burst into song.[60]

59. For more on the history of ISAE, see the discussion of its founders at http:// isae.wheaton.edu/about/founders/. The quote is from Jon Butler, "Born-Again America? A Critique of the New 'Evangelical Thesis' in Recent American Historiography," unpublished paper, Organization of American Historians, Spring 1991, as quoted in Harry Stout and Robert Taylor Jr., "Studies of Religion in American Society: The State of the Art," in *New Directions in American Religious History,* ed. Harry S. Stout and D. G. Hart (New York: Oxford University Press, 1997), p. 19. On religion and political science, see David Leege and Lyman Kellstedt, eds., *Rediscovering the Religious Factor in American Politics* (Armonk, NY: M. E. Sharpe, 1993); Kenneth D. Wald, Adam L. Silverman, and Kevin S. Fridy, "Making Sense of Religion in Political Life," *Annual Review of Political Science* 8 (2005): 121-43.

60. Noll, *Scandal of the Evangelical Mind,* p. 109; Noll, "We Are What We Sing," *Christianity Today,* 12 July 1999, http://www.christianitytoday.com/ct/1999/july12/9t8037 .html; Edith Blumhofer, *Her Heart Can See: The Life and Hymns of Fanny J. Crosby* (Grand

Beyond the hymnbook, evangelical scholars found other ways to tell the old, old story. Influenced by the post-liberal theology of Hans Frei and George Lindbeck (Yale colleagues of Paul Holmer), they recovered the arc of the Christian storyline. This recovery could be seen in the 2006 Call to an Ancient Evangelical Future, which proclaimed "the primacy of the Biblical narrative." This document urged evangelicals to "restore the priority of the divinely inspired story of God's acts in history." Shaped by N. T. Wright's five-act hermeneutic of creation/fall/Israel/Jesus/church, others have stressed the "urgency of reading the Bible as one story." By putting this five-act play at the center of human history, evangelical theologians have resisted the temptation to view America as the kingdom of God. In many cases, the return of the biblical narrative has been accompanied by a rediscovery of liturgical worship. This shift has also served as a corrective to Christian nationalism, subordinating the calendar of American civil religion to the church year. By looking to Canterbury, Rome, and Constantinople, along with Wittenberg and Geneva, evangelical scholars have learned from the great traditions. In the process, they have renewed their own tradition of American Protestantism.[61]

Rapids: Eerdmans, 2005); Blumhofer, "Biographical Sketch," on a website dedicated to Hans R. Waldvogel, http://www.hanswaldvogel.com/biography.html; Richard Mouw, introduction to *Wonderful Words of Life*, p. xiii; Carpenter, *Revive Us Again*. I was present at the author-meets-critics session for Carpenter's book.

61. Timothy Phillips and Dennis Okholm, eds., *The Nature of Confession: Evangelicals and Postliberals in Conversation* (Downers Grove, IL: InterVarsity, 1996); Stanley Hauerwas and L. Gregory Jones, eds., *Why Narrative? Readings in Narrative Theology* (Grand Rapids: Eerdmans, 1989); the 2006 "Call to an Ancient Evangelical Future" is available at http://www.aefcall.org/read.html; N. T. Wright, *The Last Word: Scripture and the Authority of God — Getting Beyond the Bible Wars* (New York: HarperCollins, 2005), p. 121; Michael W. Goheen, "The Urgency of Reading the Bible as One Story," *Theology Today* 68, no. 1 (2008): 469-83; Richard T. Hughes, *Christian America and the Kingdom of God* (Champaign: University of Illinois Press, 2009); Stanley Hauerwas, "A Christian Critique of Christian America," in *The Hauerwas Reader*, ed. John Berkman and Michael Cartwright (Durham, NC: Duke University Press, 2001), pp. 459-80; Robert Webber, *Evangelicals on the Canterbury Trail: Why Evangelicals Are Attracted to the Liturgical Church* (Waco, TX: Word, 1985); Charles W. Colson and Richard John Neuhaus, *Evangelicals and Catholics Together: Toward a Common Mission* (Dallas, TX: Word, 1995); William M. Shea, *The Lion and the Lamb: Evangelicals and Catholics in America* (New York: Oxford University Press, 2004); D. H. Williams, *Retrieving the Tradition and Renewing Evangelicalism: A Primer for Suspicious Protestants* (Grand Rapids: Eerdmans, 1999). See also Kevin Vanhoozer's *The Drama of Doctrine: A Canonical Linguistic Approach to Christian Theology* (Louisville: Westminster John Knox, 2005).

Like the Harvard fundamentalists, the evangelical intellectuals who came of age during the sixties wanted to remember and forget. Parting company with Richard Nixon, they remembered the political radicalism of their nineteenth-century forebears, rediscovering a heritage of social reform. Exploring the ambiguities of American capitalism, they agreed to disagree. Rejecting the religious nationalism of the Moral Majority and the Christian Coalition, they did not depict them as enemies. Dumping out the bathwater of evangelical anti-intellectualism, they held on to the baby of evangelical hymnody. There is no better symbol of this complicated interchange than Mark Noll's autobiographical reflections in the *Christian Century.* Recalling that in "Sunday School more than 50 years ago we used to sing, 'Deep and wide, deep and wide, there's a fountain flowing deep and wide,'" he noted that "this simple chorus comes close to describing how my mind has changed over the last four decades." Like Noll, evangelicalism has opened its mind to the wider world, while drawing on a deep well of Christian piety and thought.[62]

The Uneasy Conscience in the Twenty-First Century

Over sixty years have passed since Carl F. H. Henry wrote *The Uneasy Conscience of Modern Fundamentalism,* twenty since he came home to say goodbye. The year 2010 also marked the twentieth anniversary of my graduation from Wheaton College. Every time I return to Wheaton, my mind floods with memories. My class reunion was no exception. The 2010 homecoming verse was taken from Psalm 145: "One generation will commend Your works to another; they will tell of Your mighty acts." After spending the summer reading about post-war evangelicalism, I was ready to contemplate the past. Spotting Williston Hall (where I lived during the summer of 1988), I recalled the hours Edward Carnell spent washing dishes in the 1930s. Walking past Pierce Chapel, I remembered that William Bell Riley preached Charles Blanchard's eulogy there in 1925.[63]

Much has changed since Carl Henry criticized the *Wheaton Record* for debating the morality of the card game Rook while the nations played with fire. Six decades later, the same paper featured a story on

62. Mark Noll, "Deep and Wide," *Christian Century,* 1 June 2010, p. 30.
63. Psalm 145:4 was also the sesquicentennial verse for 2009.

incoming President Philip Ryken's global studies initiative, while *Wheaton* magazine profiled Haitian Ambassador Raymond Joseph, a member of the class of 1960. A candidate for the presidency of his nation, Joseph helped Haiti recover from a devastating earthquake. During reunions, members of the class of 1990 received a copy of Professor David Maas's *Marching to the Drumbeat of Abolitionism: Wheaton College in the Civil War*, a reminder of evangelicalism's radical past. Likewise, the exhibit area in the new science center featured a call to protect all God's creatures, discussing the importance of environmental stewardship. Clearly, Wheaton has become more socially engaged.[64]

What has happened at Wheaton has also happened to American evangelicalism. At InterVarsity's 2006 Urbana student missions conference, the program testified to a heightened concern with global poverty, HIV/AIDS, and racial reconciliation. Speaker after speaker challenged evangelicals to respond to the world's suffering. After U2's Bono appeared via satellite, thousands of Urbana goers texted the ONE campaign, illuminating the stadium with their cell phones. In a 2006 survey conducted by the National Study of Campus Ministries, 87 percent of InterVarsity staff agreed that social justice is at the heart of the gospel. In 1947 Henry lamented the "evaporation of fundamentalist humanitarianism." Such a critique could not be made today.[65]

And yet evangelicalism continues to possess an uneasy conscience, reflecting enduring tensions in American religion, politics, and culture. In the space that remains, I would like to discuss three sources of uneasiness. None is entirely new. All require the attention of evangelical scholars.

The first is the persistence of conspiratorial themes in evangelical discourse. In 2008 televangelist Bill Keller suggested that the Obama campaign logo fulfilled a Muslim prophecy predicting a sun rising in the West. In 2009 a Keller infomercial questioned the president's citizen-

---

64. Henry, *The Uneasy Conscience of Modern Fundamentalism*, p. 7; Caroline Dolman, "Wheaton Explores Global Learning," *Wheaton Record*, 1 October 2010, p. 1; Alanna Fowell Barajas, "Rebuilding Haiti," *Wheaton*, Autumn 2010, pp. 20-23; David Maas, *Marching to the Drumbeat of Abolitionism: Wheaton College in the Civil War* (Wheaton, IL: Wheaton College, 2010).

65. John Schmalzbauer, "Social Engagement in an Evangelical Campus Ministry: The Case of Urbana 2006," *Journal of College and Character* 11, no. 1 (2010), http:// journals.naspa.org/jcc/vol11/iss1/12/; Henry, *The Uneasy Conscience of Modern Fundamentalism*, p. 1.

ship, airing in a dozen television markets. At first glance, the fact that 29 percent of white evangelicals believe Barack Obama is a Muslim would seem to come out of nowhere. The same goes for the belief that Obama is the Antichrist, affirmed by a significant minority of Americans.[66] Yet a review of the evangelical prophecy literature reveals that these allegations are not new. In the 1930s, Gerald Winrod argued that Franklin Roosevelt was a Jew. So did Gerald L. K. Smith. In the 1960s, some suggested that John F. Kennedy was the Antichrist. In the 1990s, Pat Robertson advanced conspiracy theories about international bankers and the Trilateral Commission. When evangelicals talk about Obama's alleged secret Muslim identity, they are channeling their predecessors.[67]

The second cause for uneasiness is the continuing appeal of bad history. Commenting on a recent poll, historian John Fea notes that evangelical scholars seem to "have done very little to curb the Christian nation crowd." Wheaton alumnus and Bush speechwriter Michael Gerson makes a similar point in the *Washington Post*, lamenting the fact that 55 percent of Tea Party supporters believe that "America has always been and is currently a Christian nation." Instead of listening to Mark Noll and George Marsden, the evangelical community has been swayed by the writings of amateur historians David Barton and Peter Marshall.

---

66. "Is Senator Barack Hussein Obama the Fulfillment of Islamic Prophecy?" Daily Devotional, 8 August 2008, available at http://www.liveprayer.com/ddarchive3 .cfm?id=3411. Keller's organization claims to have over 2.5 million subscribers to its Daily Devotional emails. He earned a General Studies degree from Liberty University, focusing on journalism and biblical studies. See "A Prodigal Son Turns Preacher," *Liberty University News*, http://www.liveprayer.com/press/lib.htm. For more on Keller's television spots, see Justin Elliott, "New Birther Infomercial Running in Seven Southern States," Talking Points Memo, 25 September 2009, http://tpmmuckraker.talking pointsmemo.com/2009/09/new_birther_infomercial_running_in_seven_southern .php; "Growing Number of Americans Say Obama Is a Muslim," Pew Research Center report, 19 August 2010, http://people-press.org/reports/pdf/645.pdf. A poll by Harris Interactive found that 14 percent of Americans and 24 percent of Republicans believe that Obama is the Antichrist. See Nick Allen, "Quarter of Republicans Think Barack Obama Is 'the Antichrist,'" *Telegraph*, 25 March 2010. For a discussion of the flawed methodology of this survey, see Gary Langer, "Polling on Presidential Pejoratives," ABC News, 24 March 2010, http://blogs.abcnews.com/thenumbers/2010/03/polling -on-presidential-pejoratives-.html.

67. Fuller, *Naming the Antichrist*, pp. 141, 147; Pat Robertson, *The New World Order* (Waco, TX: Word, 1991); David Edwin Harrell, *Pat Robertson: A Life and Legacy* (Grand Rapids: Eerdmans, 2010), pp. 289-93. According to Harrell, Robertson's *The New World Order* sold 500,000 copies.

Their influence can be seen in the Texas State Board of Education, where both have served as consultants, and in Barton's regular appearances on Glenn Beck's radio and television broadcasts. A convert to Mormonism, Beck has also promoted the works of the late W. Cleon Skousen, a supporter of the John Birch Society who once taught at Brigham Young University. In *The Five Thousand Year Leap*, Skousen echoes British Israelism, noting that the Anglo-Saxons may have "included a branch of the ancient Israelites."[68]

A third reason for uneasiness lies in the way evangelicals have been depicted in the media and academia. In the 1920s, journalist H. L. Mencken dubbed fundamentalists the "gaping primates of the upland valleys." In the 1960s, Richard Hofstadter used evangelicals as the poster children for his *Anti-Intellectualism in American Life*. In 1993 the *Washington Post* called conservative Protestants "largely poor, uneducated, and easy to command." More recently, books like *American Theocracy* and *Republican Gomorrah* have portrayed evangelicals as a sinister force in American life. A colorful chart in *Mother Jones* offers more of the same, purporting to diagram the networks of the New Christian Right. In the *Mother Jones* version of American evangelicalism, outfits like the Chalcedon Foundation loom larger than life. In reality, most evangelicals have never heard of them.[69]

68. John Fea, "The Staying Power of Christian America," *Religion in American History*, 25 September 2007, http://usreligion.blogspot.com/2007/09/john-fea-staying -power-of-christian.html; Michael Gerson, "Christine O'Donnell's Misconception of the Constitution," *Washington Post*, 22 October 2010, http://www.washingtonpost.com /wp-dyn/content/article/2010/10/21/AR2010102104858.html; Marshall and Manuel, *The Light and the Glory*; David Barton, *America's Godly Heritage* (Aledo, TX: WallBuilders, 1993); Joshunda Sanders, "Christianity's Role in History of U.S. at Issue," *Austin American-Statesman*, 10 January 2010, http://www.statesman.com/news/texas-politics /christianitys-role-in-history-of-u-s-at-172516.html; Alexander Zaitchik, "Meet the Man Who Changed Glenn Beck's Life," *Salon*, 16 September 2009, www.salon.com /news/feature/2009/09/16/beck_skousen; Joanna Brooks, "How Mormonism Built Glenn Beck," *Religion Dispatches*, 7 October 2009, www.religiondispatches.org/archive /politics/1885/; W. Cleon Skousen, "The Mystery of the Anglo-Saxons," Appendix A, *The Five Thousand Year Leap* (Franklin, TN: American Documents, 2009), p. 226; originally published in 1981. In the 1980s, Jerry Falwell enrolled his staff in Skousen's courses. In 2010 Glenn Beck was the commencement speaker at Liberty University. On Falwell and Skousen, see Zaitchik, *Common Nonsense: Glenn Beck and the Triumph of Ignorance* (Hoboken, NJ: Wiley, 2010), p. 226.

69. H. L. Mencken quoted in Marsden, *Fundamentalism and American Culture*, p. 187; Richard Hofstadter, *Anti-Intellectualism in American Life* (New York: Vintage

How should evangelical scholars respond to these developments? When it comes to Barack Obama, they might do well to follow the example of Cathleen Falsani, who made an honest attempt to explore the president's faith. A reporter for the *Chicago Sun-Times*, Falsani took a novel approach: she asked him about his beliefs. The man she uncovered is a hybrid of liberal Protestantism and the black church. While evangelicals may disagree with Obama on theology and politics, he is not all that different from previous occupants of the White House. Of course, this may not be enough. On several occasions, televangelists Jack and Rexella Van Impe have implied that the president may be the Antichrist, mixing talk about shadowy elites with faulty biblical exegesis. Familiar with Falsani's interview, they have used it to bolster their attacks. In the end, only better eschatology will rescue evangelicalism from wild speculation about the end times.[70]

What about bad history? Addressing a popular audience, historian John Fea has written *Was America Founded as a Christian Nation?*, a careful effort to get at the role of faith in the American founding. Unfortunately, a book from Westminster/John Knox is unlikely to reach most evangelicals. Far more effective was Baylor University historian Thomas Kidd's appearance on the Glenn Beck show. A student of Marsden, Kidd bridges the gap between professional historians and ordinary evangelicals, 48 percent of whom admire Beck. In *God of Liberty: A Religious History of the American Revolution*, Kidd has written a book that appeals to both his mentors and the viewers of Fox News, depicting the founding fathers as "neither 'Christian' nor 'godless.'" Another consummate bridge builder is classical education advocate Susan Wise

Books, 1963); Michael Weisskopf, "Energized by Pulpit or Passion, the Public Is Calling: 'Gospel Grapevine' Displays Strength in Controversy Over Military Gay Ban," *Washington Post*, 1 February 1993, A1; Max Blumenthal, *Republican Gomorrah: Inside the Movement That Shattered a Party* (New York: Nation, 2009); Kevin Phillips, *American Theocracy: The Perils and Politics of Radical Religion, Oil, and Borrowed Money in the 21st Century* (New York: Viking, 2006); Frederick Clarkson, "Expanding Universe: The Religious Right's Orbits of Influence," *Mother Jones*, December 2005, pp. 44-45.

70. Cathleen Falsani, "Obama: I Have a Deep Faith," *Chicago Sun-Times*, 5 April 2004, http://www.suntimes.com/news/falsani/726619,obamafalsani040504.article. Falsani provides more excerpts from this interview in *The God Factor: Inside the Spiritual Lives of Public People* (New York: Farrar, Straus, and Giroux, 2007). Jack and Rexella Van Impe's comments on Falsani's interview are available at http://podcast.jvim.com/video/1041.mp4. They imply that Obama may be the Antichrist in a video available at http://www.youtube.com/watch?v=nI8t-Mr_9Wo.

Bauer. The author of two world history textbooks published by W. W. Norton, she is a minor celebrity at homeschooling conventions. In a recent interview, Bauer criticized Americans for spending "maybe three times as much time on American history [as] on world history," adding that "studying world history — and then studying the place of America within that framework — gives us a much more realistic view of our place in the world."[71]

The globalization of Christian scholarship has helped to demythologize the American past. While historian Timothy Larsen has explored the world of Victorian Britain, sociologist Samuel Reimer has documented the distinctiveness of Canadian evangelicalism. Neither country believes in the myth of American chosenness. The same is true of the Latino and Asian immigrants who are transforming the face of American Christianity, people such as Amos Yong. A reputational survey of 140 Pentecostal faculty members identified Yong as the leading American scholar in that tradition. Born in Malaysia to Chinese parents, he sees America much differently from his university's founder, Pat Robertson. In a book on Pentecostalism and political theology, Yong suggests that the gospel provides a "critical principle that can orient the many voices in the civic square in ways that avoid legitimizing the ideology of any state."[72]

What can evangelical scholars do about caricatures of evangelicalism? First, they can acknowledge the grain of truth in some negative

71. John Fea, *Was America Founded as a Christian Nation?* (Louisville: Westminster John Knox, 2011); " 'Glenn Beck': Founders' Friday: George Whitefield," Fox News, 17 May 2010, www.foxnews.com/story/0,2933,592997,00.html; "New Survey: Less Than 1-in-5 Support Fox News Host Glenn Beck as Religious Leader," Public Religion Research press release available at http://www.publicreligion.org/research/published/?id=372; Thomas S. Kidd, *God of Liberty: A Religious History of the American Revolution* (New York: Basic, 2010). The phrase "neither 'Christian' nor 'godless' " comes from Mark Noll's endorsement. Susan Wise Bauer's interview with Christian Book Distributors can be found at www.christianbook.com/Christian/Books/cms_content?page=972648&sp=102656 &event=1016INT|1866480|103879&action=New+Ticket.

72. Timothy Larsen, *Contested Christianity: The Political and Social Contexts of Victorian Theology* (Waco, TX: Baylor University Press, 2004); Samuel Reimer, *Evangelicals and the Continental Divide: The Conservative Protestant Subculture in Canada and the United States* (Montreal: McGill-Queen's University Press, 2003). The reputational survey is reported in Jonathan Olson, "From the Margins to the Mainstream: The Emergence of an American *Pentecostal* Intellectual Life" (unpublished MA thesis, Missouri State University, 2008); Amos Yong, *In the Days of Caesar: Pentecostalism and Political Theology* (Grand Rapids: Eerdmans, 2010), p. 249.

accounts. To be sure, Hofstadter's "paranoid style" is one of the most overused concepts in political discourse. Yet when evangelicals concoct bizarre conspiracy theories about the New World Order, it is hard not to call them paranoid. At the same time, evangelical scholars must critique inaccurate depictions of their subculture. In *Christian America? What Evangelicals Really Want*, sociologist Christian Smith does just that, demonstrating that believers are not bent on theocracy. Likewise, Lyman Kellstedt's piece on the Falwell issue agenda shows that most evangelicals did not fall in line with the Moral Majority. Of course, some did. In *The Democratic Virtues of the Christian Right*, Jon Shields argues that Christian conservatives have made good citizens, chronicling their growing civic engagement.[73]

The most important thing we can do is to mediate between worlds. In our polarized times, few Americans have regular contact with those who think differently from themselves. As Bill Bishop argues in *The Big Sort*, "the clustering of like-minded America is tearing us apart." Studies of Amazon.com purchases indicate that readers of political bestsellers almost never purchase books from the other side of the aisle. While Tea Party activists carry around Friedrich von Hayek and Ayn Rand, Progressives consult Noam Chomsky and Howard Zinn. The same is true of cable news, where it is Fox versus MSNBC. In this respect, evangelical scholars may be different. Positioned between a conservative religious subculture and an academy that leans to the left, they have frequent interchange with both sides of the political spectrum. In a country split between red and blue, they are often purple.[74]

Political scientist Amy Black spoke to this issue in *Beyond Left and*

73. Richard Hofstadter, *The Paranoid Style in American Politics and Other Essays* (New York: Vintage, 1967); Christian Smith, *Christian America? What Evangelicals Really Want* (Berkeley: University of California Press, 2002); Lyman Kellstedt, "The Falwell Issue Agenda: Sources of Support among White Protestant Evangelicals," in *Research in the Social Scientific Study of Religion*, ed. Monte Lynn and David Moberg (Greenwich, CT: JAI, 1994), pp. 109-32; Jon Shields, *The Democratic Virtues of the Christian Right* (Princeton, NJ: Princeton University Press, 2009).

74. Bill Bishop, *The Big Sort: Why the Clustering of Like-Minded Americans Is Tearing Us Apart* (New York: Mariner, 2009); Emily Eakin, "Study Finds a Nation of Polarized Readers," *New York Times*, 13 March 2004; "Partisanship and Cable News Audiences," Pew Research Center press report, 30 October 2009, http://pewresearch.org /pubs/1395/partisanship-fox-news-and — other-cable-news-audiences. See Pepperdine University Professor Craig Detweiler's *A Purple State of Mind: Finding Middle Ground in a Divided Culture* (Eugene, OR: Harvest House, 2008).

Right. Arguing that the "diversity in the body of Christ makes room for Christians to disagree," she noted that "far too many discussions of Christianity and politics end in shouting matches instead of constructive dialogue." Recently, Wheaton hosted a conversation between *Sojourners* founder Jim Wallis and economist Arthur Brooks of the American Enterprise Institute. Sponsored by the Dennis Hastert Center for Economics, Government, and Public Policy, it focused on the question, "Does capitalism have a soul?" According to Hastert Center director Seth Norton, it was a "chance to hear two people who have a spiritual common denominator address complicated issues related to economic systems." Though Wallis and Brooks did not always see eye to eye, they were gracious in their disagreement. Finding opportunity for common ground, they affirmed the religious dimensions of economic life. In so doing, they parted company with both Randian libertarians and secular statists.[75]

I saw additional evidence of such mediation at the 2010 meeting of the Society for the Scientific Study of Religion. Held in the hometown of H. L. Mencken, it included scores of evangelical sociologists, political scientists, and psychologists. Presenting papers on religion and science, the emerging church, racial discrimination, and clergy politics, they provided a twenty-first-century rebuttal to Mencken's caricature of evangelicalism. "Heave an egg out of a Pullman train window and you will hit a Fundamentalist," Mencken wrote back in 1924. Today it might be more accurate to say, "Heave an egg into a crowd of college professors and you will hit an evangelical." According to a 2006 survey, 19 percent of American faculty identify as born-again Christians.[76]

What can a school such as Wheaton College do to foster the inte-

---

75. Amy Black, *Beyond Left and Right: Helping Christians Make Sense of American Politics* (Grand Rapids: Baker Books, 2008), pp. 24, 26. Information on the debate between Wallis and Brooks can be found in the event press release, available at http://www.wheaton.edu/news/releases/09-10_releases/10.12.10_Wallis_Brooks_Debate.html. Brooks is the author of *The Battle: How the Fight between Free Enterprise and Big Government Will Shape America's Future* (New York: Basic, 2010). Wallis's most recent book is *Rediscovering Values: On Wall Street, Main Street, and Your Street* (New York: Howard Books, 2010).

76. Marsden, *Fundamentalism and American Culture*, p. 188; Neil Gross and Solon Simmons, "How Religious Are America's College and University Professors?" Social Science Research Council web forum on "The Religious Engagements of American Undergraduates." Posted on 6 February 2007, http://religion.ssrc.org/reforum/Gross_Simmons/.

gration of faith and learning? In some ways, it can do so by doing just what it has always done. From Carl Henry in the 1940s to Mark Noll in the 1980s, Wheaton has thrived amid cultural and religious tensions. If evangelicalism is a multigenerational argument, the conversation is far from over. This side of the eschaton, evangelicals should expect no end to such debate. As sociologist James Hunter writes, "faithful Christian witness is fated to exist in the tension between the historical and the transcendent," adding that there "is no place of equilibrium between these oppositions and no satisfying resolutions. In this world, the church can never be in repose." Like the larger evangelical movement of which it forms a part, Wheaton College would do well to embrace its contentious heritage, in which it continues to discover the blessings of an uneasy conscience.[77]

77. Hunter, *To Change the World*, p. 183.

CHAPTER 3

Science and Religion: Place, Politics, and Poetics

DAVID N. LIVINGSTONE

I have to confess that I am more than a little inclined to kick off this chapter on a rather downbeat note. Let me explain.

On September 16, 2008, Professor Michael Reiss, an evolutionary biologist, resigned from his post as Director of Education for the Royal Society. What brought about his removal was some observation he had made about how science teachers should treat creationist beliefs. A day or two before Reiss turned in his resignation, on September 13, Nobel Prize–winner Sir Richard Roberts of New England Biolabs had written to Sir Martin Rees, President of the Royal Society, demanding "that Professor Reiss step down, or be asked to step down, as soon as possible." "We gather Professor Reiss is a clergyman, which in itself is very worrisome," the letter went on. "Who on earth thought that he would be an appropriate Director of Education, who could be expected to answer questions about the differences between science and religion in a scientific, reasoned way?"[1] The letter enjoyed the support of several other Laureates.

Enshrined in this communiqué is the assumption that science and religion are inescapably at odds, so much so that suspicion is necessarily thrown on the scientific integrity of individuals with religious convictions. Commenting on the whole episode in the *New Scientist*, Sir Har-

---

1. Priya Shetty and Andy Coghlan, "Royal Society Fellows Turn on Director over Creationism," *New Scientist*, 16 September 2008, http://www.newscientist.com/article /dn14744-royal-society-fellows-turn-on-director-over-creationism.html. The full text of the letter appears on Richard Dawkins's website: http://old.richarddawkins.net /articles/3119-letter-from-sir-richard-roberts-asking-reiss-to/.

old Kroto, recipient of the 1996 Nobel Prize for Chemistry, observed: "There is no way that an ordained minister — for whom unverified dogma must represent a major, if not the major, pillar in their lives can present free-thinking, doubt-based scientific philosophy honestly or disinterestedly."[2] Even Richard Dawkins felt this was going a bit too far! As he put it: "Unfortunately for him as a would-be spokesman for the Royal Society, Michael Reiss is also an ordained minister. To call for his resignation on those grounds, as several Nobel-prize-winning Fellows are now doing, comes a little too close to a witch-hunt for my squeamish taste."

And here's the cause of my sense of gloom. For all the sterling work produced by a generation of historians dismantling with forensic precision the presumptive conflict between science and religion; for all their efforts to dispel the myth of inevitable and persistent internecine warfare; for all the evidence they have amassed to show the complexity of the historical record — their work has made scarcely a dent on leading scientific spokesmen, never mind popular consciousness. The idea of inexorable struggle — like a resilient virus — is proving exceptionally hard to eradicate. As Ronald Numbers has recently put it in some reflections on the corpus of historiographical revisionism: "outside a small circle of experts the turn to complexity has left most people yawning or, worse yet, unconvinced."[3]

And so it looks like I'm now caught in a double dilemma. Not only am I starting on that downbeat note I mentioned, but if Ron's right I'm also likely to make my readers yawn. For the fact is, people just do prefer simple master-narratives to complexity and complication, subtlety and sensitivity. I recall hearing the story of an old American fundamentalist preacher — Uncle Buddy Robinson — who was accused by those of a more scholarly disposition of always preaching the same sermon; he just used different texts. "Well," he once quipped, "if I can find the message where it isn't, maybe you smart fellas can find it where it is!" Contemporary pundits in the science-religion culture wars, it seems to me, are solidly in Uncle Buddy's camp. They are forever finding a science-religion feud where it isn't. And it's not just that they prefer the mono-

2. Quoted in Shetty and Coghlan, "Royal Society Fellows Turn on Director."
3. Ronald L. Numbers, "Simplifying Complexity: Patterns in the History of Science and Religion," in *Science and Religion: New Historical Perspectives*, ed. Thomas Dixon, Geoffrey Cantor, and Stephen Pumphrey (Cambridge: Cambridge University Press, 2010), p. 264.

chrome of counter-factual stereotype to the technicolor of real history; they seem to have no qualms about manufacturing, out of whole cloth, mythologies to suit their own ends. For those like me with a taste for spotting this species of myth-making, last year was a particularly good year. Let me illustrate.

Culture Wars

Jerry Fodor is a brilliant and highly distinguished philosopher of mind at Rutgers University, and a self-declared secular humanist. In February 2010 he brought out a book with fellow cognitive scientist Massimo Piatelli-Palmarini with the daring title *What Darwin Got Wrong*. In fact, Fodor had been thinking about Darwinism for several years and had been expressing some philosophical doubts about the explanatory power of natural selection in places like the *London Review of Books* and, rather more technically, in the journal *Mind and Language*.[4] It's a complex set of arguments that I don't really need to explain in detail save to say that Fodor's case draws on the distinction between intentional and extensional propositions to make the case that the idea of nature selecting *for* particular phenotypic traits of organisms to adapt them to their environment is, in the last analysis, incoherent. Selecting *for,* he insists, requires some kind of agency — of precisely the sort that mindless nature doesn't have. Selectionist accounts of organic history, he concludes, are at best *post hoc* historical narratives, rather than law-like scientific explanations. There is a lot more to it than just that, of course; and in the book with Piatelli-Palmarini, the authors devote a lot of time to biological dimensions of the story. Now let's be clear. Fodor has no problem with evolution and, what's more, assumes that "evolution is a mechanical process through and through."[5] What he is convinced about, though, is that natural selection can't be the mechanism of adaptive evolution that the ultra-Darwinians claim it is.

Reaction has certainly been something to behold. I mentioned that Fodor has no religious axe to grind. He and his coauthor describe them-

---

4. Jerry Fodor, "Why Pigs Don't Have Wings," *London Review of Books* 29, no. 20 (18 October 2007); Jerry Fodor, "Against Darwinism," *Mind and Language* 23 (2008): 1-24.

5. Jerry Fodor and Massimo Piatelli-Palmarini, *What Darwin Got Wrong* (London: Profile, 2010), p. xv.

selves as "card-carrying, signed-up, dyed-in-the-wool, no-holds-barred atheists."[6] That looks fairly clear to me. But you would not think it from the reviews. Michael Ruse, for example, ordinarily a careful commentator on these matters, had this to say in the *Boston Globe*: "At the beginning of their book, they proudly claim to be atheists. Perhaps so. But my suspicion is that, like those scorned Christians, Fodor and Piattelli-Palmarini just cannot stomach the idea that humans might just be organisms, no better than the rest of the living world. We have to be special, superior to other denizens of Planet Earth. Christians are open in their beliefs that humans are special and explaining them lies beyond the scope of science. I just wish that our authors were a little more open that this is their view too."[7] Naturally enough, Fodor didn't take too kindly to that. "Well none of that is remotely our view," he observed; ". . . there's not a scintilla of text in our book (or elsewhere) to support the accusation of creeping theism. . . . Short of trial by fire, water, or the House of UnAmerican Activities Committee, what must one do to prove one's bona fides?"[8]

For all that, Fodor's querying of natural selection has continued to be framed in the language of science-and-religion one way or the other. Robert Richards, for example, felt the need to round off his review with the observation that the authors of *What Darwin Got Wrong* "orchestrate a medley of contradictions that can delight only the ears of creationists and proponents of intelligent design." This led into a final salvo consisting of a cautionary parable from the Wilberforce-Huxley legend in which Huxley is supposed to have retorted that he "would rather have a monkey as his ancestor than be connected with a man who used great gifts to obscure the truth."[9] By finishing with that rhetorical flourish he plainly sought to throw the whole matter into the cauldron of science-religion relations.

For his part, Daniel Dennett is pretty dismissive of anybody who doesn't wholly buy into what he calls "Darwin's strange inversion" — the idea that you can have purposeless purpose, designer-less design, unintended intentions, and the like. To Dennett there's a label for those

---

6. Fodor and Piatelli-Palmarini, *What Darwin Got Wrong*, p. xv.

7. Michael Ruse, "Origin of the Specious," *Boston Globe*, 14 February 2010.

8. Jerry Fodor, "From the Darwin Wars," mss. I'm grateful to Professor Fodor for allowing me to see this yet-to-be-published piece.

9. Robert J. Richards, "Darwin Tried and True," *American Scientist* 98, no. 3 (May-June 2010): 238-42.

who don't swallow his claim that natural selection is a persuasive way to ground a theory of natural teleology: "we call them creationists," he announces. This means that atheists like Fodor and Nagel who don't think natural selection provides a good explanation for, say, the human mind are what he calls "mind creationists."[10] Elsewhere Dennett declares that because Fodor insists that the idea of design without a designer just doesn't make sense, he "sounds like Christoph Schönborn, Catholic archbishop of Vienna, the chap duped by the Intelligent Design folks. . . . Fodor ends up agreeing with the archbishop: evolution happens, but natural selection isn't how it works its magic."[11]

Comparable observations could easily be instanced. In almost his first breath on Fodor and Piatelli-Palmarini's book, John Dupré worries that "it has been, and will continue to be, picked up by the fundamentalist enemies of science."[12] Ned Block and Philip Kitcher, alleging that the authors have not responded to the many criticisms leveled at earlier versions of the argument (an unwarranted accusation in my view), quip that in this regard they "resemble creationist debaters, who . . . hear detailed refutations of their charge, and repeat their patter in the next forum."[13] Even Simon Conway Morris, who is always to be taken seriously, was concerned that, although the authors would be "horrified" by the comparison, "the tenor of their argument is uncomfortably reminiscent of 'Intelligent Design.'"[14]

If tossing Fodor's critique into the science-religion minefield is striking in these commentaries, the language that interlocutors have resorted to has been marked in no less conspicuous ways. To put it mildly, it has not exactly been characterized by scholarly moderation. Dennett wonders what could have driven Fodor to "hallucinate" so wildly.[15] Douglas Futuyma tells the readers of *Science* that the authors of *What Darwin Got*

10. Daniel Dennett, "Darwin's 'Strange Inversion of Reasoning,'" *Proceedings of the National Academy of Sciences* 106 (16 June 2009), Supplement 1, p. 10062.

11. Daniel Dennett, "Fun and Games in Fantasyland," *Mind and Language* 23, no. 1 (2008): 25-31, at 26-27.

12. John Dupré, "Review: What Darwin Got Wrong," *TPM: The Philosophers' Magazine* 50 (23 July 2010).

13. Ned Block and Philip Kitcher, "Misunderstanding Darwin," *Boston Review* (March/April 2010).

14. Simon Conway Morris, "Mindless Evolution," *Big Questions Online*, 17 August 2010, http://www.bigquestionsonline.com/columns/simon-conway-morris/mindless-evolution/.

15. Daniel Dennett, Letter, *London Review of Books*, 15 November 2007.

Wrong are "Two Critics without a Clue."[16] Samir Okasha, in the *TLS*, says that their book "is the sort of thing that gives philosophy of science a bad name."[17] To a non-biologist like me, what makes this intemperance all the more surprising, I think, is that Richard Lewontin (a Harvard geneticist who can hardly be accused of biological ignorance and who is a collaborator on the very paper with Stephen Jay Gould that people like Dennett say Fodor egregiously misunderstands) in his review for the *New York Review of Books* thought it would be wiser now to "stop talking about 'selection for.' " Of course Lewontin has misgivings about parts of Fodor's analysis, but he does wonder if "biologists should stop referring to 'natural selection,' and instead talk about differential rates of survival and reproduction."[18] I'm pretty sure Fodor would welcome that. What's clear in Lewontin's remarks, though, is the complete absence of vitriol and spleen venting that are elsewhere only too discernible.

Mistaken targets, misconstrued intentions, and misplaced scorn bear all the hallmarks of a culture war. They're the academic equivalent of misnamed friendly fire. For the fact of the matter is there's nothing friendly about it all, as my good friend and colleague Keith Bennett recently discovered. Keith is an outstanding paleo-botanist — again with no hint of any religious agenda — and the recipient of a Royal Society Wolfson Research Merit Award. Several years ago he was invited by the *New Scientist* to allow the magazine to publish a keynote lecture he had delivered at the International Paleontological Congress the previous summer at Imperial College London. The other keynote speaker was Niles Eldredge. It made the front cover of the magazine.

Here Keith presented evidence he'd gathered over many years as part of a case he mounted to argue that adaptation to environment may turn out not to be a major driver of evolutionary change. As he put it, "the connection between environmental change and evolutionary change is weak, which is not what might have been expected from Darwin's hypothesis."[19] In its place Keith proposed that evolution is

16. Douglas J. Futuyma, "Two Critics without a Clue," *Science* 328 (7 May 2010): 692-93.

17. Samir Okasha, "Whites and Blues," *Times Literary Supplement* (16 March 2010): 3-5, at 5.

18. Richard Lewontin, "Not So Natural Selection," *New York Review of Books*, 27 May 2010.

19. Keith Bennett, "The Chaos Theory of Evolution," *New Scientist* 208, no. 2782 (16 October 2010): 28-31, at 30.

non-linear and that the causes of macro-evolutionary change lie in the genetic dynamics of the relationship between genotype and phenotype. From the blogs you'd think the sky had fallen in. Jerry Coyne well nigh foamed at the mouth. A sample of his vocabulary should be enough to give a rough sense of Coyne's tone: "stupid," "thoughtless," "rotten," "hogwash," "moron," "drivel."[20] You catch the drift. Soon other bloggers were stoking the flames.

Now what interests me here is something that the commissioning editor posted on the website "Why Evolution Is True," which Coyne himself runs, in response to the diatribe. The editor said: "if Bennett is so hopelessly wrong, why was he ever invited to give the keynote (alongside Niles Eldredge)? Why did the symposium even take place? Bennett was not the only one to question the primacy of natural selection in macroevolution. . . . I was at Bennett's talk; the room was full of learned and eminent people. He took a few questions but there were no howls of protest like yours."[21] Coyne didn't respond to that. He was busy weeping, he'd already said, for the Royal Society. Sad.

To add a further footnote to this avalanche of protest, it is worth remarking that a few years earlier, Bennett had presented similar findings at the Royal Society itself. Here he concluded that it could "well be the crucial insight that evolution, after all, has rather little to do with environmental change."[22] Evolution might well be driven by mechanisms that are non-adaptive. Commentators did not experience apoplexy at the thought but engaged calmly and constructively with the proposal.

These skirmishes advertise, in one way or another, the three cuts I want to make at the whole issue of thinking about the historical relations between science and religion: place, politics, and poetics. By "place" I am referring to the different locations — both physical and social — in which debates about scientific matters, and indeed their engagements with religion, literally "take place." By "politics" I have in mind the role of political atmospherics, broadly construed, in which discussions are

20. Jerry Coyne, "Can *New Scientist* Get Any Worse on Evolution?," http://whyevolutionistrue.wordpress.com/2010/11/05/can-new-scientist-get-any-worse-on-evolution/.

21. The editor's remarks can be accessed at: http://whyevolutionistrue.wordpress.com/2010/11/09/new-scientist-defends-bad-science/.

22. K. D. Bennett, "Continuing the Debate on the Role of Quaternary Environmental Change for Macroevolution," *Philosophical Transactions of the Royal Society of London, Series B* 359 (2004): 301.

enmeshed. And if only for the sake of ornamental alliteration, I am using the label "poetics" to call attention to questions of rhetoric and idiom in the conduct of debates.

Let me initially illustrate something of what I am after, using the cases I have just mentioned, before generalizing a little more widely. The fact that things can be said at a professional meeting of paleontologists and before an audience at the Royal Society without dramatically raising temperatures while the same arguments cause screams of protest in some other public forum underscores the salience of place in scientific dialogues. What can be said, and how it is heard, is different from place to place, from site to site, from venue to venue. This suggests that in thinking about scientific controversies, and quarrels over science and religion, it is important to attend to the social and physical spaces within which altercation takes place. It is pretty clear, too, that certain scientific issues — in these cases rotating around Darwinian evolution — are freighted with cultural politics. Evolution has acquired such iconic status in latter-day culture wars that it has come to embody political investments of many different kinds. This reminds us that science and religion both operate in wider political arenas that shape debates in distinctive ways. The unrestrained language of trashing to which Fodor and Piattelli-Palmarini have been treated, and Jerry Coyne's loose-lipped tirade in his belittling of Keith Bennett, suggest, to me at any rate, that rhetorical style counts for as much as, maybe more than, calm careful scrutiny of arguments in controversial scientific matters. And so I want to argue that place, politics, and poetics should be accorded more attention in efforts to get a handle on the encounters between science and faith.

Beyond Conflict?

Before I turn to these, though, I need to issue a health warning. I am far from convinced that greater sophistication, scholarly care, historiographical nuance, and the like have much chance of making a blind bit of difference to public presumption about inherent warfare between science and religion. So far, despite the outstanding work of figures such as John Hedley Brooke in particular, that seems to be the case.[23]

---

23. John Hedley Brooke, *Science and Religion: Some Historical Perspectives* (Cambridge: Cambridge University Press, 1991).

One of the reasons, of course, is that stereotype and superficiality prevail, not least among the leading publicists. Terry Eagleton refers to this species of scientific polemic against religion as Yeti theology and finds it in abundance in the writings of Christopher Hitchens and Richard Dawkins — Ditchkins for short. According to Eagleton, Ditchkins — and their admirers such as Daniel Dennett — persistently commit the "blunder of believing that religion is a botched attempt to explain the world which is like seeing ballet as a botched attempt to run for a bus."[24] As he bitingly put it in a review for the *London Review of Books*: "Imagine someone holding forth on biology whose only knowledge of the subject is the *Book of British Birds*, and you have a rough idea of what it feels like to read Richard Dawkins on theology." The claim can be generalized. "The more they detest religion," he observes, "the more ill-informed their criticisms of it tend to be. If they were asked to pass judgment on phenomenology or the geopolitics of South Asia, they would no doubt bone up on the question as assiduously as they could. When it comes to theology, however, any shoddy old travesty will pass muster."[25] The fact is, of course, neither phenomenology nor South Asian geopolitics can move books at the rate that Richard Dawkins does. Complexity is hard to advertise; caricature has always enjoyed good sales.

It is the same on the other side too, of course. I do not need to elaborate. But since I have quoted Eagleton against the cultured despisers of religion, it is perhaps apt to refer to him on why certain versions of fundamentalism turn out to be the mirror image of the new atheism: "when reason becomes too dominative, calculative, and instrumental, it ends up as too shallow a soil for a reasonable kind of faith to flourish. As a result, faith lapses into a kind of irrationalism . . . turning its back on reason altogether. . . . Fundamentalism is among other things the faith of those driven into zealotry by a shallow technological rationality which sets all the great spiritual questions cynically to one side, and in doing so leaves those questions open to being monopolized by bigots."[26]

And here is one reason why the dismantling of the conflict thesis in scholarly circles is passing the public by. Conflict mythology serves the interests of partisans only too well. It can be deliberately used to excite

---

24. Terry Eagleton, *Reason, Faith, and Revolution* (New Haven: Yale University Press, 2009), p. 50.

25. Terry Eagleton, "Lunging, Flailing, Mispunching," *London Review of Books*, 19 October 2009, p. 32.

26. Eagleton, *Reason, Faith, and Revolution*, pp. 148-49.

controversy — religious or scientific. As Geoffrey Cantor reminds us, Arthur Keith used it in the 1920s "to infuriate the clergy" and in "much the same way Richard Dawkins, Peter Atkins, and others have in our own day evoked the power and authority of science to attack religion."[27] For that matter, so did Thomas Henry Huxley with his rhetorical gibe that it was only "old ladies, of both sexes, [who] consider [*The Origin of Species*] a decidedly dangerous book."[28] Comparable taunts in our own day obviously boost sales, make for feisty radio and television, and provide colorful courtroom drama. Of course, I do not mean to reduce the whole thing to just these considerations. But, like all myths, its survival against the historical odds suggests the conflict fable continues to perform some function in today's culture. Those who want to trade in the currency of hostility have high investments in projecting their own struggles onto the past.

Chris Fleming and Jane Goodall have some telling things to say about the way in which what they call "the culture-shock myth" of Darwin's work "functions as a rhetorical strategy in our own time." According to them, those intent on seeing Darwin's idea as inherently dangerous, and Darwin himself as the generator of turmoil, confusion, and anxiety, present "a picture of civilization before Darwin as held in a state of intellectual childhood, incapable of thinking its way toward the great truths."[29] And herein lies conspicuous irony. What connects both sets of propagandists — ultra-Darwinians and polemical creationists — is what Merryl Wyn Davies calls "absolute pan-galactic certainty" about the truth of their claims.[30] It calls to mind the famous remark by Conor Cruise O'Brien, commenting on years of violence and conflict, that "Ireland was inhabited, not really by Protestants and Catholics, but by two sets of imaginary Jews."[31] Each side believes it holds the tablets of stone. It's much the same in the modern science-religion culture wars. And here's the irony, nicely pinpointed by Michael Ruse, for war-

27. Geoffrey Cantor, "What Shall We Do with the 'Conflict Thesis'?" in Dixon et al., eds., *Science and Religion*, p. 294.

28. Thomas Henry Huxley, *Man's Place in Nature and Other Essays* (London: Dent, 1911), p. 299.

29. Chris Fleming and Jane Goodall, "Dangerous Darwinism," *Public Understanding of Science* 11 (2002): 259-71, at 259, 267.

30. Merryl Wyn Davies, *Darwin and Fundamentalism* (Cambridge: Icon, 2000), p. 58.

31. Conor Cruise O'Brien, *States of Ireland* (London: Hutchinson, 1972), p. 309.

mongers like Richard Dawkins in the science-religion arena: "The paradox is that Dawkins should be more modest. He stresses that we are the product of Darwinian evolution, and hence there is no good reason to think we have the power to penetrate into the mysteries of the universe. Our abilities are to get out of the jungle and live on the plains. In a way, the Darwinian is back-to-back with Saint Paul: we peer through a glass darkly."[32]

The flourishing of the conflict fable, of course, is not for want of far more compelling ways of thinking about the subject. Laying aside the conflict model's equally troublesome *alter ego* — namely, that sweetness and light have always prevailed between religion and science — two alternative narratives have had their attractions for me. The first is rooted in the writings of the recently deceased Yale historian, Frank Miller Turner. In a number of important contributions, Turner argued that the so-called Victorian conflict between science and faith should be reconceptualized as a *social* struggle (rather than an intellectual battle) between two opposing forces in Victorian society, namely, an older elite (the clergy) and an emerging newer elite (the scientists). What looks like a conflict between scientific findings and theological dogma is to be understood rather as a competition for cultural power in society between two sets of "professionals," as it were, each with vested interests.[33] Seen in this light, the way in which figures such as Thomas Henry Huxley resorted to talk of the "scientific priesthood," "lay 'sermons,'" "hymns to creation," "the church scientific," and the like can be seen as part of a strategy to wrest power from the older clerical brigade.

A different, but no less socially grounded hermeneutic was put forward by the radical historian of science and psychotherapist, Robert M. Young. Young's tactic is to emphasize neither intellectual conflict nor social competition between science and religion in Darwin's era, but rather to draw attention to what he sees as profound continuities between theological and scientific belief-systems. His argument is subtle and sophisticated; but the gist of it goes something like this. During the early decades of the nineteenth century, the existing social order was

32. Michael Ruse, review of Richard Dawkins, *The God Delusion*, in *Isis* 98 (2007): 814-16.

33. I have in mind Frank Miller Turner, "The Victorian Conflict between Science and Religion: A Professional Dimension," *Isis* 69 (1978): 356-76; and Frank Miller Turner, "Rainfall, Plagues and the Prince of Wales: A Chapter in the Conflict of Religion and Science," *Journal of British Studies* 8 (1974): 45-65.

justified in the conventional language of Christian theodicy.[34] The hierarchical state of society and its class structure were rationalized as the expression of God's will. A stanza from Cecil Frances Alexander's famous hymn "All Things Bright and Beautiful" captures it nicely:

The rich man in his castle,
The poor man at his gate,
God made them, high or lowly,
And ordered their estate.

As the nineteenth century wore on, according to Young, this earlier theodicy erected on natural theology was progressively replaced by a secular theodicy grounded in Darwinian natural selection. Now the social order was rationalized, not in terms of divine purpose, but in the language of selection and struggle. The polymath Patrick Geddes, writing in 1925, captured the transformation when he spoke of the "substitution of Darwin for Paley": "the place vacated by theological and metaphysical explanation," he proposed, "has simply been occupied by that suggested to Darwin and Wallace by Malthus in terms of the prevalent severity of industrial competition."[35]

As it happens, I am not myself entirely persuaded by either of these re-readings despite their imaginative recasting of the story. I applaud the way in which they set the whole issue in its broader social and political setting. But even so, I do not think they are fine-grained enough to capture the complexity of the relations between science and religion even for the Victorian era. And so I want to complicate the story in other ways. In large part this desire stems from my allergy to large abstractions — like "science" and "religion." At the very least these need pluralizing — and in every instance of thinking about the "relationship," we ought to ask "which science, whose faith?" For the fact is that the encounters between particular scientific claims and particular faith traditions display what I would call different *flash points* and operate in different *trading zones*. By "flash points" I mean those matters — different from tradition to tradition, from place and place, from time to time —

34. See Robert M. Young, *Darwin's Metaphor: Nature's Place in Victorian Culture* (Cambridge: Cambridge University Press, 1985).

35. Patrick Geddes, "Biology," in *Chambers's Encyclopaedia* (Edinburgh: Chambers, 1925), p. 164.

which have been seen to cause tension in the engagement of faith traditions with science. By "trading zones" I refer to those arenas of engagement where the interface between science and religion has facilitated fruitful intellectual exchange.

Let me illustrate. So far as flash points are concerned, the list of potential candidates is a lengthy one, and a few examples must suffice. In Britain and the United States, a recurrent, though not universal, source of contention has centered on questions of teleology and natural theology. Richard Dawkins insists that Darwin's theory of evolution has shattered what he calls the illusion of design by showing that apparent purpose is nothing more than the product of hum-drum, natural causes. This, of course, is only the last in a long sequence of scientific assaults on teleology. French advocates of a more radical enlightenment in the eighteenth century, such as Diderot and d'Holbach, attacked the Newtonian moderates and pushed for an all-embracing naturalism. Their stance stood in marked contrast to Newton's Unitarian defense of a purposive cosmic order and Voltaire's commitment to providential deism. Design was also an issue for Islamic engagements with science. Because traditional Kalam arguments from design remained important, what has been called the "more ideological forms" of Darwinism and materialism, alongside philosophical positivism and social Darwinism, brought discord.[36] By contrast, arguments from design are apparently not characteristic of Jewish thought on the subject. At the same time, *within* traditions, different stances could be adopted. The flourishing of natural theology in seventeenth-century England represented one Christian response to what were perceived to be the dangers of a mechanistic atomism; by contrast, later writers as diverse as Thomas Chalmers and John Henry Newman did not hesitate to identify theological reservations about the teleological argument. Newman never cared for the design argument because he was never able to see its logical force; Chalmers thought it could never lead to Christian theism.[37]

---

36. Ekmeleddin İhsanoğlu, "Modern Islam," in *Science and Religion around the World*, ed. John Hedley Brooke and Ronald L. Numbers (Oxford: Oxford University Press, 2011), pp. 148-74.

37. See John Hedley Brooke, "Modern Christianity," in Brooke and Numbers, eds., *Science and Religion around the World*, pp. 92-119. See also the discussions in Michael Ruse, *Darwin and Design: Does Evolution Have a Purpose?* (Cambridge: Harvard University Press, 2004).

Other flash points could readily be elaborated. The links between natural philosophy and the tradition of natural magic were more troublesome for some traditions than for others. For Jews, it is said, Talmudic bans on magic were critically important, and later Maimonides sought to undermine astrology. In traditions united by a canonical text, the development of the science of textual criticism could create major difficulties for orthodox believers. In other times, places, and settings, different issues dominated the science-religion skyline. Among these we might refer to the questioning of divine miracle by the idea of omnipresent natural law; the subversion of free will in deterministic projects that conflated mind and brain; the challenges that new theories of matter posed to some understandings of the Eucharist; the materialistic ethos of certain strands of scientific reductionism; the use of scientific research to support various forms of eugenics. All these — and doubtless many more — have been flash points for certain groups in certain places at certain times in science's dialogue with religion. This realization forces us to acknowledge the complexities of scientific-religious narratives and should curb any inclination to universalize particulars.

Flash points in one mode, of course, may surface as trading zones in another. Such zones of exchange, of course, are not restricted to the Judeo-Christian tradition, but in the interests of space I'll restrict my few examples to it. If their commitment to teleology made some religious believers resistant to certain forms of scientific explanation, in other spaces natural theology could act as a stimulus to scientific inquiry. The idea of a divinely designed natural world was foundational to the natural history of writers John Ray and William Derham during the seventeenth and eighteenth centuries. For them, the belief that living things were divinely adapted to their natural environments fostered their inquiries into plant and animal life. The treatises produced by figures like these were thus both theological and scientific at the same time. The doctrine of humanity's fall from grace and the theology of original sin could likewise serve as a trading ground for scientific and theological exchange. Advocates of the new experimental philosophy of the sixteenth and seventeenth centuries frequently took with great seriousness the adverse implications of these particular Judeo-Christian doctrines for human rationality — what has judiciously been called "the wounding of reason." Recognition of this fallen condition kindled a sense that mechanisms needed to be put in place to overcome the epistemic consequences of original corruption

87

and its legacy of human depravity.[38] New observational instruments, measuring devices, experimental apparatuses, and warranting procedures were all espoused in hopes of introducing greater rigor into knowledge-acquiring enterprises. In this trading zone, productive exchanges could take place between theological thinking about the epistemic implications of fallen humanity and technological developments in scientific instrumentation.

The belief of the monotheistic religions that all human beings are descended from Adam has also fostered intellectual traffic between theological conviction and scientific inquiry. The search for Adam's language, efforts to elucidate human racial differentiation, attempts to examine whether the human race is of monogenetic or polygenetic origin, explorations of the relationship between the world chronologies of different regional cultures, inquiries into how emerging archaeological artifacts should be interpreted — stances on all of these subjects were hammered out on the terrain of humankind's Adamic ancestry.[39] The character of reading practices has also been a ground on which science and religion have traded wares. Shifts in how the book of Scripture was read had a critical effect on ways of reading the book of nature during the early modern development of science. The demise of allegorical approaches to Bible reading, Peter Harrison suggests, had knock-on consequences for the tradition of interpreting the natural order through emblems and symbols. In this case literalism, which in a later era could disrupt science's relationship with theology, had a positive impact on the development of scientific theory.[40]

Given the range of these engagements, it is fairly clear that the complexity of the historical relationships between science and faith cannot be reduced to simple models of conflict or cooperation. So I want to return to the three matters I mentioned earlier — place, politics, poetics — that I believe might be profitably highlighted in thinking about science-religion encounters.

38. Peter Harrison, *The Fall of Man and the Foundations of Science* (Cambridge: Cambridge University Press, 2008).

39. I have discussed this in *Adam's Ancestors: Race, Religion and the Politics of Human Origins* (Baltimore: Johns Hopkins University Press, 2008).

40. Peter Harrison, *The Bible, Protestantism and the Rise of Natural Science* (Cambridge: Cambridge University Press, 2001).

Putting Science in Its Place

Scientific theories do not diffuse evenly across the face of the earth. And Charles Darwin's theory of evolution is no exception. Consider how it was encountered in a number of different locations at the time. Take Charleston, South Carolina. John McCrady (1831-1881; mathematician and naturalist with interests in marine invertebrates) remained a life-long opponent of Darwin's theory — as did his colleagues at the Charleston Museum. They remained devotees of the Harvard paleontologist Louis Agassiz, who believed that life had been created in a number of different centers of creation across the globe. To them animals were created in and for the environments in which they were found. In New Zealand, in contrast, Darwinism was welcomed and the controversies that elsewhere attended the arrival of natural selection were — by and large — conspicuously absent.

To understand just why these venues responded so differently to Darwin's proposals we need to consider the cultural politics prevailing in the two locations. Among the Charleston naturalists, Darwin's ideas about human origins and species transmutation were profoundly troubling to naturalists such as McCrady, who was dedicated to the idea of racial superiority. Closely following his teacher, Louis Agassiz, he insisted that the different races constituted different species. Each race had a separate point of origin, and any blurring of its transcendental individuality was both biologically and socially repugnant. McCrady thus repeatedly insisted that it was simply impossible to conceive that the white and black races could have descended from the same origin. To him, Darwin's theory of species transmutation was nothing less than a subversive threat to Southern culture. The scientific circle that rotated around the museum shared McCrady's reading. Edmund Ravenel, for example, declared that the laws of nature could not be obliterated by abolitionists. John Holbrook, Francis Holmes, and Lewis Gibbes actively connived with Samuel George Morton, the Philadelphia medical practitioner, to marginalize monogenist opposition to their thoroughgoing racialized science. In this cultural setting Darwin's theory was seen to challenge the very foundations of the social order. The meanings attributed to his theory were shaped by its implications for racial politics, post-bellum anxieties about the fragmentation of Southern culture, and attitudes towards the liberalizing politics of Reconstruction.[41]

41. See Lester D. Stephens, *Science, Race, and Religion in the American South: John*

Half a world away in New Zealand, things were different. Whereas McCrady read Darwinian evolution as subversive of racial hierarchy, here Darwin's theory was read as underwriting the runaway triumphs of white colonialism. A set of public lectures presented at the Colonial Museum introduced the inhabitants of Wellington to Darwin's theory of evolution in 1868-69. As the speaker, William Travers — botanist, lawyer, and politician — read Darwin, he discerned a theory with immediate implications for race history. Just as the European rat, honeybee, goat, and other invader species had displaced their New Zealand counterparts, so the "vigorous races of Europe" were wiping out the Maori. It was a law of nature: in the struggle for existence, whenever a "white race comes into contact with an indigenous dark race on ground suitable to the former, the latter must disappear in a few generations." Nor was this law of nature to be lamented. The historic successes of European culture meant that "even the most sensitive philanthropist may learn to look with resignation, if not with complacency, on the extinction of a people which, in the past, had accomplished so imperfectly every object of man's being."[42] In reading natural selection through the lens of race relations, Travers was simply bringing to Darwin's text the long-standing colonial conviction that the Maori were fated for extinction by nature. The view was widely shared, for the New Zealand encounter with Darwin's theory and the meanings that were read in it were shaped by the contingencies of settler-Maori politics and the desire to enlist enlightened science in the service of colonial policy.

Place and politics were no less important among the scientists who circulated around the St. Petersburg Society of Naturalists in late-nineteenth-century Russia. The very principle that made Darwinian theory attractive to Wellington audiences, namely struggle, was precisely what most perturbed the Russian scientists. Here Karl Kessler instigated a tradition of research dedicated to identifying what he called mutual aid — cooperation — in evolutionary history. He was profoundly critical of what he called "the cruel, so-called law of the struggle for existence," and sought ways of reasserting the survival value of cooperation, not least in harsh environments. Later that idea was championed

---

Bachman and the Charleston Circle of Naturalists, 1815-1895 (Chapel Hill: University of North Carolina Press, 2000).

42. William T. L. Travers, "On the Changes Effected in the Natural Features of a New Country by the Introduction of Civilized Races," *Transactions and Proceedings of the New Zealand Institute* 2 (1869): 299-313.

by Peter Kropotkin, who elaborated in detail on the role of mutual aid in biological and social history alike. This viewpoint, of course, fitted Russian collectivist ideology at the time — an ideology deeply critical of Thomas Malthus, whose atomistic conception of society had already been castigated as a cold, soulless, mechanistic product of English political economy.[43] As Daniel Todes has recently put it: "political supporters of the two most important classes, rich landlords and peasants, spoke the language of communalism — stressing not individual initiative and struggle, but the importance of cooperation within social groups and the virtues of social harmony."[44]

Science and Religion: Place, Politics, Poetics

If scientific theories can take on different meanings in different venues, so can works dealing with the relationship between science and religion. Consider the fate of John William Draper's *History of the Conflict between Religion and Science* (which came out in 1874) in Turkey. The work was translated by the Ottoman author Ahmed Midhat and provided with exegetical commentary at key points. This work has recently been scrutinized by Alper Yalcinkaya, who makes the telling point that the so-called conflict between science and religion at the time was intimately connected to another conflict — between religion and religion. In his translation, Midhat stage-managed Draper's thesis to present it as a contribution to the clash between Islam and Christianity. Again and again Midhat underscored hints in Draper's text of a more positive stance toward science among Muslim writers so as to develop an apologia for Islam's compatibility with science compared with Christianity. Whether it was praising the contributions of the so-called Saracens, identifying the scientific potentials in Islamic fatalism, or retrieving the insights of Averroes, Midhat used Draper to exonerate Islam and at the same time to confirm "the conflict between Christianity and science, thus providing Ottoman Muslims with a weapon against the missionaries." What this means is that, as Yalcinkaya notes, "Representations

43. See Daniel Todes, *Darwin without Malthus: The Struggle for Existence in Russian Evolutionary Thought* (New York: Oxford University Press, 1989), ch. 2.
44. Daniel Todes, "Global Darwin — Contempt for Competition," *Nature* 462 (5 November 2009): 36-37.

of and disputes around science and religion need to be analyzed within their own contexts."[45]

In the light of these considerations, it is understandable that what I am calling the poetics of science and religion is likely to take different shapes in different settings. What I mean is that the rhetorical stances adopted by interlocutors are conditioned by the venues in which encounters take place. The reason is that location and locution are intimately connected.

Allow me to illustrate something of these intertwinings by dwelling finally on the ways in which one Christian tradition — Presbyterianism — engaged with Darwin's proposals during the final decades of the nineteenth century. What soon becomes clear is that, even within this single theological community, marked differences of stance and rhetoric are discernible in different places. What could be said in one venue would not be tolerated elsewhere. Consider.

The Presbyterian Knox College in Toronto launched its own monthly journal in 1883. Its editorial manifesto pointed to Darwinian evolution as a subject that demanded the attention of every serious church member. The rhetorical tone in which the conversation was conducted here is what I want to call attention to. It was ameliorative. Writers worked hard to absorb the theory of evolution, and even to rethink certain aspects of theology in its light. Acrimonious opposition, literalistic readings of Scripture, and an unyielding faith in a fixed creation are certainly conspicuous — but only by their absence. In 1886 an article for the magazine entitled "Biology and Theology" told readers that "the Biology of today is inseparable from the theory of evolution." Evolution was "a law, a method of operation," and a "purely a scientific question." And the biologist "uses this theory as a 'working hypothesis,' exactly in the same way that the chemist uses his atomic theory."[46] Another writer, William Hunter, did not shirk the implications of Darwinism for human descent: "Man is not less a work of art, because he is gradually formed," he insisted. Readers, he urged, should not "be alarmed if we see in the lower animals manifestations of some of the higher emotions which were once supposed to belong exclusively to man."[47] What is striking

---

45. M. Alper Yalcinkaya, "Science as an Ally of Religion: A Muslim Appropriation of 'the Conflict Thesis,'" *British Journal for the History of Science* 44, no. 2 (2011): 6, 2.

46. W. Dewar, "Biology and Theology," *Knox College Monthly* 4 (February 1886): 150-56.

47. W. A. Hunter, "Evolution and the Church," *Knox College Monthly* 13 (May 1895): 591-602.

is the accommodating language that contributors to the *Knox* magazine used in reflecting on Darwin. Even on matters of human origins, there is a marked absence of hostility.

What was it that facilitated the Knox College fraternity's inclinations toward rapprochement with Darwinian biology? In some measure it stemmed from their creative dialogue with their Scottish heritage over the potentials of Baconian induction. In contrast to Canada's most resolute anti-Darwinian, Sir John William Dawson — who gloried in a Baconian resistance to speculation and conjecture — the Knox College Professor Robert Y. Thomson threw off Baconian shackles to defend the value of *a priori* theorizing; as he put it, by way of example: "Kepler could never have discovered that the heavenly bodies move in elliptical orbits, had the idea of an ellipse not been already in his mind."[48] The extent to which these Toronto theologians could free themselves from Bacon's clutches facilitated their engagement with evolutionary conjectures.

Just as important, I think, was their turn to the idea of progressivism that gripped textual critics examining the development of the biblical documents. Of course, the tradition of biblical criticism long pre-dated Darwin's intervention. But my point is that, at Knox College, evolutionary thought-forms delivered a vocabulary that facilitated the pursuit of the idea that the biblical text and divine revelation had themselves evolved. And it fostered the application of the notion of historical development in various arenas.

Something of this surfaces in an article entitled "Evolution of Scripture" by Rev. John Thompson. Here he portrayed the Hebrew Bible as "a wonderful study in evolution." To him it had "evolved and grew in connection with the history of our race."[49] Here the idea of evolutionary transformation opened up a zone of exchange with textual history that could be exploited. And others followed suit.

The rhetorical stance that the Knox Presbyterians adopted toward Darwin stands in marked contrast to the way in which evolution was talked about among Southern Presbyterians — one of whom, James Woodrow (uncle of Woodrow Wilson), was dismissed in 1886 from his post in the Southern Presbyterian Theological Seminary in Columbia, South Carolina, for advocating the theological and scientific propriety

48. R. Y. Thomson, "The Evolution in the Manifestation of the Supernatural," *Knox College Monthly* 8 (1890): 293-318.

49. J. Thompson, "Evolution of Scripture," *Knox College Monthly* 13 (1895): 363-72.

of Darwin's theory of species change.[50] The Southern Presbyterians' orthodox keeper of its sacred flame, Robert L. Dabney, wasn't persuaded. He had long harbored doubts about geology, urging that its claims about the age of the earth fell far short of demonstrated truth. To Dabney it was simply impossible to believe *both* in Scripture *and* in evolution. John Lafayette Girardeau, then a professor at the Columbia Seminary and leader of the opposition to Woodrow in the 1880s hearing, thought the whole business boiled down to a contest "between Dr. Woodrow's hypothesis and the Bible as our church interprets it: between this scientific view and our Bible — the Bible as it is to us."[51] Again, George Armstrong, clergyman, former professor of chemistry and geology, and architect of the resolution that outlawed evolutionary theory in Southern Presbyterianism, voiced his opposition to Woodrow with the observation: "We say these teachings of evolution are dangerous errors, because they endanger the plenary inspiration of the scriptures."[52]

Doctrinal though these debates seemed to be, dwelling as they did on the character of Scripture, the cultural politics of race relations in the American South were critically important. Antebellum Southern Presbyterians had long regarded the Bible as the foundation of Southern social order. During the 1850s that happy coalition came increasingly under threat with the rise of antislavery sentiments. Crucial to the Southern Presbyterians was the conviction that a plain, literal reading of the Bible provided ample justification for the institution of slavery and racial segregation. They saw abolitionism as a rationalistic assault on the integrity of Scripture and the Christian character of Southern culture. The Bible was thus appealed to as a means of resisting a host of perceived Yankee evils, including radical democracy, emancipation, higher criticism, and modern science.

Woodrow's chief critic — Dabney — was already well known for his opposition to public education on account of its trend toward social leveling and for his belief that abolitionism was the product of atheistic theories of human rights. To him slavery was plainly taught in Scrip-

50. On the general subject, see Monte Harrell Hampton, " 'Handmaid' or 'Assailant': Debating Science and Scripture in the Culture of the Lost Cause" (PhD thesis, University of North Carolina at Chapel Hill, 2004).

51. John L. Girardeau, *The Substance of Two Speeches on the Teaching of Evolution in Columbia Theological Seminary, Delivered in the Synod of South Carolina, at Greenville, S.C., Oct. 1884* (Columbia, SC, 1885).

52. Geo. D. Armstrong, *Evolution: The Substance of Two Lectures* (Norfolk, VA, 1885).

ture, and abolitionist attacks on that institution were assaults on the unadulterated Word of God, literally understood. With such convictions, Dabney was constitutionally allergic to theories of evolution that played metaphorical with plain Scripture. In these circumstances any attempt to read the Genesis narrative in poetic voice so as to accommodate Darwinian evolution was widely denounced. A literalist biblical hermeneutic was the foundation stone of Southern culture, and the Presbyterians were not going to let it crumble to accommodate the speculations of some fanciful theory about one species transmuting into another.

The rhetorical register in which the encounter with Darwin was transacted in Edinburgh could not have been different. In October 1874 Robert Rainy, the newly appointed Principal of New College, took up "Evolution and Theology" as the subject of his inaugural address. To Rainy, Darwin's theory was theologically irrelevant. Indeed, he was remarkably casual even about the idea of human evolution. "The application of theories of Evolution to the origin of man . . . is a point regarding which the theologian . . . may be perfectly at ease."[53] Because he was always sensitive to his ecclesiastical constituency, his insistence on evolution's theological neutrality at New College in 1874 is indicative of a general lack of panic about the subject among Scottish Presbyterians by the final quarter of the nineteenth century.

As the century wore on, more and more theological voices were added in support. Robert Flint worked hard to develop an evolutionary natural theology. Accordingly he urged that the "law of heredity," the "tendency to definite variation," and the "law, or so-called law, of natural selection" could all be read as expressions of divine purpose.[54] The United Presbyterian clergyman Henry Calderwood was similar. A supporter of the evangelistic activities of Moody and Sankey in Edinburgh, and an enthusiast for the Scottish philosophy of common sense, Calderwood took up the Chair of Moral Philosophy in Edinburgh in 1868. Calderwood welcomed evolution as a *bona fide* scientific theory: "Evolution stands before us as an impressive reality in the history of Nature."[55]

This accommodation to Darwin's proposals is conspicuous. But to un-

---

53. Robert Rainy, *Evolution and Theology: Inaugural Address* (Edinburgh, 1874).
54. Robert Flint, *Theism* (Edinburgh, 1877).
55. Henry Calderwood, *Evolution and Man's Place in Nature* (London, 1893), p. 340.

derstand it, we need to set it alongside other matters that were testing the patience of Scottish Presbyterian culture at the time. For during the 1870s and 1880s the Darwinian issue paled in significance beside the protracted heresy trial of William Robertson Smith, which made headline news; it would end in Smith's dismissal from his chair at the Free Church College in Aberdeen. What sparked off the row were Smith's entries for the ninth edition of the *Encyclopedia Britannica*, which revealed his acceptance of German higher criticism. Later he would produce an immensely influential historical anthropology entitled *The Religion of the Semites* (1889). Here he urged that a primitive sense of communal unity found expression in a ceremonial meal — the precursor of the Christian Eucharist. But it was a meal with a difference; the items on the menu were provided through ritual cannibalism. Revitalization of the tribe's sense of belonging was secured — as George Davie pungently expresses it — through wolfing down "the gobbets of throbbing flesh, newly-killed, of their fellow-tribesmen."[56] That got the attention of none other than Sigmund Freud! Indeed, even he felt that Smith's ideas about cannibalistic nostalgia were a bit too much! Not surprisingly, Smith's application of his theory to the Old Testament shocked the Free Church to its core. Smith's biblical anthropology was infinitely more threatening than the idea of species transformation. Whatever Dan Dennett may think now about something he calls "Darwin's dangerous idea," to the Scottish Presbyterians it was pretty tame compared with what Robertson Smith had to offer. And that profoundly shaped the rhetorical cadence of the Presbyterian encounter with Darwin in Edinburgh.

That very winter, 1874, when Rainy was opening his arms to evolutionary possibilities, across the Irish Sea J. L. Porter, professor of biblical criticism at the Presbyterian College in Belfast, delivered his opening address. Here he spoke ominously of the "evil tendencies of recent scientific theories" — evolution in particular — which threatened to "quench every virtuous thought." He stood "prepared to show that not a single scientific fact has ever been established" from which the deadly dogmas of Huxley and Tyndall could be "logically deduced."[57]

As Porter's evaluations suggest, Darwin's fate among Belfast Pres-

56. George Elder Davie, "Scottish Philosophy and Robertson Smith," in *The Scottish Enlightenment and Other Essays* (Edinburgh: Polygon, 1991), p. 131.

57. J. L. Porter, *Theological Colleges: Their Place and Influence in the Church and in the World; with Special Reference to the Evil Tendencies of Recent Scientific Theories. Being the Opening Lecture of Assembly's College, Belfast, Session 1874-75* (Belfast, 1874).

byterians was markedly different from his reception by their Edinburgh counterparts. Why? On Wednesday, 19 August 1874, the *Northern Whig* enthusiastically announced the coming of the "Parliament of Science" — the British Association — to Belfast. The meeting was being welcomed to the city as a temporary respite from "spinning and weaving, and Orange riots, and ecclesiastical squabbles." Nevertheless, "some hot discussions" were predicted "in the biological section," between advocates of human evolution and those "who believe there is a gulf between man and gorilla."[58] That year's president was the pugnacious Irish physicist John Tyndall. His truculent performance did not fall short of expectations; all "religious theories, schemes and systems," he thundered, "must . . . submit to the control of science, and relinquish all thought of controlling it."[59] The gauntlet had been thrown down.

So began Belfast's winter of discontent. Events moved quickly. The next Sunday, Tyndall's presidential address was the subject of a fractious attack by Rev. Professor Robert Watts at Fisherwick Church in downtown Belfast. Watts, the Assembly's professor of systematic theology, was already spitting blood on account of the fact that the Association had turned down his offer of a paper congenially calling for "peace and cooperation between Science and Theology." He delivered it the following Monday in Elmwood Church. Now Tyndall's mention of Epicurus galled him even more; that name had "become a synonym for sensualist," and Watts baulked at the moral implications of adopting Epicurean values.[60] The full details of his address appeared the next week in the church's weekly newspaper, *The Witness*, and a pamphlet, which sold 5,000 copies within a month, soon followed.

During that winter the Presbyterians put together a set of weekly lectures on the relationship between science and religion to stem any tide toward materialism that Tyndall's attack might trigger. Eight theologians and one scientist (David Moore of the Glasnevin Botanical Gardens in Dublin) took part.[61] The series was intended to enable

58. *Northern Whig,* Wednesday, 19 August 1874.

59. John Tyndall, *Address Delivered before the British Association Assembled at Belfast* (London, 1874).

60. Robert Watts, "Atomism — An Examination of Professor Tyndall's Opening Address before the British Association, 1874," in *The Reign of Causality: A Vindication of the Scientific Principle of Telic Causal Efficiency* (Edinburgh, 1888).

61. These were drawn together under the title *Science and Revelation: A Series of Lectures in Reply to the Theories of Tyndall, Huxley, Darwin, Spencer, Etc.* (Belfast, 1875).

the church's leadership to regain control of the debate. It was nothing less than a concerted effort to set the terms in which conversation about evolution in Ulster had to be conducted. Tyndall's rhetoric had made it virtually impossible for mediating voices to be heard. Watts was crystal clear: "According to Moses, the several species were brought into existence by distinct creative acts, not mediately through the utilization of previously existing organisms modified and adapted to new ends and habitats." The whole tenor of the Mosaic account, he insisted, was in "antagonism to our modern evolutionists."[62]

By now, Watts had grown entirely disillusioned with the Edinburgh New College network, and he actively cultivated links instead with Princeton Theological Seminary. In introducing a student to the Princeton campus he wrote to the theologian B. B. Warfield in 1893: "I am greatly pleased to find that our young men have turned their eyes to Princeton instead of Edinburgh."[63] In an earlier letter he had concluded: "I dread the influence of the Scotch Theological Halls."[64] He had in mind figures such as Marcus Dods, A. B. Bruce, and, of course, Robertson Smith, whose critical scholarship he found outrageous. Dods for his part was appalled and quipped that Watts was "one of those unhappily constituted men who cannot write unless they are angry."[65]

In different venues — Toronto, Columbia, Edinburgh, Belfast — Darwin was talked about in different ways, for in each place different cultural politics pertained. Place, politics, poetics. Without attending to these I think it is impossible to come to grips with what Darwinism was taken to mean and how the encounter with evolution was negotiated. Wider implications are surely to be drawn, as we saw from our initial reflections on more recent engagements. Debates on science and faith always need to be located — physically, politically, and culturally. And what is true for the pronouncements of others in science-religion debates has self-referential implications for those in the academy with their own religious convictions. For we, too, are located; and, if history

62. Robert Watts, "The Huxleyan Kosmogony," in *The Reign of Causality*, pp. 215-50, at 236.

63. Letter, Robert Watts to B. B. Warfield, 5 October 1893, Warfield Papers, Archives, Speer Library, Princeton Theological Seminary.

64. Letter, Robert Watts to B. B. Warfield, 13 October 1890, Warfield Papers, Archives, Speer Library, Princeton Theological Seminary.

65. Cited in Robert Allen, *The Presbyterian College Belfast, 1853-1953* (Belfast: William Mullan, 1954), p. 182.

is anything to go by, we are all too apt to mistake the particular for the transcendental, cultural forms for theological principles, contingency for necessity. For that reason faith traditions, if they are to remain vibrant rather than moribund, need to be in constant, critical dialogue with themselves.

Trading in the tired monochrome categories of conflict or cooperation, I suggest, is both historically dishonest and socially irresponsible. But whether attending to the subtleties of place, politics, and poetics has any chance of making a difference in the marketplace of contemporary cultural superficiality, I must leave for you to judge.

CHAPTER 4

On the Theology of the Intellectual Life

John Webster

In order to lay out a theology of the intellectual *life*, it is necessary first to expound a theology of the *intellect*, because to understand how to exercise a power we need to understand its nature; and to lay out a theology of the intellect it is necessary to say a little about the object and task of *theology*.

The object of Christian theological inquiry is God and all things in relation to God. This integral object can be broken down into two topics. First, theology is inquiry into God in himself, into the eternal, perfect, and eternally blessed life of God the Holy Trinity in his inner works. Second, and derivatively, theology is inquiry into the economy, that is, into the outer works of God as creator, reconciler, and perfecter of creatures, and so into the unfolding of created realities as they come from and return to God. Even though these two topics can never be disentangled, there is a proper material order to be followed in treating them. God in himself precedes the economy, for he is the uncreated creator who wholly transcends the creation of which he is the principle and which derives its being entirely from him. Yet within this order, neither topic can be left to one side: not God, for creatures are unintelligible without reference to the one by whom all things were made; and not creatures, for the uncreated one is indeed the creator of heaven and earth, to be considered also in his outer works.

It follows from this that theology is comprehensive in scope; it is the science of all things. Theology is about everything; but it is not about everything about everything, but about everything in relation to God. For theology, this "in relation to God" is fundamental to understanding any created reality. The being and activities of creatures can be adequately understood only when understood in their relation to the one by whom they were made and are preserved. Part of the task of a theology of created realities is thus to offer an evangelical metaphysics — an account of the nature of things that derives from the gospel's announcement of God as the origin, preserver, and end of creatures. A theology of the intellectual life is an element in this theological-metaphysical task.

What is the special responsibility of theology in this matter? Theology is a work of the regenerate mind directed by God toward God; it fulfills its vocation as it is instructed by the divine Word and illuminated by the Holy Spirit. Theology, that is, comes to know as it is taught and enlightened by God. Properly undertaken, theology relies on the presence of Word and Spirit, sent by the Father's love to heal the ignorance of creatures and conduct them into knowledge of the truth. The presence of the Word and the Spirit is communicative, bringing about in finite minds a creaturely replication of God's infinite knowledge of himself and all things. This communicative presence — these loving divine missions that, through the embassy of the prophets and apostles, generate knowledge — is what is meant by revelation. God himself speaks and sheds abroad his light, and so knowledge arises in the creaturely realm: "You have been anointed by the Holy One," the apostle John writes with some astonishment, and "you all have knowledge" (1 John 2:20).

As theology receives this divine instruction, how does it build up an account of the natures of created things, including the created intellect? Here are two accounts of that process, one rather formal in tone, a second that is more direct in its use of primary Christian language.

First, theology seeks to understand created things in terms of their *principles*.[1] By principles we mean those realities and powers by virtue of which other things exist and can be known. "Principles" are thus "foundations"; to know things in terms of their principles is to trace them back to the prior realities on which they rest and by which they are shaped. In Aristotelian terms, this is "knowledge by causes": we come to know *that* something is, *what* it is, and *how* it is by tracing its cause, that from which it comes and by which it is held in being. The idiom of principles and causes proved deeply attractive to some classi-

---

1. On this, see K. L. Schmitz, "Analysis by Principles and Analysis by Elements," in *Graceful Reason: Essays in Ancient and Medieval Philosophy Presented to Joseph Owens CSSR*, ed. L. P. Gerson (Toronto: PIMS, 1983), pp. 315-30.

cal Christian thinkers, especially the medieval and post-Reformation scholastics, above all because it enabled theology to articulate a set of profound metaphysical and spiritual convictions: realities other than God are not free-standing, self-subsistent realities; such realities do not have their being in themselves and do not persist of themselves, but owe being and persistence to the being and action of another; to understand such realities we must therefore make reference to the one from whom they come and on whom they depend. In short, the idiom of principles and causes is a way of spelling out the metaphysics of creation and createdness.

It is important not to allow the formality of the idiom to distract or frustrate us, for it is simply an abstract rendering of the spiritually perceived and wholly delightful truth that all created things come from God's generosity. God's generosity is his love turned outward to bestow being on that which is not; it is the abundance with which he who alone has life in himself purposes, makes, and preserves all things. The movement of divine love is the principle and cause of creatures and their movements; to come to know those creatures is to come to know that movement by which their movements are moved.

This takes us to the threshold of a second, more *material* description of the same matter. All created things, including created intellect, are to be understood in terms of the history of fellowship between God and creatures. This history is the long, complex, yet unified movement of God's giving, sustaining, and consummating created life. Created reality is as it participates in this history with God. It is a history with three principal moments, which correspond to the three great external divine works. There is, first, the moment of creation; God the Father, maker of heaven and earth, brings creatures into being out of nothing and bestows on them their several natures. To human creatures he gives a nature that is not fully formed, one that unfolds over time, that is enacted. There is, second, the moment of reconciliation. Human creatures reject the vocation that their given nature entails, and seek to be what they are not: self-originating, self-sustaining, self-perfecting. Yet such is the goodness of the creator that creatures are not permitted to ruin themselves. God destines the creature for perfection, and God is not hindered. In the history of covenant grace, at whose center lies the incarnation of the Word and which embraces creatures now in the Spirit's quickening power, God arrests the creature's plunge into destruction and turns the creature back to himself. And so there is, third, the moment of consummation, inaugurated but awaiting completion, in which the creator ensures that creatures reach their end.

All created reality is caught up in and determined by this history. For the Christian gospel, there is no secularity, no nature and time that is not referred wholly to God, because there is nothing other than God that is not a creature, and there is no creature that is not shaped by the works of God. This being so, metaphysical ambition is not only permitted but required of Christian theology: it is obligated to search the gospel for an account of the nature of things. Modern theology has commonly shied away from this task, persuaded by its opponents that the territory of the metaphysics of nature and history is territory over which theology has lost control and can claim no jurisdiction. By consequence, theology has often contented itself with a reduced role, restricting itself at best to a theology of the benefits of Christ, at worst to a science of Christian piety. The gospel concerning Jesus Christ permits no such retractions, because its scope is universal. "In him all things in heaven and on earth were created . . . all things have been created through him and for him. He himself is before all things . . . he is the beginning, . . . so that he might come to have the first place in everything" (Col. 1:16-18). Because Jesus Christ is this one — the *archē*, "the author and restorer of all things," as Calvin has it[2] — Christian theology will have much to say about the things of which he is author and restorer, including created intellect; to this we now turn our attention.

The Created and Creative Intellect

To talk of created intellect, we must observe the proper order of things and begin by talking of God's intellect in which created intellect has its principle and cause.

God is pure intelligent being, in whose mind is all knowledge and wisdom. The divine intellect is infinite: unrestricted in the scope of its knowledge, and knowing all things not by laborious acquisition but in a simple act of intuition. God's uncreated intellect differs qualitatively, not merely by extent, from the intellect of creatures. The mind of God, says Augustine, is "so greatly abounding in knowledge" as to be

2. John Calvin, *The Epistles of Paul the Apostle to the Galatians, Ephesians, Philippians and Colossians* (Edinburgh: Oliver and Boyd, 1965), p. 311 (on Col. 1:18).

"exceedingly wonderful and very astonishing."[3] Yet, though the incommensurability of divine and human intellect is fundamental, it is not all that is to be said. The God whose intellect is boundlessly exalted is also author and teacher of finite intelligence. By virtue of God's work of creation and preservation, there exists a certain correspondence between the intellect of God and the intellect of creatures; there is an element in the being of the creature that is a coordinate to God's own mind. Further, it is to this creaturely element that God addresses himself, for he who knows himself and all things also wills to *be known* by creatures, to become at his own behest and by his own instruction an object of created intelligence. If this is so, what is to be said of the created intellect by which God wills to be known?

Intellect is essential to human creatures (and not just to those human creatures who consider themselves "intellectuals," for the intellectual life is simply a modification and intensification of something true of all human creatures). The intellect is the human creature's power of apprehension. It is the capacity for the kind of knowledge, understanding, and thought that differentiates humans from beasts and that is intrinsic to all our dealings with reality. Our relations to us, to the material, animal, and social worlds, and ultimately to God all take place by virtue of our possession of an intellectual nature.

But *how* do we possess it? We have this intellectual nature as *creatures*. Creatureliness is basic; we have our being and exercise its powers in a particular way, namely, not in ourselves but by virtue of God's being and activity. We live, move, and have our being in him. This does not mean that we are not really alive, that we lack substance or endurance. It means that the substance that we have — including the *intellectual* substance that we have — is of God. Two things follow from this.

First, to have intellect is necessarily to stand in relation to God; the very possession of intellect locates us *coram Deo*, before God. This is because to *have* this capacity is to *have received* this capacity, to be — as Calvin once more puts it — "clothed and ornamented with God's excellent gifts."[4] Created intellect is an endowment, not just pure nature, and its possession places us in relation to the one by whom we are endowed. This relation is one in which God is not only the ultimate origin of created intellect but also the one by whose quickening and empowering intellect is sustained.

3. Augustine, *Confessions*, trans. Rex Warner (New York: Penguin, 2001), XI.31.
4. John Calvin, *Institutes of the Christian Religion*, II.2.15.

Second, to have intellect is to exist under a particular determination or vocation. Intellect is a capacity for activity; "possession" and "exercise" belong together. To have intellect is not just to possess a property but to execute a movement. Yet what kind of movement? A movement that is moved from beyond itself, though no less our own movement because of that. The movement of creative intellect is moved by God so that not only the origin but also the exercise of intellect has God as its principle. This does not mean that the work of created intellect is not our performance; it means that the condition for our performance is God's work on us and in us. Calvin again: God "fills, moves, and quickens all things by the power of the . . . Spirit," and does so not in violation of the integrity of the creature but "according to the character that he bestowed upon each kind by the law of creation."[5]

So much by way of general description. What may be said in more detail about the created intellect at work?

Created intellect works *discursively.* It does not understand intuitively, in an instant, but comes to understand by a process of learning. Aquinas put this in formal terms, by saying that the intellect of creatures is a "passive power," in the sense that its operation proceeds as a movement from potentiality to actuality.[6] God's intellect has no potentiality; it is a pure, fully realized act of understanding. Not so with creatures: creaturely intellectual activity is a matter of *acquiring* knowledge, *coming* to understand, *reaching* judgments. Created intellect takes time.

Alongside this, however, it is important to recognize that this coming to understand is not a process in which the intellect has nothing to do, as if objects of knowledge simply impress themselves on the intellect. Created intellect is not a purely receptive medium; quite the contrary. As Aquinas again puts it, "there has to be an intellectual agency which by an abstractive process makes things actually open to understanding."[7] Coming to understand is a work, not a simple surrender. But what kind of work? Perhaps we might say something along these lines.

Created intellect is awakened to activity by sense experience: we see, hear, and touch things, becoming aware of their presence to us. The intelligibility of these realities happens as we move beyond mere con-

---

5. Calvin, *Institutes of the Christian Religion,* II.2.16.

6. Aquinas, *Summa Theologiae,* trans. Timothy Suttor, vol. 11, *Man* (Cambridge: Cambridge University Press, 2006), Ia.79.2.

7. Aquinas, *Summa,* Ia.79.3.

sciousness of their surface phenomena: the color of beech leaves in early spring, the fine tracery of the tree's branches. By the intellect's operation we begin to assimilate a pattern, to generalize and compare, to abstract from sensible particulars; in short, to understand what something is: a beech tree. This act of intelligence is not "poetic"; it is, certainly, an act of "making" but not of "making up." Say it is an act of establishing an intelligent relation to something that precedes the intellect, something that is inherently intelligible. Intellect discerns intelligibility, follows the intelligible as the law by which it operates. This discernment takes stable form by representation: the intellect forms an idea of the reality that endures beyond the instant of apprehension and that enables us to rehearse and reproduce that reality, to preserve things in thought, and by the operation of memory to retrieve them.

This, in the crudest terms, is the intellect's work of making things actually intelligible. The intellect, of course, does not do its work in isolation from other elements of our creatureliness. It is inseparable from the body, for though intellect is not executed by any specific bodily organ, it is not executed apart from the body's acts: to know, I must breathe. Further, the intellect sits alongside the emotions or passions, those movements of inclination toward or aversion from realities that present themselves before us, and alongside the will, the power of appetite that impels us in a certain direction. We are intellectual creatures in and with our being embodied, emotional, and volitional creatures. But within that complex, intellect has the task of governance. Human creatures fulfill their nature when their performance of themselves is ordered by knowledge, and knowledge is seated in the intellect. The intellect directs the body, the emotions, and the will, restraining them from taking command, and ensuring that they are fixed on proper objects. Intellect apprehends the law of our nature, which we are to love, seek, and embody.

In such ways the gift of created intellect fulfills its vocation. But vocation can be resisted, and given powers can become instruments of ingratitude and treason against our nature and its loving creator. How does this happen? What sorrow and damage are brought about when intellect becomes vicious and depraved?

Fallen Intellect

In making the turn from considering created intellect to considering the intellect in its fallen state, two matters should orient our reflections. First, however grave the depravity of the intellect, it is not something absolute and must be enclosed within and limited by the more primary reality of the intellect's regeneration. The deformation of the intellect is never more than an interim reality, an interval between the intellect's integrity at creation and its perfection in the world to come; its defection from its calling has already been arrested by the Word and the Spirit. There is a vicious intellect, and there is intellectual vice; but, even more, there is "the new self, which is being renewed in knowledge according to the image of its creator" (Col. 3:10). God remains the intellect's Lord. Second, we would be unwise to think of the depravity of the intellect as a peculiarly modern occurrence, a collateral effect of the naturalization of our view of ourselves. It assumes peculiar modern forms, such as the association of the intellect with pure human spontaneity and resistance to the idea that the movement of the mind is moved by God. But these are instances of perennial treachery; if our intellects are depraved, it is not because we are children of Scotus or Descartes or Kant, but because we are children of Adam.

What intellectual defect do we inherit and repeat? Sin is betrayal of our created nature and refusal to live out the vocation that that nature entails. Life in, with, and under the creator involves three elements: glad consent to the nature and powers that in his love the creator has bestowed on us; use of our given powers in ways that move us to our creaturely fulfillment; fellowship with the creator. To take these in turn: (1) Unlike beasts, human animals have a conscious, deliberate, and consensual relation to our nature. We are not simply instinctual creatures; we are reflectively aware of our nature, and so we are able to make it our own rather than merely act it out in an unconscious way. This power is the freedom in which we possess our nature; it is the power of awareness of and consent to being the sort of creatures that we have been made to be. (2) Having our nature in this way, we are to perform it. Our nature has a teleological structure; to possess it is to be required to engage in a movement in which our nature is fulfilled. Our given powers are powers to fill out our nature in certain ways and not in others, to give ourselves this, not that, shape. Not all uses of our powers lead to the fulfillment of our nature; some are wicked and destructive. Once again, we must deliberate and direct ourselves. (3) As we fill out our nature by deploying our powers, we do so in relation to God. This means that we are to use our powers in accordance with the purpose of the creator and in dependence upon the creator's grace. Only in relation to him can creatures come to enjoy their good.

The children of Adam do not do these things. They despise and oppose their given nature and fail in their vocation. The freedom to consent becomes the freedom to dissent, to act against the purpose of the creator. We give ourselves permission to use our powers to fill out our nature in ways that the creator has not left open to us; as we take that permission, we come to think of ourselves as grand beings, rich and fascinating makers of possibilities. And so we edge ourselves away from life in obedience to the creator's purpose and reliance on the creator's goodness; we fall into evil self-responsibility. In all of this, we cannot, of course, unmake our own nature: even the most depraved exercise of creaturely powers cannot undo the work of the creator. But we can disrupt the performance of our nature and indulge ourselves in the belief that we have brought something original into being. Yet what is that self-made nature? Nothing but corruption, a vain essay in the unmaking of ourselves. Adam gains nothing from the fall except guilt, and what he loses is very great.

How is the intellect caught up in the corruption of Adam's children?

As with our created nature in general, so with our intellectual nature: sin cannot eradicate what God has made. But the performance of our intellectual nature is deeply distorted, and our movement toward perfection halted in its tracks. We may listen to Calvin's instruction on this point. Calvin firmly resists any notion that our intellectual powers are destroyed by the fall: "something of intelligence and judgment remains as a residue," he writes; creatures retain a power of perception and "some sort of desire to search out the truth"; even sinners continue to be captivated by love of truth. Yet the intellect is gravely damaged; it is "weak," "plunged" into such "deep darkness" and so "corrupted" that all that we see of created intellect are "its misshapen ruins" *(deformes ruinae)*. Intellect as a capacity or disposition remains, even though in severely impaired form; what is lacking is the intellect's purposeful and well-directed execution of itself. It "cannot come forth effectively" *(efficaciter emergere nequeat)*, Calvin says; the "longing for truth, such as it is, languishes before it enters upon its race because it soon falls into vanity. Indeed, the human mind, because of its dullness, cannot hold to the right path but wanders through various errors and stumbles repeatedly, as if it were groping in darkness, until it strays away and finally disappears. Thus it betrays how incapable it is of seeking and finding truth."[8]

After the fall, the intellect descends into what the apostle calls "futility," a failure to run its proper course. Of the many symptoms of this futility, we may select one to which the Christian tradition has often drawn attention, namely, curiosity.

We have grown accustomed to consider curiosity either innocent or virtuous. For the earlier Christian tradition, however, curiosity is a vice. It is vicious because it is a corruption of the virtue of *studiousness*. By studiousness we mean the strenuous application of the powers of creaturely intellect in order to come to know. Indeed, studiousness is an element in all the works of intelligence, being basic to the implementation of our intellectual nature. The intellect's power is known in its eager, assiduous, concentrated deployment. Yet there is a measure of ambivalence in studiousness. From one angle it is itself a good, because in pursuing knowledge it puts to work the powers of our created nature. But in pursuit of that good, intellectual powers must be applied properly, that is, to fitting objects, in due measure, and for fitting ends. Such is the intellect's futility after the fall that this does not happen; studiousness is corrupted into curiosity.

Curiosity happens when intellectual activity is commanded by crooked desire. We may note some of its manifestations. (1) Curiosity applies the power of the intellect to improper objects; it is the intellect reaching beyond what is legitimate, and so refusing to give consent to the limitations of created intelligence. Curiosity, Augustine says, "snaps the reins of prohibition under the pressure of the desire to know as God knows."[9] Curiosity is the intellect defying divine limitation and exceeding divine permission; in it, the intellect seeks to be unbounded, and precisely so fails to fulfill its created nature. (2) Curiosity directs the power of the intellect to knowing created realities without reference to their creator. The curious intellect stops short at corporeal properties of things, lingering too long over them and not allowing them to steer intelligence to the creator. Curiosity is greedy for "new experiences

---

8. Calvin, *Institutes*, II.2.2.

9. Augustine, *The Literal Meaning of Genesis*, in *The Works of St. Augustine*, vol. 13, *On Genesis*, ed. John E. Rotelle, trans. Edmund Hill (Hyde Park, NY: New City Press, 2002), XI.40.

through the flesh," Augustine once again says,[10] and its very eagerness halts the movement of intelligence. (3) Curiosity is a deformation of the proper manner in which created intellect is called to operate. Curiosity involves inordinate appetite for new knowledge — a craving for intellectual novelty that is addictive and that swamps intelligence. As such, it is indiscriminate intellectual greed. Curiosity craves the excitement of acquiring new knowledge, caring nothing for the worth or otherwise of the objects of intelligence. Moreover, curiosity is entangled with pride. Gratification of an inflamed appetite expands our pleasure in our own powers and makes us satisfied with ourselves. Curiosity does this, and so erodes the lowliness of spirit and teachableness that must accomplish the proper exercises of the mind. (4) Finally, curiosity pursues knowledge for improper ends: perhaps to increase self-esteem, or to accomplish some evil purpose, or to feed a prurient appetite for the new.

Curiosity is a telling instance of the intellect's declension and disarray in the wake of the fall. But like all such instances of intellectual defect, it is decisively countered by the mercy of God in the reconciliation and regeneration of the mind. How is this so?

Adam bequeathed to his heirs futility of mind, darkness of understanding, and alienation from the life of God because of ignorance (Eph. 4:17-18). These vices and deformities are beyond any repair that creatures might of themselves attempt. Such is the intellect's incapacity that mere exhortation to temperance will not suffice; nor will rules for the direction of the mind or patterns of formation through catechesis have of themselves any permanent effect, because they are powerless against the alienation from the life of God that lies at the core of our intellectual disarray. What is needed, the apostle tells us, is renewal in the spirit of the mind (Eph. 4:23). This no creature can effect; but God can do so, and has done so in the loving missions of the incarnate Son of God and the outpoured Spirit.

It is the mission of the incarnate Son to put an end to the enmity between God and the creatures of God, to effect reconciliation. At the behest of the Father, and in fulfillment of the Father's unshakeable purpose of fellowship with his human creation, the Son of God takes to himself the creature's fallen condition in all its squalor and shame. In taking it to himself, he takes it away, freely submitting in his own person

---

10. Augustine, *The Confessions of St. Augustine*, trans. Albert C. Outler (1955; repr., Mineola, NY: Dover, 2002), X.35.

to its destruction, and so actually destroying it, making it the "old" nature. And more: in our stead he lives the true life of the creatures of God, gathering us to himself so that we come to be new creatures in him. In all this, he constitutes and effects the "new" nature by reconciliation. Because he is who he is — the one "in [whom] all the fullness of God was pleased to dwell" — he "reconcile[s] to himself all things" (Col. 1:19-20). This "all things" includes in its scope the created intellect: those who were "once estranged and hostile in mind . . . he has now reconciled in his fleshly body through death" (Col. 1:21-22). By virtue of the Word made flesh, that is, there arises a new created intellectual nature.

It is the mission of the Holy Spirit to realize and preserve this new intellectual nature. The Holy Spirit is the Lord and giver of life; he so works upon and in reconciled creatures that the new nature comes to be their own. Intellectual dispositions that had fallen asleep are awakened at the Spirit's approach; powers that had ebbed away and dissipated are restored and concentrated; desires that had scattered into chaos are directed to what is good and holy. And so the intellect begins once again to move, and by the breath of the Spirit there arises a new intellectual *life* corresponding to the new intellectual nature. We now turn to some reflections on the characteristics of this new intellectual life.

The Regenerated Mind

So far we have examined three components of a Christian theology of the intellect: the nature and operation of created intellect; the intellect's devastation as a consequence of our disloyalty to God; the reconciliation and regeneration of the intellect by the works of the Son and the Spirit. Christians engaging in intellectual work do so in the realm of regeneration, as those to whom the Holy Spirit has imparted a new principle of intellectual life, new powers, and a new vocation. What does the living of this life look like? What human forms does it take? Before sketching the outlines of an answer, three preliminary matters should be dispatched.

First, when we turn to speak of living the intellectual life, we do not cease to speak of the grace of God. Life in the realm of regeneration conforms to the character of creaturely being, namely, that we have life and movement as we are vivified and moved by God. The first law of intellectual life is, therefore: "All this is from God" (2 Cor. 5:18).

Second, in the intellectual life this "from God" does not eliminate but establishes and sustains our proper intellectual nature and movement. As he imparts a new principle to the intellect, the Spirit makes the intellect alive and active. This is perhaps hard for us to see, because we have been schooled into the assumption that divine and human action are in competition, so that to speak of the Spirit's moving of the mind is to erode the mind's own work. Not so: God the Spirit moves not extrinsically, as an alien causal power, but intrinsically, as the mover of our movement. Only by God's moving does the intellect move; but by God's moving the intellect does, indeed, move. The second law of intellectual life is, therefore: God "is at work in you, enabling you both to will and to work" (Phil. 2:13).

Third, the life into which we have been born anew awaits consummation; and so the intellectual life of believers, though regenerate, is not yet brought to completion. Christian intellectual life participates in the comprehensive alteration of our state by God; it is "born . . . of God" (John 1:13). But the new principle that this establishes does not instantaneously propel the intellect to perfection; rather, it sets the intellect within the history of sanctification in which, by the empowerment and illumination of the Spirit, believers have to inhabit and actively to fill out the new nature given to them. They do this by a double process of detachment and appropriation: detachment, because they need to separate themselves from the old nature that is no longer their own; appropriation, because they need to *make* their own the new nature that *is* their own. How does this happen in the sphere of the intellect?

In the realm of regeneration, the basic elements and operations of created intellect remain: its discursive character, its making things intelligible by representation, and so on, continue unaltered. Yet there is much that is new. The renewal of the intellect effects an entire alteration of the manner or conduct of the intellectual life. Life in Christ and the Spirit brings with it a characteristic way of understanding the life of the mind, one that distinguishes it from other ways of living that life. A number of matters present themselves for reflection:

(1) There is in the performance of regenerate intellectual life a pervasive sense that this life has emerged out of a decisive alteration of our condition and capacities. Persons engaging in this life are deeply mindful that the life of their natural intellectual existence has been broken; that they have been brought forth "by the word of truth" (Jas. 1:18), awakened and enlightened by the Spirit; in short, converted. This sense

is to suffuse all intellectual activity, generating a distinctive mode of intellectual life. It manifests itself as a set of the mind that takes the form of gratitude — that what was once in ruins is now being rebuilt, that fallen ignorance is being checked and overcome, that exhausted and damaged natural powers are made to live and act again by a second gift of the creator.

(2) Regenerate intellectual life exhibits teachableness. It takes place in the domain and active presence of the divine instructor, by whose instruction intelligence is healed. Can human intellect be taught of God and retain its dignity and proper energy? Kant opposed enlightenment and tutelage, considering the latter to be servility and lack of resolution in the life of reason. To look for intellectual direction from another is to say, "I need not trouble myself, I need not think."[11] But for regenerate intellectual life, this is not so; in the school of divine instruction, intelligence *flourishes*. It does so because the one who teaches is not some hostile dictatorial pedagogue, but the loving, creative divine wisdom that repairs intelligence. His teaching heals and restores. "Those who are diseased in soul," says Clement of Alexandria, "require an instructor to cure our maladies, and then a teacher, to train and guide the soul to all requisite knowledge"; and such we have in the divine instructor who "guides the sick to the perfect knowledge of the truth."[12]

(3) The performance of regenerate intellectual life requires the exercise of both intellectual and moral virtues. The required intellectual virtues are simply the mind's natural powers, given by the creator and renewed and strengthened by regeneration. Without their exercise, the intellectual life will not happen. Alongside this, regenerate intellectual life also requires the exercise of certain moral and ascetical virtues. The operation of redeemed intelligence calls for powers in addition to intelligence; it stipulates that we become certain kinds of persons. We do this not by self-cultivation but by the Spirit's cultivating work; what the Spirit effects is a set of character that becomes the moral and spiritual climate within which the life of the intellect can prosper. Here are a couple of examples:

(a) The intellectual life requires a concentration of the will on intel-

---

11. Kant, "What Is Enlightenment?" in *Kant on History*, ed. L. W. Beck (New York: Macmillan, 1963), p. 3.

12. Clement of Alexandria, *Paedogogus*, http://www.ccel.org/ccel/schaff/anf02.vi .iii.i.i.html (accessed 18 June 2013), I.1.

lectual vocation and ready compliance with its requirements. Serious and sustained intellectual resolve is necessary; this work cannot be entered upon casually and cannot be pursued indolently, intermittently, or in a distracted way. The necessary resolve includes being prepared for the losses that will most likely be sustained: of bodily ease, perhaps, or of society, or of easy acceptance of much that surrounds us. And the resolve also entails acceptance of the sheer labor of acquiring facility with the means and skills of intellectual life. Such resolve is rarely natural to us; to exercise it, we must become pliable and obedient; and pliability and obedience are matters of the Spirit's grace.

(b) The intellectual life requires the ruling and right use of the body, a regime in which care for the body serves and does not hinder the intellect's vocation. We may shy away from talking of the subservience of the body, considering the body a great good and scolding earlier Christians for failing to realize the fact. The body is a good, and its care is a duty; but its goodness consists principally in its service of other goods, of which the intellectual life is one. And so — again under the Spirit's superintendence — intellectual activity demands discipline of the body in such matters as food, speech, rest, and movement.

The examples indicate the kind of virtues that issue from conversion and shape intellectual disposition. To do its work well, the intellect needs to be unimpeded; but because we are still climbing out of our sinful selves, many impediments loiter around inside us, and we often cherish them. Moral and ascetical virtues are a way in which the Spirit moves us to remove such encumbrances and make intelligence ready for truth.

(4) Regenerate intellectual life is conducted with calm awareness and embrace of the limitations and opportunities of its present situation, and therefore undertaken *freely*. We are where we are, in our own bit of the history of human culture, in certain institutions, and in the society of certain others; we are not elsewhere. Either nostalgia for where we are not, or bitter hostility to where we are, is fruitless. But because the principle of our intellectual life is the presence of God in his Word and Spirit, we are given a liberty both from and for our circumstances. Our present condition constrains us: certain resources have been forgotten or are difficult of access; common prejudices hold us back; questions press themselves on our attention with great insistence; habits of thought may hold us in their thrall. Yet the same situation also affords opportunities, opening up possibilities we would otherwise not enjoy,

prompting us in unexpectedly fruitful ways. In all this, regenerate intellectual life must prove its freedom. Heeding the gospel's instruction, it can adopt an uninhibited posture toward its setting. It does not think of that setting as fate, sweeping everything before it; it can seize the opportunities without being bound by the limitations. It can, therefore, take place in a manner that allows that the present is the object of both God's judgment and God's provision, not resigning itself to the sour thought that the present is all there is.

(5) Regenerate intellectual life devotes itself to the study of created things in order to ascend to contemplation of God, for in contemplation of God lies our true happiness. There are two objects of intellectual consideration: creatures and God. We study creatures in the natural and social sciences and the humanities — "creatures," note, not nature or society or human culture, as if these were complete in themselves and did not refer us to God. For the regenerate intellect there are no secular studies, because there is nothing that is not to be traced to God as its principle. Say, therefore, that in our study of natural and social and cultural objects we study the "works of God"; that is, we treat such objects of inquiry as objects that have their own natural integrity but that in that very integrity point us to the creator. The fallen mind, trapped in curiosity, does not permit study of creatures to prompt consideration of the creator; instead, it arrests the movement of intelligence by fastening on natural surfaces and does not penetrate to the depth beneath the created sign. Regenerate studiousness, by contrast, inquires into creatures — with ardent attention, respect, and well-tempered delight — in order to be drawn also to knowledge of God. Created things, Augustine says, are "stepping stones to immortal and everlasting things."[13] To study them as such is not to pass over them inconsiderately, as vain and shallow matters scarcely fitting for the regenerate mind; it is, rather, to study them in such a way that intelligence is stretched out to God. "The ultimate fulfillment of the human intellect is divine truth," Aquinas tells us; "other truths enrich the intellect by their being ordered to divine truth."[14]

---

13. Augustine, quoted in Aquinas, *Summa*, IIa IIae. 180.4.
14. Aquinas, *Summa,* IIa IIae. 180.4.

John Webster

The Gift of Thought

For Christian faith, the intellect and its operations are not pure natural elements but created realities, to be explicated by reference to God's loving work of origination, preservation, reconciliation, and perfection. Only as we are brought to know that divine charity is the setting in which we enact ourselves do we come to understand our own nature, including our intellectual nature. But God's charity and its formation of our lives are only indirectly perceptible, known only in the course of making our answer to divine grace. Because this is so, Christians cannot escape a measure of estrangement from their neighbors who do not make the Christian confession; the estrangement is such that those neighbors may sometimes view Christian conceptions of the intellectual life with amusement, disdain, or even hostility. There is no surprise in this: it is an axiom of Christian faith that "the mind that is set on the flesh is hostile to God" (Rom. 8:7), and Christians trying to map the world with a firm eye on their confession will endure a share of that hostility. It is important to respond to this state of affairs prudently: neither anxiously nor with belligerent zeal, but with tranquil confidence that the gospel outbids the world; with modesty, because the gospel can look after itself; and with charity, because the gospel seeks our neighbor's good and not just our neighbor's defeat. To this end, calm exposition of first principles serves the gospel best. The truth will establish itself; we must simply let it run on its own path.

CHAPTER 5

Christianity and the Contemporary Challenge

ELEONORE STUMP

Without doubt, there are things in contemporary academic culture that are hostile to Christianity and opposed to any attempt to integrate Christian beliefs with academic work. One challenge to the integration of Christianity and learning therefore comes from those who reject Christianity and are outsiders to the faith.

But another important challenge to Christianity in the academy actually comes from those who identify themselves as Christian. The problem here is that on a whole range of issues that matter deeply to religious believers Christians no longer speak with one voice, if they ever did; and the internal dissension can be more destructive than any external attack. Some years ago, one embittered conservative Catholic professor at a Catholic university complained to me that there were no longer any Catholics — apart from himself — in his department. The complaint was perplexing because there were a number of Catholic priests in his department, and I said so. "You call those priests Catholic?" he said bitterly; "I feel about them the way Cromwell felt about the Irish: shoot them all, and let God sort them out." He did not say how those priests felt about him. But it is fair to suppose that they did not regard him as an ally in their program for the integration of Christian faith and learning. So a second challenge to Christianity in the academy comes from the internal dividedness of the Christian community itself.

In this essay, I want to discuss both the external and the internal challenge to the integration of faith and learning. I will begin with the external challenge that comes from the outsiders who think that the attempt to integrate Christian commitment with learning is pernicious to the goals of higher education. Then I will turn to the challenge posed by the lack of philosophical and theological consensus on the part of the Christian community itself.

The External Challenge

Many non-Christian academics ask whether it is even possible for scholarship and Christian conviction to mix. On the face of it, this might seem to be a foolish question. Widespread atheism among intellectuals is a fairly recent phenomenon in the Western tradition, and scholarship of all sorts has been characteristic of Christianity almost from its inception. So for most of Christian history, everyone would have supposed that there is an obvious answer to the question whether Christianity and scholarship can mix: Yes, it can!

Since the Enlightenment, however, many people have supposed the right answer is "No, it can't!" and it isn't so hard to see why they think so. The Enlightenment believed that all reputable learning is a *universal or generically human* enterprise. This belief is part of a view sometimes called "modernism." In academia, modernists have thought, we should put aside all our particularities — of gender, race, nationality, religion, social class, age — and enter into the project of learning just as the generic human beings we are.

Modernists have also thought that there is a certain hierarchy to academic disciplines. Science is at or near the top, as the paradigm of what academic learning should be; and theology is at or near the bottom. For the modernist, the sciences represent our ideal of learning; and since theology is so far from using the scientific method, theology falls seriously short of the ideal. On these views, any reputable learning has to operate in the way science does; and it has to be a generically human enterprise, which makes no allowances for the particularities among human beings.

And that is why modernists thought Christianity and reputable academic work do not mix. On modernist views, mixing Christianity with scholarship just wrecks the scholarship. The combination of Christianity and scholarship will not operate according to the rules of science; and Christian scholarship is not a generically human enterprise, able to be engaged in by everybody regardless of their particularities. Recent years have seen the rise in academia of what we call "postmodernism." Postmodernists reject much of the picture of the modernists. The academic good news of the day, according to the postmodernists, is that the false views of modernism have been shattered. There is now a new view of scholarship, and even of science and the methods by which scientists work. According to many postmodernists, science, even in its celebrated achievements, shows the effects of human biases, self-interest, and politics. And so all learning, even scientific research, is done in the context of culture and politics; none of it is universal or generically human.

Consequently, postmodernists repudiate the modernist ideal of generically human learning. For postmodernists, it is only pretense to present any scholarship as generically human in character; all of it is done from the vantage point of one human particularity or another. And, of course, the main particularity the postmodernists thought characterized much of academic work in the past is the particularity of Eurocentric white males. Postmodernist views have generated a great deal of debate. There are still some people who embrace the old modernist ideal of universal, generically human learning and who refuse to concede the postmodernist charge that the academy has not lived up to that ideal in the past. There are also people who still embrace the modernist ideal but who are willing to grant that the academy has fallen short of it; they acknowledge that the academy has privileged one particularity, as the postmodernists claim. And then there are people who accept postmodernism. They reject the modernist ideal entirely and argue that particularist learning is all there is. These people want many different particularities and viewpoints represented in the academy, and they tend to see them as all equally legitimate.

There are not too many people who still believe in the modernist ideal and think that the academy has lived up to it. Most academics see that view as flying in the face of overwhelming evidence against it. So I will leave it to one side. In the current climate on American campuses, it no longer seems a viable option. The two remaining views are apparently these, then. We can hold on to the old modernist ideal but grant that the academy has failed to live up to it. That is, we can acknowledge that academia has largely reflected the particularity of Eurocentric white males, but we can hold nonetheless that the modernist ideal is still the right one. In that case, we will also think that the academy just needs to try harder to live up to that ideal and enforce it. Alternatively, we can repudiate the modernist ideal altogether and accept postmodernism.

Then we will argue for the right of other particularities to engage in learning from their own, equally legitimate perspectives.

In this debate, some Christian academics have adopted postmodernism and have seen in it an opportunity for Christianity to flourish in academia, as it hasn't done for many years. Although it is a position with which I am going to disagree, it is an important and thoughtful point of view, held by a growing number of eminent Christian academics; and so I want to look at it in some detail.

On the postmodernist view, there is no such thing as universal, generically human learning or scholarship. And since there isn't, all learning, all scholarship, has to be particularist and perspectival. According to postmodernism, we need to acknowledge this fact. But if all learning and scholarship represent just one perspective and one human particularity, then there is no basis for anyone to claim that Christianity itself is not an allowable particularity. Christianity is as allowable as any other particularity and perspective.

One person who adopted this position in earlier work is the well-known Christian philosopher Nicholas Wolterstorff. He argued that everyone in the academy is engaged in particularist work. And he made some recommendations for doing this particularist scholarship well. He said that "those who self-consciously engage in particularist perspectival learning must always face in two directions[:] . . . reflection with the members of their own communities . . . [and] conversation with those who represent other perspectives, so as both to share insight and submit to correction." "The goal," he said, "is thereby to arrive at a richer, a broader, a more accurate perspective. This . . . is what should replace that old but impossible [modernist] ideal of generically human learning."[1]

On a view such as this, the answer to the question whether Christianity and scholarship can mix is a definite affirmative, but that affirmative answer does not mark a return to the old modernist worldview represented by a Christian thinker such as Augustine, for example. Instead, the idea is that Christianity and scholarship can legitimately mix, because *all* scholarship is only perspectival, and Christianity is one perspective among others. Proponents of a particular perspective should engage in reflective dialogue with the proponents of other perspectives;

---

1. Nicholas Wolterstorff, *Educating for Shalom*, ed. Clarence W. Joldersma and Gloria Goris Stronks (Grand Rapids: Eerdmans, 2004), p. 190.

and Christians, like everybody else, should be prepared to alter some of their beliefs in consequence of that dialogue.

Many people suppose that this is the view that is dominant in the academy. They think that the modernist ideal of universal, generically human learning has been seen to be a mistake by almost everyone who isn't a hide-bound conservative. To them, modernism looks like an Enlightenment illusion, about as palatable now as the notion that the Europeans brought civilization to the savages.

I am not convinced that this impression of the current climate of opinion in the academy is correct. For example, the acclaimed philosopher Kwame Anthony Appiah argues eloquently against the particularism of postmodernism in his impressive book *In My Father's House*. For Appiah, something like a failure to accept the idea that there is a universal, generic human nature, in learning and elsewhere, is at the heart of all racism. In discussing the nineteenth-century Pan-Africanist Alexander Crummell, Appiah argues that those who make race a basis for grouping human beings into particularities are still racists of one sort or another, even if their intentions are benevolent rather than oppressive. He sums up his argument:

> Americans need . . . to escape from some of the misunderstandings in modern discourse . . . epitomized in the racialism of Alexander Crummell. . . . Because the intellectual projects of our one world are essentially everywhere interconnected, because the world's cultures are bound together now through institutions, through histories, through writings, [Crummell in fact] has something to teach [not just Africans, as he thought, but rather] the one race to which we *all* belong.[2]

Whatever we may think of Appiah's position here, a different problem for particularism can be readily seen by considering Appiah the man. He was born in Africa to a British mother and an African father, related to the royal household of Ghana. He was raised in Africa and educated in Britain. His family was important in African politics; but he himself is employed at an Ivy-League university in the U.S. Now, if Appiah were to engage in particularist learning, what particularity

2. Kwame Anthony Appiah, *In My Father's House* (New York: Oxford University Press, 1992), p. 27.

would he belong to? How would he identify his particularity of race? Of nationality? For that matter, why suppose, for example, that gender or race constitutes one particularity? As Appiah himself points out,[3] the experiences of American blacks are vastly different from the experiences of blacks in Africa, and African blacks themselves have a myriad of different languages, traditions, and histories. So it is not easy to decide what constitutes a person's particularity.

In addition, the case postmodernists make against modernism is often actually not an argument against modernism as an ideal; it is rather just an argument that modernism didn't live up to its own standards. Consider, for example, the criticism made by some postmodernists that the dominance found in modern universities has been secured by power and not by the discovery of truths that any impartial person would accept. This criticism isn't attacking modernism as a theory; it is complaining that academia was only pretending to a universalism it had no interest in living up to. I can't make this point better than Appiah does, so I will simply quote him:

> It is characteristic of those who pose as [postmodernists] . . . to use the term *universalism* as if it meant *pseudouniversalism*, and the fact is that their complaint is not with universalism at all. What they truly object to . . . is Eurocentric hegemony *posing* as universalism. Thus, while the debate is couched in terms of the competing claims of particularism and . . . [modernism], the actual ideology of universalism . . . is even tacitly accepted.

That postmodernism at least sometimes tacitly (and inconsistently) accepts universalism can be seen by considering the claim of some postmodernists that we should argue for the right of all particularities to engage in learning from their perspective. But how does one argue for that right if one also rejects universalism? Isn't the claim that there is such a right a claim that we think all impartial people interested in truth ought to accept, no matter what their own perspectives are? And in that case, aren't we supposing that universalism holds at least when it comes to the right of particularities to be heard?

What can a postmodernist say about Nazis, or Stalinists, or those who were supporters of apartheid, none of whom supports the right of

---

3. Appiah, *In My Father's House*, ch. 1.

other particularities to be heard in the academy? Shall we admit them as yet another set of particularities that have a right to be heard? But, of course, what characterizes their position is precisely that they won't admit that other particularities are of equal value or deserve an equal hearing. So to admit them to the academy as one particularity among others is just to refuse them admittance. On what grounds, however, could a particularist rule out some particularities as unacceptable?

Furthermore, some of the recommendations some postmodernists put forward for dialogue also seem tacitly universalist; that is, they are recommendations intended for all rational people regardless of their particularities. So, for example, consider Wolterstorff's line that "those who engage in particularist perspectival learning must always face in two directions[:] . . . reflection with members of their own communities . . . [and] conversation with those who represent other perspectives." If particularist learning is the only kind, however, then on what basis can one correct one's own point of view?

Any given postmodernist who isn't a hermit will, of course, know that her perspective isn't shared by everybody. But for postmodernism, there can be only a great and non-converging pluralism in the academy. Someone else's criticism of one's own position will just represent the point of view of the criticizer's perspective, a perspective not shared by the recipient of the criticism. There can't be any non-particularist criticism if postmodernism is right. Criticism by one particularist of another particularist's position, then, seems to have not much more than the status of autobiographical report. It expresses the particularism of the criticizer, and it invites only the response, "Well, of course, you would think that; you're an X" (where X is some particularity). What room is there, then, for correcting one's position, on particularist accounts?

As far as that goes, on postmodernist views, what reason is there for engaging in any dialogue with those in particularities other than one's own? We might say, as some postmodernists do, that some perspectives are more accurate than others. But on what basis can postmodernists make such a claim? If the only kind of learning possible is perspectival and particularist, then unless we can somehow step out of our own particularity and function as universalists, how can we find any perspectives more accurate than our own? The fact that the postmodernist agenda has placed a value on dialogue that it seems unable to support is one of the reasons, I think, for Appiah's claim that postmodernism tacitly and inconsistently accepts universalism.

On postmodernism, then, it is hard to see how a perspective could ever reform or correct itself. By the same token, it is hard to see how we from within whatever particularity we inhabit could ever criticize another perspective. Consider, for example, those in Pakistan arguing in favor of laws against blasphemy; they want the law to punish severely utterances that strike them as irreligious. Their views seem to me both false and pernicious. But according to particularism this view of mine has to be understood as resulting from the particularity to which I belong. The Pakistanis defending blasphemy laws belong to a very different particularity. They will hardly be surprised to learn that someone who occupies my particularity is criticizing their position. But if particularism is all there is, on what basis can the critical views of my particularity be shown to be right and the views of their particularity be shown to be wrong, or the other way around? Any argument to such a conclusion will itself be only the expression of some particularity.

Although postmodernism is intended to empower those who have been marginalized in the past, it is not compatible with a robust program of social justice. If there is no acceptable basis for a person in one particularity to criticize the views of someone in a different particularity, it is hard to see how postmodernism can do much except support the status quo.

But what about the promise that postmodernism seemed to hold for Christianity? What about the hope that with the rejection of modernism academia will again be a place where Christians can function as Christians? If Christianity is one particularity among others, Christians have as much right to participate in the academy as representatives of any other particularity. Christians are as entitled to be part of academia as the representatives of *their* particularity.

But if we look at the Christianity of Augustine, or Anselm, or Aquinas, or Luther, or Calvin, or Kierkegaard, their Christianity is bolder and more demanding than this Christian particularist stance. It isn't content with being an allowable particularity. It claims to be true, and true for everybody everywhere. What is wrong with the views of the atheist, on Augustine's views, is not that the atheist doesn't see Christianity as an allowable particularity, but that he doesn't acknowledge Christianity as true. Augustine certainly would have repudiated the idea that he was entitled to engage in learning as a person coming from one particularity among others. He had more in mind, I suppose, taking his world by storm, with a passionate conviction that Christianity provided the truth that was sought or half-seen elsewhere.

Augustine's sort of passion isn't in good repute among at least some postmodernists, who see in it only arrogance. But I mention Augustine's attitude in order to point out that there are two ways of looking at things here. Postmodernists might see Augustine as arrogant; but he, on the other hand, might see a particularist Christianity as compliant with the demands of secularism. And this much, at any rate, seems right. If we approach Christianity as postmodernists of the sort I have been addressing here do, then at least some of the activities that have been central to Christianity in the past no longer are acceptable. As one particularity among others, Christianity is no more in a position to criticize or reject other particularist perspectives than they are to repudiate Christianity. It is hard to see what room this approach leaves for prophetic denunciations of governments, ascetic rejections of mainstream culture, or social reform. For the same reasons, missionary work is hard to render compatible with a particularist approach to religion. Postmodernists might find this an advantage of their position, since missionary activity is not in favor with this group. But the spread of Christianity throughout the world has been a preoccupation of Christianity from its beginning to now. So for all these reasons, some general and some specially related to Christianity, I myself do not accept the position of the postmodernists.

What are we left with, then? Postmodernists think that if we reject postmodernism, we are left with only two possibilities. We can stubbornly maintain that the academy *has* lived up to the standards of modernism and blind ourselves to the very apparent dominance of white Eurocentric males in academia. Or we can grant that academia didn't live up to modernist standards but insist that, if we would only try harder, academia would exemplify these standards now. Both *these* alternatives to postmodernism constitute attempts to preserve the old modernism, with only this difference between them: that one is an obstinately blind conservatism and the other is a hopelessly optimistic conservatism. But I would like to suggest that there is one more alternative. To see this alternative, it helps to have a political analogy. So consider the formerly communist nations in Eastern Europe. Those nations were engaged in a great social experiment to see if the extended human family could live according to the Marxist maxim: "From each according to his ability; to each according to his need." What should we *now* think about Marxism given the history of that social experiment in those communist countries? There are some obstinately blind communist conservatives who still believe that those communist nations were in fact living up to Marxist ideals. Then there are some hopelessly optimistic communist conservatives who acknowledge that Marxism failed in those countries but insist that, if people in those countries only tried harder, Marxist goals could be achieved there. And then there are people who think that Marxism failed in those countries and that that failure proves that unbridled capitalism is what makes society run well. But, of course, these are not the only possible responses to the history of Marxism in those countries. There is one more position possible.

If we accept Christ's emphasis on alleviating the suffering of the poor, we might think that the Marxist maxim "From each according to his ability; to each according to his need" ought to govern all our social interactions. But as Christians we might also have a considerable appreciation of the depth and power of evil in all human beings. The great communist social experiment in Europe, we might think, was a disaster and would always be a disaster because of the human proclivity to serious wrongdoing. In this respect, then, we would be rejecting Marxism. But it wouldn't follow that we accepted some nineteenth-century version of capitalism. We might think that the human sinfulness amply demonstrated by the failure of European communism simply requires a much more indirect route to establishing the Christian goal of living in a socially just way. And so we might conclude that only the checks and balances of true democracy could bring us close to the kind of society in which any hopes for decent treatment of the poor could be achieved. *This* is yet another possible response to the history of communism in Europe.

We can think of the debate over modernism and postmodernism in academia in ways analogous to this. What is missing from the list of alternatives in the contemporary debate over modernism and postmodernism is the analogue to this last response to the history of European communism. On *this* position, we should accept the ideals of modernism, but we should acknowledge that the academy did not live up to those ideals. We should grant that the academy was in fact dominated by white Eurocentric males who supposed that their interests and worldviews constituted the norm for all human beings and who treated others in biased or unjust ways. What their failure to implement the ideals of modernism shows us is just what the failure of communism in Europe shows us: the power of moral evil, which can distort not only our hearts but our minds as well.

It does not follow, however, that we ought to adopt the academic analogue to unbridled capitalism. We do not need to abandon hope that there is a universalist standard by which all particularities can be judged and corrected. There is a more indirect way to circumvent the distorting power of moral evil than the direct route taken by modernism. We can put our hope instead in the checks and balances of true intellectual democracy. The political view that seems the most promising as a response to the failure of communism in Europe has an analogue here among the responses to the failure of modernism in the academy.

If we accept this position, then we will be adopting the ideals of modernism. We can even hold, consistent with these ideals, that Christianity is a large part of the truth that ought to be accepted universally, by all human beings, regardless of their particularity. But we will also accept that the best way to strive for the ideals of modernism is to follow the particularist path and let competing particularities in the academy argue it out. Like postmodernism, then, this view favors encouraging many particularities in the academy; but, unlike postmodernism, this view favors encouraging many particularities just because it sees doing so as the best road to the ideals modernism hoped for. So I think that Christians should not accept postmodernism. The passionate insistence of an Augustine on the authoritative truth of Christianity seems to me right, even today. But what we ought to be keenly aware of, from the history of our failures and the accusations of the adversaries of modernism, is the power of human moral evil to corrupt the mind. The worst of human evil is that it makes us self-deceived about our own failures.

This point is brought home with memorable eloquence by the great nineteenth-century abolitionist and former slave Frederick Douglass. It is worth quoting him at some length:

> I love the pure, peaceable, and impartial Christianity of Christ; I therefore hate the corrupt, slaveholding, women-whipping, cradle-plundering, partial and hypocritical Christianity of this land. . . . I am filled with unutterable loathing when I contemplate the religious pomp and show, together with the horrible inconsistencies which everywhere surround me. . . . The man who wields the blood-clotted cowskin during the week fills the pulpit on Sunday, and claims to be a minister of the meek and lowly Jesus. . . . He who sells my sister for purposes of prostitution stands forth as the pious advocate of purity. He who proclaims it a religious duty to read the Bible denies me the

right of learning to read the name of the God who made me. . . . The warm defender of the sacredness of the family relation is the same that scatters whole families, sundering husbands and wives, parents and children, sisters and brothers, leaving the hut vacant and the hearth desolate. . . . The slave auctioneer's bell and the church-going bell chime in with each other, and the bitter cries of the heart-broken slave are drowned in the religious shouts of his pious master.[4]

Douglass's fearsome denunciation and the scalding scorn of his true Christianity make vivid a point Augustine put in a much paler way in a different context. The church, Augustine said, needs its accusers, even its enemies; they help the church find its way to the one absolute objective truth that holds for all people everywhere. When it comes to the external challenge to the integration of Christian faith and learning, therefore, Augustine seems to me right. Only if we begin with the faith that there is a creator who made us and the world in which we live will any of us ever really reach the truth about ourselves and our world. So we ought to reject postmodernism and retain the hope of modernism that there is one truth that holds universally for all human beings. But then we must also take into account the potent ability of moral evil to yield self-deception. Human evil has the power to warp understanding in the service of self-interest. The only safety here is to join ranks with the postmodernists and welcome diverse perspectives, especially those critical of our own. The external challenge to Christianity in the academy is consequently wrong and yet still a blessing.

The Internal Challenge

By contrast, although the internal challenge to Christianity in the academy stemming from divisions in the Christian community is wrong-headed, I certainly wouldn't call it a blessing as well.

One source of the division within the Christian community in the academy, I think, stems from the fact that many Christians have become embarrassed or even repulsed by the distinction between orthodoxy and heresy. They no longer want to judge any views heretical, even

4. "Narrative of the Life of Frederick Douglass," in *The Classic Slave Narratives*, ed. Henry Louis Gates Jr. (New York: Mentor, 1987), pp. 326-27.

though they also reserve the right to reject or disdain other people also claiming to be Christians.

I myself think, however, that the appropriate response to the divisions within the Christian community in the academy should be just the opposite. The distinction between orthodoxy and heresy is good, useful, and important for the Christian community, but dismissal and rejection of the holders of heretical views is a serious mistake.[5]

To see the point here, think about what heresy is. The distinction between orthodoxy and heresy requires more than just supposing that some beliefs pertaining to a religion are true and others aren't.

Religions have an order or structure to them; so does any worldview, however secular. Among the claims taken to be true by a particular religion or worldview, some will be central to it, and others will not. The claims that constitute orthodoxy in a religion or a worldview are its central claims, not its peripheral claims. Only a denial of a claim central to a religion or a worldview can count as a heresy.

The importance and usefulness of the distinction between orthodoxy and heresy, so understood, can be seen by considering what happens when we reject it. If we reject it, there is a danger that the denial of *any* of the claims taken to be true in a worldview will seem equally as serious as the denial of any other. For example, at the death of Mao Tsetung, one of the groups competing for power was called "the Whatever Faction," because the members of that group were committed to maintaining as true, and compulsory for all Chinese to believe, anything Mao said, whatever it was. The history of Christianity is studded with cautionary examples manifesting similar confusion. In the fourteenth century, authorities in the Catholic Church fought bitterly with some Franciscan friars about the appropriate length of Franciscans' cloaks. And at Marseille in 1318 the Catholic authorities burned to death four Franciscan friars because of their views about the length of Franciscan cloaks. A recognition by all participants to the dispute that beliefs about the length of cloaks are not central to the faith would have kept that fight from disintegrating into the shameful spectacle it became.

So there are beliefs central to the Christian faith, just as there are beliefs central to a secular worldview such as Maoism. A person who identifies himself as a Maoist but who also believes in unrestrained capi-

---

5. Some of the material in this section is taken from my "Orthodoxy and Heresy," *Faith and Philosophy* 16 (1999): 487-503.

talism is a heretical Maoist. And, of course, the analogous point holds for Christian belief, too. Some Christian beliefs are orthodox, and others are not; some are heretical.

The important question for my purposes, however, is this. Supposing that there is a good distinction between orthodoxy and heresy, how should those who hold orthodox beliefs react to those who hold heretical beliefs? If the distinction between orthodoxy and heresy is good and useful, what about the notion of a heretic? In my view, the notion of *heretic* should be discarded for any purpose other than historical description.

That's because a heretic is generally supposed to be someone who is worthy of being thrown out of the community of believers because of his heresy. But it is a great mistake to suppose that one can make a legitimate inference from the appropriateness of rejecting a belief to the appropriateness of rejecting the person who holds that belief. Someone might hold a belief that no reasonable people would consider orthodox; and yet that person might be worthy of being admired by the community of the orthodox for religious and moral excellence.

To see what I mean, consider the story of William Hunter in *Foxe's Book of Martyrs*. In that story, Hunter is persecuted for heretical beliefs by the church authorities of his time. I won't tell you what Hunter's heresy was, just in case it might not strike you as heretical. But use your imagination and pick some theological position that in your own view is not only theologically beyond the pale but philosophically illiterate as well. Imagine that to be Hunter's heresy, and in my view you won't be far off the mark. I should also point out that *Foxe's Book of Martyrs* isn't generally considered the best authority on the history of martyrs; but if the story it tells about Hunter isn't accurate in all its details, there is some story just like it somewhere in the history of Christianity that is accurate.

According to the story, William Hunter was a nineteen-year-old apprentice in England during the reign of Queen Mary; and he was convicted of heresy by the Catholic authorities then in power. The authorities gave Hunter every opportunity and every incentive to recant. The bishop put him in stocks, imprisoned him, and even tried to bribe him with the offer of a job and a large sum of money; in the end, the bishop just threatened him with execution if he didn't recant. But the teenager was as oblivious to threats as to bribery, and he maintained his position steadfastly. When he was finally condemned to be burned to death as a heretic, he comforted his weeping mother by telling her, "For the little pain I shall suffer, which shall soon be at an end, Christ has promised me, mother, a crown of joy. Should you not be glad of that?" And he was burned to death with the words of Psalm 51 on his lips: "a broken and a contrite heart, O God, thou wilt not despise."[6] Perhaps his theology was hopeless; but, as for the man himself, who among us is worthy to sit beside him?

In my view, this story, and many others like it, shows that it is a wretched mistake to judge a person's character or his standing with God on the basis of a judgment that some of his Christian beliefs are heretical. As Hunter's story illustrates, a person can hold a belief that is heretical and yet be someone whose Christian excellence is far beyond our own. So although a heretical belief is worthy of rejection, it is a mistake to think that the person holding that belief is therefore also worthy of rejection.

It is an even more lamentable mistake, in my view, to suppose that coercion of any sort should be used to suppress heretical beliefs. As the history of the Catholic Church shows, it is not possible to have a community that uses coercion against beliefs it wants to eliminate without making that practice known to those in the community. The result is that, even if the beliefs that community is trying to protect are all true, the coercive practices of that community will nonetheless undermine love of truth.

Those who hold orthodox beliefs will realize that it is prudent for them to do so, so that whatever love of truth brings them to orthodox beliefs, their acceptance of those beliefs will also be motivated by prudential considerations. Those who are undecided about orthodox beliefs will weigh their beliefs with mingled concern for truth and for their own well-being. And those who pride themselves on their unwillingness to let prudential considerations motivate their beliefs will be more inclined to reject than to accept the truth of orthodox beliefs, because to accept them in such a community is not to love the truth but to yield to pressure. Even those who reject orthodoxy, then, will evaluate orthodox beliefs with some self-regarding concern — for ensuring their independence of political pressure — and will be more inclined to the role of rebel than to the seeking of truth.

So in virtue of choosing coercive means to try to protect truth, a com-

6. *Foxe's Book of Martyrs*, ed. Marie Gentert King (New York: Pyramid, 1968), p. 235.

munity does serious damage to the love of truth. This is bound to be a concern for any society, but it is disastrous for the Christian community.

So although it is important, good, and useful to work hard at distinguishing orthodox from heretical beliefs, we ought to value love of truth above success in finding it. We also need to distinguish between rejecting beliefs and rejecting the persons who hold them; we need to recognize that the value of a person is not identical to the value of the beliefs she holds, not even the theological beliefs. If we were clear on these points, the internal challenge to Christianity based on divisions within the Christian community would be at least significantly diminished.

Conclusion

So here is what I want to say by way of a very brief conclusion about both the external and the internal challenge to the integration of faith and learning in the academy.

As modernism maintains, there is one universal truth that holds for all people, regardless of their particularities, and Christian faith is part of that truth. It can therefore certainly be integrated with any other academic pursuit of truth. But this integration will go best in a pluralistic environment, in which both truth and orthodoxy are sought but adversaries and heretics are protected.

It was one of the tragedies of Mao Tse-tung's life that he took those who disagreed with him as his enemies and persecuted them; he used force to bring the views of his adversaries into agreement with his own. This policy was ultimately disastrous to him. The result of it was that he undermined some of the very things he gave his life to promote. The history of Christianity has been marked by analogous tragedies. The periodic failure of Christian authorities to heed Augustine's advice and see Christianity's adversaries and heretics as good for the church led to betrayals by the church of the very things Christianity is committed to loving.

I would say therefore that, even in the academy, for the integration of faith and learning, it is crucial for Christians to love and protect those they take to be their enemies.

CHAPTER 6

Modern Physics and Ancient Faith

STEPHEN M. BARR

Is there a conflict between religion and science? It depends what religion one is talking about. In this essay, religion means biblical religion. I speak from a Catholic perspective, but everything I will say applies also, I think, to the mainstream of Protestantism and Judaism. I will argue that there is no conflict between religion so understood and science. What there is, and long has been, is a conflict between religion and scientific materialism.

Scientific materialism is not a part of science, although it often wraps itself in the mantle of science. It is, rather, a philosophical theory. It says that the ultimate reality is matter, and everything that exists and everything that happens can therefore be explained by the laws of physics and blind chance. However, there is more to it. For some, scientific materialism is a passionately held ideology with a mission. That mission is to free people's minds from superstition in all its forms, but especially in the form of religion. Religion thus plays for some materialists the role of a needed enemy, the struggle against which contributes to the larger meaning and purpose of their lives. It is necessary to their worldview, therefore, that there be a conflict between science and religion.

There are three elements in this supposed conflict: a historical claim, a philosophical claim, and a scientific claim. The historical claim is that religious people and institutions have generally been hostile to science and have tried to suppress it. Here, the trial of Galileo is often invoked. The philosophical claim is that there is an inherent incompatibility between the religious and scientific outlooks. Science is based on natural explanations of phenomena, while religion is based on the supernatural. Science is based on reason, while religion is based on dogma, faith, and mystery, which are seen as inimical to reason. The scientific claim is that the actual discoveries of science since the time of Copernicus have given us a picture of the world that ever more diverges from the picture that religion painted of it. In other words, materialism has a standard interpretation of the history of scientific discovery as debunking religion. I have called this materialism's "story of science."

Science vs. Religion: The Historical Claim

Let us begin with the historical claim. A standard account of scientific history has it that after the great achievements of the ancient Greeks, the rise of Christianity snuffed out the further development of science and mathematics for a thousand years. Christians were interested in gaining the next world, not in understanding this one; in the supernatural, not the natural. Supposedly, science did not revive until the West began to throw off the shackles of religion in the Renaissance, and when it did, it was immediately attacked by the church, as in the case of Galileo. The emancipation from religion and the development of a rational scientific outlook accelerated during the Enlightenment. The decisive battle came with Darwin, a battle that is still being bitterly fought.

The foregoing is a very common view of scientific history, but it is extremely distorted. First of all, Christianity and Judaism were not based on supernaturalism, if one means by that a rejection of the idea of a natural order. Indeed, scholars tell us that the book of Genesis contains an attack on pagan supernaturalism and superstition. For example, when Genesis said that the Sun and Moon were lamps placed by God in the heavens to light the day and night, it was countering the pagan religions that worshiped the Sun and Moon. When it said that human beings are made in the image of God and are to exercise "dominion" over the animals, Genesis was countering the paganism in which people worshiped and bowed down to animals or to gods made in the image of animals.

In paganism, the world was imbued with supernatural and occult forces and populated by deities of every kind — gods of war, gods of the ocean and of the earth, goddesses of sex and fertility, and so forth. But Jews and Christians taught that there was only one God who was to be sought not *within* Nature, not within its phenomena and forces, but outside of Nature, a God who was indeed the Author of Nature. In this way, biblical religion helped to strip the physical world of the supernatural. It helped make the world into a natural world, and thus clear the ground for the later emergence of science.

The biblical religions, then, taught that there is a natural order, which came from God. It is this very orderliness of the universe that points to its Creator. The Christian writer Minucius Felix, writing around AD 200, had this to say:

> If upon entering some home you saw that everything there was well-tended, neat, and decorative, you would believe that some master was in charge of it, and that he was himself much superior to those good things. So too in the home of this world, when you see providence, order, and law in the heavens and on earth, believe that there is a Lord and Author of the universe, more beautiful than the stars themselves and the various parts of the whole world.[1]

Note that he does not point to the miraculous, but to the providence, order, and law in the universe, as evidence of God. The classic Jewish and Christian argument was that if there is a law there must be a Lawgiver. Of course, God was the Lawgiver to Israel — the first books of the Bible are called the Torah, or Law — but he is the Lawgiver also to the cosmos itself. In the book of Jeremiah, God says, "Only if I had not established my covenant with day and night and the ordinances of heaven and earth, would I reject the offspring of Jacob and of my servant David" (Jer. 33:25-26). Psalm 148 tells of the Sun, the Moon, the stars, and the heavens obeying a divinely given "law that cannot pass away" (Ps. 148:6).

If, indeed, the biblical religions upheld the idea of a natural order and a lawful universe, then what about the accusation that the rise of Christianity brought an end to the glorious science of the ancient world? It is simply false. The golden age of Greek mathematics and science ended two hundred years before the birth of Christ. One of the last great scientists of antiquity was the astronomer Ptolemy, who died around AD 165, when Christians were still a small and persecuted sect. Moreover, the attitudes of early Christians toward science were not different from

---

1. Minucius Felix, *Octavius*, trans. William A. Jurgens, in *The Faith of the Early Fathers*, vol. 1 (Collegeville, MN: Liturgical, 1970), p. 109.

those of their pagan neighbors, according to the distinguished historian David C. Lindberg.[2]

The decline of scientific knowledge in Western Europe between AD 500 and AD 1000 was owing to the general cultural, economic, and political collapse brought on by barbarian invasions. But in the eleventh century Western Europeans began to acquire the scientific works of the ancient Greeks through contact with the Byzantines and Arabs. This led to a great hunger for this learning among both clergy and laity, and led to a massive effort to translate these works into Latin. The medieval universities were founded largely as places where this newly recovered knowledge could be studied. These universities were, for the most part, founded under church auspices, received much church patronage and protection, and were staffed largely by clerics. And science, which in those days was called "natural philosophy," held an honored place in their curricula: indeed, in medieval universities the study of natural philosophy/science was a prerequisite for the study of theology.

The historian Edward Grant has emphasized that the founding of the medieval universities gave to science for the first time a stable institutional basis.[3] Before that, science had been supported by wealthy or powerful individuals who happened to have an interest in it, and it was therefore a hit-or-miss affair. But in the medieval universities a stable community of scholars was created that studied scientific questions continuously from generation to generation. By the end of the Middle Ages there were about a hundred universities in Europe, and their graduates numbered in the hundreds of thousands, creating a scientific public from whose ranks scientific talent could emerge. Without the scientific community and the scientific public created by the medieval universities, the Scientific Revolution would not have had the soil in which to germinate.

The science taught in medieval universities was naturalistic — indeed, as I noted previously, it was called "natural philosophy." So the church was not at all hostile to the study of nature. The attitude of the medieval church was typified by the fourteenth-century scientist and theologian Jean Buridan, who said that when confronted by new phe-

2. David C. Lindberg, *The Beginnings of Western Science* (Chicago: University of Chicago Press, 1988).

3. Edward Grant, *The Foundations of Modern Science in the Middle Ages* (Cambridge: Cambridge University Press, 1996).

nomena, we should seek "appropriate natural causes."[4] Another leading medieval scientist and theologian, Nicolas Oresme, said that in explaining strange new phenomena, "There is no reason to take recourse to the heavens, . . . or to demons, or to our glorious God as if He would produce these effects directly, [any] more . . . than [he would] those effects whose [natural] causes we believe are well known to us."[5]

When Galileo was forced to recant, it was not because the Catholic Church was upholding a supernatural view of the physical universe. On the contrary, the Aristotelian-Ptolemaic theory of astronomy that the Catholic Church favored was just as naturalistic as the Copernican theory that it condemned. The condemnation of Galileo was a terrible blunder, but not a rejection of science per se. This is shown by the words of Cardinal Bellarmine himself, the head of the Roman Inquisition during what is sometimes called Galileo's "first trial." In a famous letter, Bellarmine said, "If it were demonstrated that [the Sun were really motionless and the Earth in motion] we should have to proceed with caution in interpreting passages of Scripture that appear to teach the contrary, and rather admit that we do not understand them than declare something false which has been proven to be true."[6] However, Bellarmine went on to say that he had "grave doubts" that such a proof existed and that "in case of doubt" one must stay with the traditional interpretation of those passages of Scripture. It should be noted that, as a matter of fact, a genuine proof that the Earth moves was not available in Galileo's time. There were hints and evidence that pointed in that direction, but really conclusive evidence was not available until decades later.

The Galileo case was an aberration — an exception to the rule. The church has always had a favorable attitude toward science. I would like to concentrate on the Catholic Church's record, in particular, because the Galileo case is seen as typifying that record, and this is central to the myth of a general science-religion conflict. One fact that dramatically illustrates the true historical relation of the Catholic Church to science is the large number of priests who made significant contributions to sci-

4. Quoted in Edward Grant, *God and Reason in the Middle Ages* (Cambridge: Cambridge University Press, 2001), p. 197.

5. Quoted in Ronald L. Numbers, "Science without God: Natural Laws and Christian Beliefs," in *When Science and Religion Meet*, ed. David C. Lindberg and Ronald L. Numbers (Chicago: University of Chicago Press, 2003), p. 267.

6. Quoted in Giorgio de Santillana, *The Crime of Galileo* (Chicago: University of Chicago Press, 1955), pp. 99-100.

ence all the way from the thirteenth century to the twentieth. I would like to list a few noteworthy examples. (Good articles on each of the scientists below can be found in the *Dictionary of Scientific Biography*.)[7] This is a largely untold story and quite a remarkable one. The list is somewhat long. But we Catholics have our litanies. What follows is a litany of priest-scientists.

In the Middle Ages, one starts with the great Dominican scholar St. Albert the Great, the teacher of St. Thomas Aquinas. St. Albert did original work in botany and zoology. The *Dictionary of Scientific Biography* calls his work *On Vegetables and Plants* "a masterpiece for its independence of treatment, its accuracy and range of detailed description, its freedom from myth, and its innovation in systematic classification."

Robert Grosseteste, bishop of Lincoln, studied the refraction of light and came up with a geometrical theory of how lenses magnify images that was essentially correct.

Thomas Bradwardine, archbishop of Canterbury, showed that Aristotle's ideas on the relation of force and motion were not self-consistent and developed his own mathematical theory of this relation. His theory was wrong, but it was one of the first attempts to give a mathematical formula to describe a physical process.

Jean Buridan, mentioned above, developed the idea that objects in motion continued in motion because of a property imparted to them that he called "impetus." This anticipated Newton's First Law of Motion and the modern concept of momentum.

The greatest of the mediaeval scientists was Nicolas Oresme, bishop of Lisieux. His contributions to mathematics and physics were far ahead of his time. He was the first to have the idea of plotting physical quantities on a graph. He used such graphs to calculate the distance traveled by an accelerating object. He proposed that the speed of a falling body is proportional to the time it has fallen, which is correct and anticipates Galileo's famous "law of falling bodies." And he argued that the apparent motion of the stars could be explained by the Earth's rotation on its axis, and the analysis by which he refuted common physical objections to this theory was correct and quite sophisticated.

The man who is credited with writing the book that sparked the Sci-

---

7. Charles Coulston Gillespie, ed., *The Dictionary of Scientific Biography* (New York: Scribner, 1970-80).

entific Revolution, Nicolas Copernicus, was himself a Church official, though not a priest.

The Scientific Revolution exploded in the 1600s, and there we find the Catholic clergy in the thick of important research.

Four Jesuit astronomers are particularly noteworthy. Christoph Scheiner discovered sunspots independently of Galileo and made the most detailed studies of them. Grimaldi discovered, named, and carefully investigated the extremely important phenomenon of the "diffraction of light." Giovanni Riccioli discovered the first binary star and made the first maps of the Moon's surface. Niccolo Zucchi built the first reflecting telescope, fifty years before Newton, who is usually credited with doing so.

Marin Mersenne, a Minimite friar, was the discoverer of many of the basic facts about sound, waves, and vibration that are taught in college physics courses today, and he has therefore been called the "father" of the science of acoustics. He also played a crucial role in organizing scientific activity on the continent of Europe. His convent became a meeting place of famous scientists, and his correspondence with other scientists was an important means by which they learned of each other's work. The *Dictionary of Scientific Biography* calls him one of the "architects of the European scientific community."

Benedetto Castelli, a Benedictine priest and student and friend of Galileo, is regarded as the founder of the science of hydraulics. Buonaventura Cavalieri, a student of Castelli, made crucial contributions to the development of calculus, which were later acknowledged by Leibniz himself.

Blessed Niels Stensen, who eventually became a Catholic bishop, made fundamental discoveries in anatomy, but his most important work was in geology. He was the first to explain the origin of fossils and of sedimentary rock. His theory of geological strata allowed people to begin to understand the history of the Earth. He is usually listed first among the founders of the science of geology.

One of the leading biologists in the world in the 1700s was Lazzaro Spallanzani, whose experiments disproving the theory of spontaneous generation were the basis of those later performed by Louis Pasteur. Rene-Just Haüy is called the father of crystallography. Giuseppe Piazzi, head of the Palermo Observatory, discovered the first known asteroid in 1801. Angelo Secchi, one of the founders of modern astrophysics, pioneered the use of spectroscopic methods in astronomy and developed a classification of stars that is the basis of the classification still used today.

The Czech priest Bernhard Bolzano did groundbreaking work on the foundations of calculus in the early decades of the nineteenth century. The Austrian monk Gregor Mendel is, of course, famous as the discoverer of the laws of heredity and the founder of the science of genetics. Equally important, but less known to the public, is the fact that one of the two founders of the Big Bang theory was a Belgian priest and physicist named Georges Lemaître. And, finally, Julius Nieuwland, a professor of chemistry at the University of Notre Dame, made breakthroughs that led to the first synthetic rubber, neoprene.

Obviously, had the Catholic Church been hostile to science there would not have been so many distinguished priest-scientists — many of them the founders of whole branches of science — over a nearly unbroken span of eight hundred years.

So much for the idea that religion has been an enemy of science. But was science an enemy of religion? Certainly that was not the view of most of the great founders of modern science who were themselves religious, men such as Copernicus, Brahe, Kepler, Galileo, Boyle, Newton, and Ampére. The two greatest physicists of the nineteenth century, Michael Faraday and James Clerk Maxwell, were deeply devout, even by the standards of that time. Indeed, it seems that most scientists were religious believers, up to about the middle of the nineteenth century.

However, as I mentioned earlier, one of the main claims of scientific materialists is that the actual discoveries of science over the last four hundred years have debunked many religious beliefs and rendered the religious conception of the world incredible. This version of scientific history is what I have called the materialist's "story of science." This story has five major themes, which we will examine critically in the remainder of this essay.

Materialism and the Story of Science

The first theme is the overturning of the religious cosmology. We now know that we do not live at the center of a cozy little cosmos, but in what Bertrand Russell called a "backwater" of a vast universe.[8] The Earth is but a tiny planet orbiting an insignificant star, near the edge of an or-

---

8. Bertrand Russell, *Religion and Science* (1935; repr., London: Oxford University Press, 1961), p. 222.

dinary galaxy that contains a hundred billion other stars, in a universe with more than a hundred billion other galaxies.

The second theme is the overthrow of design. Religious believers saw God's handiwork all around them in the world. Whether it was the starry heavens or the beauties of living things, they saw the magnificent productions of Nature as having been fashioned by the hand of God. Science, however, showed that they were the result of impersonal laws and blind chance. Genesis spoke of God placing the Sun and Moon in the firmament. Astrophysics shows us instead that they condensed from swirling clouds of gas and dust under the attraction of gravitational forces. Darwin showed how the intricate structures of living things could arise from natural selection operating upon random mutations. When Napoleon asked Laplace why God was never mentioned in his treatise on celestial mechanics, Laplace famously replied that he "had no need of that hypothesis."[9] The laws of physics and the laws of probability had taken the place of God.

The third theme is what Stephen Jay Gould called "the dethronement of man."[10] With the Earth but an infinitesimal speck in the limitless ocean of space, and the human race but a chemical accident, we can no longer believe ourselves to be the uniquely important beings for whom the universe was created. Indeed, not only is humankind not the purpose of the universe or Nature, but Nature has no purposes. Modern physics has banished teleology.

The fourth theme, which goes back to Newton, is the discovery of physical determinism. The laws of Nature were discovered to form a closed and complete system of cause and effect. Every physical event — including our bodily movements — could be understood as arising inevitably from the past state of the universe in a way that is precisely determined by the mathematical laws of physics. As Laplace said two hundred years ago, if the state of the world were completely known at one instant of time, its whole future development could in principle be calculated down to the smallest detail.[11] If this were true, it would raise serious difficulties for the Jewish and Christian doctrine of free will.

9. Quoted in James R. Newman, "Laplace," in *Lives in Science, a Scientific American Book* (New York: Simon and Schuster, 1957).

10. Stephen Jay Gould, *Full House: The Spread of Excellence from Plato to Darwin* (New York: Harmony, 1997), pp. 17-18.

11. Pierre Simon Marquis de Laplace, *A Philosophical Essay on Probabilities* (New York: Dover, 1951), pp. 4-5.

This leads to the fifth and final theme of the materialist's story, the emergence of a completely mechanistic view of humankind. Already in the seventeenth century it was widely suggested that animals could be understood as machines or automata. The more radical thinkers of the Enlightenment extended this view to human beings. Today, with the processes of life understood in terms of chemistry, and the brain understood to be a complex biochemical computer, this view seems close to triumphing.

The story that I have just outlined should not be lightly dismissed. Many reasonable people, not all of them hostile to religion, find this interpretation of scientific history plausible. And it must be admitted that much in scientific history up to about one hundred years ago lent itself to this interpretation. Moreover, the startling developments in physics in the twentieth century only reinforced this view. People saw dramatic discoveries, like Einstein's theory of relativity and quantum theory, as demonstrating once again that all traditional or familiar or intuitively obvious notions are naïve and fated to be cast aside. Science as debunker, it seemed, was continuing on its relentless course.

However, this view of twentieth-century science is misleading. It is true that science debunked many ideas in the twentieth century, but what it chiefly debunked, I will now argue, was the materialist's old "story of science." People usually don't recognize this, because they see what they expect to see and extrapolate from the past storyline. But the discoveries of the twentieth century threw some twists into the plot. Those plot twists have, in the view of many, invalidated every lesson that the materialist wished us to draw from scientific history.

What are those twentieth-century plot twists? I will describe five of them, which correspond to the five themes that I mentioned.

The first theme, you will recall, was the overturning of the religious cosmology. Supposedly, biblical religion taught that humankind was at the center of the universe. However, this isn't really so. The idea that space has a geometrical center entered Western thought, not from the Bible, but from pagan Greek science, specifically Aristotle and Ptolemy. There was, however, one point of cosmology that biblical religion did introduce and insist upon, and that has radically distinguished it from the beliefs of ancient pagans and modern materialists. That point was not about space and whether it has a center, but about time and whether it had a beginning.

Almost all ancient Greek philosophers, including Plato and Aristotle, believed in an eternal universe. It was the Bible — indeed, its very first words — that introduced the idea of a beginning. Both the Fourth Lateran Council in 1215 and the First Vatican Council in 1870 spoke of God creating the world "from the beginning of time," "*ab initio temporis.*" Modern atheists, on the other hand, have generally been quite uncomfortable with the idea of a beginning.

Until about eighty years ago, it seemed that scientific discoveries were all pointing against the Jewish and Christian view. In Newtonian physics it was natural to assume that the time coordinates, like the space coordinates, stretched in an unbroken line from minus infinity to plus infinity. The discovery of the law of conservation of energy gave further support to the eternity of the world, for it said that energy could neither be created nor destroyed. Chemists discovered that the quantity of matter also does not change; and we therefore find the eminent chemist Svante Arrhenius saying in 1911: "The opinion that something can come from nothing is at variance with the present-day state of science, according to which matter is immutable."[12] Thus almost every scientific indication a century ago was that space, time, matter, and energy had always existed and always would. There was little to suggest a beginning.

The first hint of a beginning came with Einstein's theory of general relativity. In the 1920s Alexander Friedmann, a Russian mathematician, and Georges Lemaître, a Belgian priest and physicist, independently proposed mathematical models of the universe based on Einstein's theory, in which the universe was expanding from some initial explosion, which Lemaître called "the primeval atom" and which is now called the Big Bang. Meanwhile, astronomers were discovering that galaxies are flying apart as if from an explosion. The Big Bang theory was slow to be accepted, however, partly because of prejudice against the idea of a beginning. The physicist Walter Nernst declared, "To deny the infinite duration of time would be to betray the very foundations of science."[13] As late as 1959, a survey showed that most American astronomers and physicists still believed in a universe with no beginning.[14] However,

---

12. Quoted in Pope Pius XII, "The Proofs for the Existence of God in the Light of Modern Natural Science," address to the Pontifical Academy of Sciences, 22 November 1951.

13. Quoted in Robert Jastrow, *God and the Astronomers* (New York: Norton, 1992), p. 104.

14. Stephen G. Brush, "How Cosmology Became a Science," *Scientific American*, August 1992, pp. 62-70.

since the 1960s, the evidence for the Big Bang has grown stronger and stronger, so that it is no longer seriously questioned by scientists.

Over the decades, many speculative theories have been proposed that attempt to salvage the idea of an eternal universe. All of them have serious difficulties, either with the Second Law of Thermodynamics or with a powerful theorem recently proved by the physicists Borde, Guth, and Vilenkin.[15] And so, while we cannot be absolutely certain that the universe had a beginning, present theory strongly favors the idea that it did.

The second theme of the materialist's story was the overthrow of design. Whereas the ancient argument was that the lawfulness of Nature required a Lawgiver, now it was argued that the laws of nature constituted in themselves, and by themselves, a sufficient explanation of reality. This brings us to the second plot twist in the story of science. This twist was a basic shift in perspective.

Physics starts by finding regularities in nature and mathematical rules that accurately describe them. At a later stage, these rules are found to follow from some deeper and more general laws, which usually require more abstract and abstruse mathematics to express them. Underlying these, in turn, are found yet more fundamental laws. This deepening has led to an increasing unification of physics. Whereas, in the early days of science, Nature seemed to be a grab bag of many kinds of phenomena with little apparent relation to each other, it later became clear that the laws of physics make up a single harmonious mathematical system.

Moreover, physicists have increasingly looked, not just at tangible physical phenomena, but also at the form of the deep mathematical laws that underlie them. They began to notice that those laws exhibit a great richness and profundity of mathematical structure, and are indeed of remarkable mathematical beauty. As time went on, the search for new theories became guided not just by detailed fitting of experimental data, but also by aesthetic criteria. A classic example was the discovery of the Dirac Equation in 1928. As Dirac was looking for an equation to describe the behavior of electrons, he hit upon a piece of mathematics that struck him as beautiful. "[It] was a pretty mathematical result," he said; "I was quite excited over it. It seemed that it must be of some importance."[16]

---

15. A. Borde, A. Guth, and A. Vilenkin, "Inflationary Spacetimes Are Incomplete in Past Directions," *Physical Review Letters* 90, no. 151301 (2003).

16. Quoted in Abraham Pais, *Inward Bound: Of Matter and Forces in the Physical World* (Oxford: Oxford University Press, 1986), pp. 290-91.

This led him to his great discovery. Dirac at one point even said that it was more important "to have beauty in your equations" than to have them fit the experimental data. The great Werner Heisenberg made this statement: "in exact science, no less than in the arts, [beauty] is the most important source of illumination and clarity."[17]

The same quest for mathematical beauty dominates the search for fundamental theories today. One of the leading theoretical particle physicists in the world today, Edward Witten, trying to explain to a skeptical science reporter why he took superstring theory so seriously, said in frustration, "I don't think I've succeeded in conveying to you its wonder, incredible consistency, remarkable elegance, and beauty."[18]

All of this has changed the context in which we think about design in Nature. When the questions physicists asked were simply about particular sensible phenomena, like stars, rainbows, or crystals, it may have seemed out of place to talk about them, however beautiful they were, as being fashioned by the hand of God. They could be accounted for satisfactorily by the laws of physics. But now when it is the laws of physics themselves that are the object of curiosity and aesthetic appreciation, and when it has been found that they form a single magnificent edifice of great subtlety, harmony, and beauty, the question of a cosmic designer seems inescapable.

In 1931, Hermann Weyl, one of the great mathematicians and mathematical physicists of the twentieth century, gave a lecture at Yale University in which he said the following:

Many people think that modern science is far removed from God. I find, on the contrary, that it is much more difficult today for the knowing person to approach God from history, from the spiritual side of the world, and from morals; for there we encounter the suffering and evil in the world, which it is difficult to bring into harmony with an all-merciful and almighty God. In this domain we have evidently not yet succeeded in raising the veil with which our human nature covers the essence of things. But in our knowledge of physical nature

17. Werner Heisenberg, *Across the Frontiers*, trans. Peter Heath (New York: Harper & Row, 1974), p. 183.

18. Quoted in John Horgan, *The End of Science* (New York: Addison-Wesley, 1996), p. 69.

we have penetrated so far that we can obtain a vision of the flawless harmony that is conformity with sublime reason.[19]

The third theme of the materialist's story was the "dethronement of man." A classic statement of this view was given by Steven Weinberg in his book *The First Three Minutes*. He wrote:

> It is almost irresistible for humans to believe that we have some special relation to the universe, that human life is not just a farcical outcome of a chain of accidents, . . . but that we were somehow built in from the beginning. . . . It is very hard for us to realize that [the entire Earth] is just a tiny part of an overwhelmingly hostile universe. . . . The more the universe seems comprehensible, the more it also seems pointless.[20]

However, in the last few decades there has been a development that suggests a very different estimate of our place in the universe. This plot twist was not a single discovery, but the noticing of many so-called anthropic coincidences.[21]

The term "anthropic coincidence" refers to some feature of the laws of physics or of the structure of the universe that seems to be just what is needed for life to be able to evolve. In other words, if these features were not there or were slightly different, the universe would be thoroughly lifeless.

A well-known example concerns the strength of the so-called strong force, which holds atomic nuclei together. Had it been a few percentage points weaker, a certain critical atomic nucleus called deuterium would not have been able to hold together, and as a result the whole process by which all the different elements are synthesized in the Big Bang and in stars would have been fatally disrupted. On the other hand, had it been a few percentage points stronger, it has been argued that other disasters

---

19. Hermann Weyl, *The Open World: Three Lectures on the Metaphysical Implications of Science* (New Haven, CT: Yale University Press, 1932), pp. 28-29.

20. Steven Weinberg, *The First Three Minutes: A Modern View of the Origin of the Universe* (Glasgow: William Collins, 1977), p. 148.

21. P. C. W. Davies, *The Accidental Universe* (Cambridge: Cambridge University Press, 1982); J. D. Barrow and F. J. Tipler, *The Cosmological Anthropic Principle* (Oxford: Oxford University Press, 1986).

would have happened. So the strong force seems delicately balanced or "fine-tuned" to make life possible.

In the last forty years many such anthropic coincidences, especially in physics, have been identified. The most obvious interpretation of them is that we were indeed "built in from the beginning," in Steven Weinberg's phrase, and that the universe, far from being "overwhelmingly hostile" to us, as he asserted, is actually amazingly, gratuitously hospitable.

There is a way to explain these anthropic coincidences in a purely naturalistic manner, called the multiverse idea. I regard the multiverse idea as very reasonable, and I think it may explain some of the anthropic coincidences. But, even if that is so, I think the anthropic coincidences strongly underline something that is highly significant. And that is that not *any old* laws of physics would have led to a universe that could generate life. Rather, the laws must be very special *in one way or another*. They may be special in being fine-tuned, or they may be special in giving rise to a multiverse — because they do have to be special to produce a multiverse. But if the laws of nature had to be special to allow life to arise, it suggests that whatever Mind conceived those laws intended that life — including human life — would arise.

The fourth theme was the determinism of physical law, which seemed to contradict the idea of free will. All the laws of physics discovered before the twentieth century — those of mechanics, gravity, and electromagnetism — were deterministic in character. If anything seemed solidly established in science, it was physical determinism. However, in the 1920s, determinism was swept away in the quantum revolution. According to the principles of quantum mechanics, even complete information about the state of a physical system at one time does not uniquely determine its future behavior; it only sets probabilities for what will happen.

This was a huge shock to physicists. Indeed, one of the hallmarks of an exact science is its ability to predict outcomes. Several of the founders of quantum mechanics, including de Broglie, Einstein, and Schrödinger, did not accept the loss of determinism. Einstein famously rejected it with the statement that "I, at any rate am convinced that He [God] does not throw dice."[22] There have been various attempts to restore determinism

---

22. Albert Einstein, letter to Max Born (4 December 1926), in *The Born-Einstein Letters*, trans. Irene Born (New York: Walker, 1971).

to physics by modifying, reformulating, or reinterpreting quantum theory, but none of them is fully satisfactory. The most significant of these attempts is the so-called many-worlds interpretation of quantum mechanics, which has certain technical problems and is in any case too wild in its implications for most physicists to accept. So far, at any rate, it seems unlikely that the old classical determinism will be restored.

To quote Hermann Weyl again, from the same 1931 lecture:

> We may say that there exists a world, causally closed and determined by precise laws, but . . . the new insight which modern [quantum] physics affords . . . opens several ways of reconciling personal freedom with [the laws of nature]. It would be premature, however, to propose a definite and complete solution of the problem. . . . We must await the further development of science, perhaps for centuries, perhaps for thousands of years, before we can design a true and detailed picture of the interwoven texture of Matter, Life, and Soul. But the old classical determinism of Hobbes and Laplace need not oppress us longer.[23]

We now turn to the fifth and final theme of the materialist's story, the completely mechanistic view of humankind. Here the human mind debunks itself. The scientific mind looks into itself and sees nothing there except complex chemistry and neurons firing. However, here again, the story is not so simple. Here again the plot has twisted. Two of the greatest discoveries of the twentieth century cast considerable doubt upon, and some would say refute, the contention that the human mind can be explained as a mere biochemical machine.

The first of these discoveries is — again — quantum mechanics. In the traditional interpretation of quantum mechanics — also called the "Copenhagen," "standard," or "orthodox" interpretation — one must, to avoid paradoxes or absurdities, posit the existence of so-called observers whose minds cannot completely be described by physics. This led Eugene Wigner, a Nobel laureate in physics, to state flatly that materialism is not "logically consistent with present quantum mechanics."[24]

---

23. Weyl, *The Open World*, pp. 54-55.

24. Eugene P. Wigner, "Remarks on the Mind-Body Question," in *The Scientist Speculates*, ed. I. J. Good (London: Heinemann, 1961), reprinted in Eugene P. Wigner, *Symmetries and Reflections: Scientific Essays* (Woodbridge, CT: Ox Bow, 1979), p. 176.

And it led another great physicist, Sir Rudolf Peierls, to say, "The premise that you can describe in terms of physics the whole function of a human being . . . including its knowledge and its consciousness is untenable. There is still something missing."[25]

Beyond Materialism: Faith, Physics, and the Human Mind

It is not possible to explain adequately in a few pages what leads some people to draw such conclusions. But I can say some words that may give the gist of what is involved. Quantum theory involves probabilities at a very fundamental level. Probabilities can be said to depend on someone's state of knowledge. Someone with complete knowledge has certainty, whereas someone with incomplete knowledge may only have probabilities. So, it is argued, quantum theory, being inherently a probabilistic theory, can be formulated only with reference to knowledge and therefore "knowers" — traditionally called "observers." As Peierls put it, "You see, the quantum mechanical description is in terms of knowledge, and knowledge requires *somebody* who knows."[26] It turns out that if one tries to describe this "observer" as if he or she were a physical system, and therefore describable by quantum mechanics, one runs into difficulties, in fact a kind of infinite regress.

Admittedly, the view I am describing, though a traditional one with a distinguished pedigree, is highly controversial. However, all the rival ideas that have been proposed over the decades are equally controversial and plagued with difficulties. The controversy over how to interpret quantum theory will not be resolved any time soon — perhaps ever. But even if it is not, the fact will remain that there is an argument against materialism that comes from physics itself, an argument that has been advanced and defended by some leading physicists and has never been refuted.

Another discovery that arguably points to something nonmaterial about the human mind is a revolutionary theorem in mathematical logic proved in 1931 by the Austrian logician Kurt Gödel, one of the greatest mathematicians of modern times. Gödel's Theorem concerns the inher-

---

25. Quoted in P. C. W. Davies and J. R. Brown, *The Ghost in the Atom: A Discussion of the Mysteries of Quantum Physics* (Cambridge: Cambridge University Press, 1986), p. 75.
26. Quoted in Davies and Brown, *The Ghost in the Atom*, p. 24.

ent limitations of mechanical systems of computation — and therefore of computers. It was recognized fairly quickly that Gödel's Theorem might have something to say about whether the human mind, at least in the way it does mathematics, is just a computer. Gödel himself was convinced that the human mind is not just a computer. Indeed, he called materialism a "prejudice of our time."[27] However, he never developed in detail, at least in print, the argument against materialism based on his own theorem. That was first done by the Oxford philosopher John R. Lucas. In 1961, Lucas wrote,

> Gödel's theorem seems to me to prove that Mechanism is false, that is, that [human] minds cannot be explained as machines. So has it seemed to many other people: almost every mathematical logician I have put the matter to has confessed similar thoughts, but has felt reluctant to commit himself definitely until he could see the whole argument set out, with all objections fully stated and properly met. This I attempt to do.[28]

Both Gödel's Theorem and Lucas's argument are quite subtle, but we can state the gist of them as follows. Gödel's Theorem implies that a computer program that is known to reason soundly can be outwitted (in a precise sense that I shall not describe) by someone who understands how it is put together. Lucas observed that if a man is *himself* a computer program, then by knowing how his own program is written he could outwit himself, which is a contradiction.

This argument was widely attacked, but it has been vigorously defended in recent times by the eminent mathematician Sir Roger Penrose.[29] The argument remains very controversial. Nevertheless, the fact remains that an argument exists that has been accepted as sound by some leading mathematicians, including it seems the great Kurt Gödel himself, to the effect that the human mind is more than a mere computer.

27. Hao Wang, *A Logical Journey: From Gödel to Philosophy* (Cambridge, MA: MIT, 1996), p. 198.

28. John R. Lucas, "Mind, Machines, and Gödel," in *The Modeling of Mind*, ed. K. M. Sayre and F. J. Crossen (Notre Dame, IN: University of Notre Dame Press, 1963), p. 255.

29. Roger Penrose, *The Emperor's New Mind* (Oxford: Oxford University Press, 1989); *Shadows of the Mind: The Search for the Missing Science of Consciousness* (Oxford: Oxford University Press, 1994).

Where does all this leave us? After all the twists and turns of scientific history, we who are Christians or Jews look around and find ourselves in very familiar surroundings. We find ourselves in a universe that seems to have had a beginning. We find it governed by laws that have a grandeur and sublimity that bespeak design. We find many indications in those laws that we human beings were built in from the beginning. We find that physical determinism, which had seemed to disprove the freedom of the human will, has been overthrown. And we find that the deepest discoveries of modern physics and mathematics give hints, if not proof, that the human mind has something about it that lies beyond the power of either physics or mathematics to describe.

CHAPTER 7

The Future of Theology amid the Arts: Some Reformed Reflections

JEREMY S. BEGBIE

The ferment of "theology and the arts" shows no signs of waning. It burgeons in colleges, universities, and churches. Theological Internet-watchers observe its fast-expanding presence, and publishers are beginning to see it as a serious niche market. In this essay, I want to home in on just one feature of this encouraging groundswell of interest, especially noticeable in recent years — what appears to be a distinct unease or awkwardness about Protestantism, and especially of the Reformed variety. Undoubtedly it would be easy to exaggerate this, but I doubt if I am the only one to have had the sense at many discussions that although Christians of this ilk are usually welcome at the table, the best they can do is catch up with the profounder and unquestionably more fruitful wisdom of others — which by and large means those of a Roman Catholic, Anglo-Catholic, or Orthodox persuasion.

The reasons are not hard to see. The weaknesses of the Reformed tradition have been regularly rehearsed: an exaggerated fear of idolatry, an excessive suspicion of the arts (a "frigid Philistinism"),[1] a tendency to suspect all images, a paucity of reflection on beauty, a frequent inability to take physicality seriously, and so on — the territory is familiar to

---

1. The phrase is Trevor Hart's; Trevor A. Hart, "Protestantism and Art," in *The Blackwell Companion to Protestantism*, ed. Alister E. McGrath and Darren C. Marks (Oxford: Blackwell, 2006), pp. 268-86, at 268.

I am very grateful to Tanner Capps, David Taylor, Bo Helmich, Suzanne McDonald, Kevin Vanhoozer, and James K. A. Smith for their valuable comments on earlier drafts of this essay.

any who explore the field. To be sure, much scholarship has questioned the caricatures and sought to straighten the record.[2] But this has not prevented many in the Reformed stream, not least evangelicals, from assuming that the theological grass will be greener elsewhere — especially in modern Roman Catholic writing, or in the pre-Reformation wisdom of Aquinas, Dionysius, or Augustine.

This eagerness to move outside one's camp is surely in many ways healthy. When I first put my toe in the Christianity and arts river in the early 1980s, I recall three main currents of writing available: the Roman Catholic (drawing on Maritain, Rahner, and others), the liberal Protestant (looking especially to Tillich), and the Dutch Neo-Calvinist (Rookmaaker, Seerveld, with Nicholas Wolterstorff sitting a little to one side). Serious dialogue between these seemed relatively rare. Today, the currents converse and mingle freely, often pulling others into the mix: artistic Reformed evangelicals are nowadays as likely to get their inspiration from Hans Urs von Balthasar and Henri de Lubac as they are from Rookmaaker or Seerveld.[3] This crisscrossing of perspectives has undoubtedly borne immense fruit. However, amid the ecumenical conviviality I am inclined to think that shame about parts of the Reformed inheritance has been overplayed and that the riches this tradition can hold before the wider church with regard to the arts are too easily overlooked. Indeed, I believe that in some respects the tradition is sorely needed in the present conversations.

This is not, of course, to imply that the critical wisdom in this area belongs solely to the Reformed Churches, or that its traits and concerns are wholly absent elsewhere. In any case, the tradition itself is

2. See, e.g., Paul Corby Finney, ed., *Seeing beyond the Word: Visual Arts and the Calvinist Tradition* (Grand Rapids: Eerdmans, 1999); William A. Dyrness, *Visual Faith: Art, Theology, and Worship in Dialogue* (Grand Rapids: Baker, 2001); Randall C. Zachman, *Image and Word in the Theology of John Calvin* (Notre Dame, IN: University of Notre Dame Press, 2007); Christopher R. Joby, *Calvinism and the Arts: A Re-Assessment* (Leuven: Peeters, 2007); David VanDrunen, "Iconoclasm, Incarnation and Eschatology: Toward a Catholic Understanding of the Reformed Doctrine of the 'Second' Commandment," *International Journal of Systematic Theology* 6, no. 2 (April 2004): 130-47; Belden C. Lane, *Ravished by Beauty: The Surprising Legacy of Reformed Spirituality* (Oxford: Oxford University Press, 2011).

3. For one account of the "state of play" in theology and the arts (as of 2007), see William A. Dyrness, "The Arts," in *The Oxford Handbook of Systematic Theology*, ed. John B. Webster, Kathryn Tanner, and Iain R. Torrance (Oxford: Oxford University Press, 2007), pp. 561-79.

hugely complex and varied. I harbor no assumptions about being able to identify a single monolithic Reformed theology and have no interest in defending all that has emerged within the tradition. (It is perhaps worth adding that I have never been a member of a Presbyterian or centrally Reformed Church or denomination.) Still less am I interested in shoring up what some would say is a waning Protestantism. I am concerned, rather, with certain casts of mind — conceptual concerns and strategies, especially insofar as they arise from close attention to the theological dimensions of biblical texts — that are more typical of the Reformed tradition than any other and that I believe deserve to be heard in the current debates. If, as some think, we are witnessing a modest resurgence of interest in "Calvinism" (in the United States at least),[4] perhaps that can provoke us to ask whether some of these casts of mind might have more to offer the current conversations about faith and art than has often been supposed. In this connection, a remark of Trevor Hart about the relevance of strands of Reformation thinking is worth quoting:

> In an age where, for many, aesthetic experience has effectively substituted itself for religious faith as a perceived window onto "spiritual" realities . . . we may find that Reformation perspectives possess a curious freshness, reminding us of things which some theological approaches to art (not least some in the Protestant tradition) appear to have forgotten or broken faith with.[5]

I want to explore this "curious freshness" with respect to elements of the Reformed heritage. I will focus on just three areas of interest I find prominent in much contemporary writing about theology and the arts, at popular, semi-popular, and academic levels: beauty, sacrament, and language.

---

4. *Time* magazine spoke of New Calvinism as one of "10 Ideas Changing the World Right Now." David Van Biema, "The New Calvinism," *Time Magazine Online*, 12 March 2009, http://www.time.com/time/specials/packages/article/0,28804,1884779_1884782 _1884760,00.html. See also Collin Hansen, *Young, Restless, Reformed: A Journalist's Journey with the New Calvinists* (Wheaton, IL: Crossway, 2008). Whether this does represent a major shift or movement is a moot point. James K. A. Smith, "Barna Report on the 'New Calvinism,'" blog entry (2010), http://forsclavigera.blogspot.com/2010/11 /barna-report-on-new-calvinism.html.

5. Hart, "Protestantism and Art," p. 270.

The Allure of Beauty

After seasons of exile, the theme of beauty seems to be enjoying something of a comeback. In artistic circles there are signs of an energetic interest, and philosophy has seen a steady stream of studies.[6] Among theologians it is proving ever more popular. Impatient with what Edward Farley calls "the new problematic of beauty" engendered in particular by the eighteenth century's "relocation of beauty from an external property to a human sensibility,"[7] many want to reinstate it by speaking of it as integral to the created world, and perhaps to the identity of God.[8] Hence the appeal of Balthasar's theological aesthetics, of Augustine and Aquinas on beauty,[9] and the increasing fascination with Jacques Mari-

---

6. See, e.g., Elaine Scarry, *On Beauty and Being Just* (Princeton, NJ: Princeton University Press, 1999); Bill Beckley and David Shapiro, *Uncontrollable Beauty: Toward a New Aesthetics* (New York: Allworth, 1998); Arthur C. Danto, *The Abuse of Beauty: Aesthetics and the Concept of Art* (Chicago: Open Court, 2003); Glenn Parsons and Allen Carlson, eds., *Functional Beauty* (Oxford: Oxford University Press, 2008); Roger Scruton, *Beauty* (Oxford: Oxford University Press, 2009); Brett Ashley Kaplan, *Unwanted Beauty: Aesthetic Pleasure in Holocaust Representation* (Urbana: University of Illinois Press, 2007); Alexander Nehamas, "The Return of the Beautiful: Morality, Pleasure, and the Value of Uncertainty," *The Journal of Aesthetics and Art Criticism* 58, no. 4 (Autumn 2000): 393-403; Alexander Nehamas, *Only a Promise of Happiness: The Place of Beauty in a World of Art* (Princeton, NJ: Princeton University Press, 2007).

7. Edward Farley, *Faith and Beauty: A Theological Aesthetic* (Aldershot: Ashgate, 2001), p. 33.

8. See, e.g., Bruno Forte, *The Portal of Beauty: Towards a Theology of Aesthetics* (Grand Rapids: Eerdmans, 2008); Richard Harries, *Art and the Beauty of God: A Christian Understanding* (London: Mowbray, 2000); David Bentley Hart, *The Beauty of the Infinite: The Aesthetics of Christian Truth* (Grand Rapids: Eerdmans, 2003); John Milbank, Graham Ward, and Edith Wyschogrod, *Theological Perspectives on God and Beauty* (Harrisburg, PA: Trinity, 2003); Aidan Nichols, *Redeeming Beauty: Soundings in Sacral Aesthetics* (Aldershot: Ashgate, 2007); Patrick Sherry, *Spirit and Beauty: An Introduction to Theological Aesthetics* (London: SCM, 2002); Daniel J. Treier, Mark Husbands, and Roger Lundin, eds., *The Beauty of God: Theology and the Arts* (Downers Grove, IL: IVP Academic, 2007); Richard Viladesau, *The Beauty of the Cross: The Passion of Christ in Theology and the Arts from the Catacombs to the Eve of the Renaissance* (Oxford: Oxford University Press, 2005); Richard Viladesau, *Theological Aesthetics: God in Imagination, Beauty, and Art* (New York: Oxford University Press, 1999), ch. 4.

9. See, e.g., John Milbank, "Beauty and the Soul," in Milbank et al., eds., *Theological Perspectives on God and Beauty*, pp. 1-34; Carol Harrison, "Taking Creation for the Creator: Use and Enjoyment in Augustine's Theological Aesthetics," in *Idolatry: False Worship in the Bible, Early Judaism and Christianity*, ed. Stephen C. Barton (London: T&T Clark, 2007), pp. 179-97.

tain.[10] Along with this often goes an almost immediate association of the arts with beauty; to care about the arts, it is assumed, is to care about beauty, and vice versa.

To call any of this into question might seem very odd, even bizarre — especially in a culture so obviously in need of beauty, and when Protestant Christians habitually neglect beauty in favor of the other two "transcendentals," truth and goodness. Nevertheless, I believe it is worth sending some friendly warning shots across the bow of this fashionable theological steamer. The first is a formal point about the assumed mutual entailment of beauty and the arts. It may well be that beauty (variously defined) can and should be considered a desirable quality in the arts. But to suppose that the presence of or aspiration toward beauty is a necessary condition for something to be considered *as* art is much more debatable, as is the stronger view that the arts are to be distinguished from other cultural activities and products by their investment in beauty. It is not hard to think of exemplary art that most would not call beautiful (e.g., paintings by Max Beckman; Stravinsky's *Le Sacre du Printemps*), and not hard to find a significant concern for beauty in other fields — say, in mathematical physics. Prior to the eighteenth century the links between what we now call the arts and beauty were not nearly as strong as is often presumed; certainly, this goes for most of the classic theologies of beauty. Thus I have a certain sympathy with Reformed philosopher Nicholas Wolterstorff when he questions a simple correlation of art and beauty (and the cluster of ideas that tend to be associated with this correlation),[11] and with Calvin Seerveld from a Dutch Neo-Calvinist perspective, who is also strongly opposed to any automatic coupling of the two.[12] Exercising

---

10. Rowan Williams, *Grace and Necessity: Reflections on Art and Love* (London: Continuum, 2005); Matthew J. Milliner, "The New Maritainians" (2010), at http://www.thepublicdiscourse.com/2010/05/1307; John G. Trapani, *Poetry, Beauty, and Contemplation: The Complete Aesthetics of Jacques Maritain* (Washington, DC: Catholic University of America Press, 2011).

11. For Wolterstorff, "aesthetic excellence" is characterized by unity, internal richness, and "fittingness-intensity." He believes that beauty (which he understands in terms of proportion, consonance, brightness, and affording pleasure upon contemplation) is not the necessary and sufficient condition of aesthetic excellence. We judge many works of art as aesthetically excellent that we would not normally judge as beautiful — and still regard them as works of art. Nicholas Wolterstorff, *Art in Action: Toward a Christian Aesthetic* (Grand Rapids: Eerdmans, 1980), pp. 156-74, esp. pp. 161-63.

12. Calvin Seerveld, *Rainbows for the Fallen World: Aesthetic Life and Artistic Task* (Toronto: Tuppence, 1980), pp. 116-25.

a little caution here means that we will be much more likely to notice that when Balthasar expounds a "theological aesthetics" he is not principally concerned with the arts (though he certainly engages the arts at length) but with beauty as a dimension of theology;[13] or that when David Bentley Hart writes so eloquently about "aesthetics," he has in mind largely the beauty of God and God's creation (he makes only fleeting references to the arts).[14]

The second point concerns the controls shaping our concepts of beauty. The Reformed tradition is well known for its stress on the noetic effects of the fall, its insistence that human sin does not rise to the neck and suddenly halt just below the cerebellum — our conceptual categories require a continual re-formation by the Spirit to be conformed to the pattern of Christ, this reconfiguration being internal to the dynamic of redemption. In this light, I suggest that if we *are* to speak of beauty as belonging to God and/or the created world, and conceive it (provisionally at least) according to some version of the so-called "great theory"[15] — where beauty is said to be characterized, for example, by proportion and consonance of parts, brightness or radiance, perfection or integrity, and as granting pleasure upon contemplation — these strands will need to be subject to a constant reshaping through the church's repeated return to God's reconciling self-disclosure.[16]

It is this alertness to theological criteria grounded in the self-identi-

---

13. Hans Urs von Balthasar, *The Glory of the Lord: A Theological Aesthetics*, vol. 1: *Seeing the Form*, trans. Erasmo Leivà-Merikakis (Edinburgh: T&T Clark, 1982), p. 118.

14. Hart, *The Beauty of the Infinite*.

15. See Wladyslaw Tatarkiewicz, "The Great Theory of Beauty and Its Decline," *Journal of Aesthetics and Art Criticism* 31 (1972): 165-80.

16. Balthasar properly insists that it is to the economy of salvation that we must go to discover God's beauty (and thus the ultimate measure of all beauty), since the incarnation, death, and raising of Jesus display God's love in its clearest and most decisive form; here, above all, we witness the mutual self-surrendering love of Father and Son in the Spirit for the healing of the world. Balthasar urges that we "ought never to speak of God's beauty without reference to the form and manner of appearing which he exhibits in salvation-history." And later: "God's attribute of beauty can certainly . . . be examined in the context of a doctrine of the divine attributes. Besides examining God's beauty as manifested by God's actions in his creation, his beauty would also be deduced from the harmony of his essential attributes, and particularly from the Trinity. But such a doctrine of God and the Trinity really speaks to us only when and as long as the θεολογια does not become detached from the οικονομια, but rather lets its every formulation and stage of reflection be accompanied and supported by the latter's vivid discernibility." Balthasar, *The Glory of the Lord*, vol. 1, pp. 124, 125.

fication of God that needs be borne in mind when reading the Reformed theologian Karl Barth on beauty.[17] Barth could not bring himself to speak of beauty as a "perfection" of God: beauty is rather the form of God's glory in his self-revelation; it is that about God's self-presentation which attracts rather than repels, which redeems, persuades, and convinces, which evokes joy rather than indifference. If we judge Barth over-cautious, we should not do so without first heeding his anxiety about an "aestheticism" that would turn a pre-set notion of beauty into an absolute to which the God of Jesus Christ is expected to conform.[18]

In very compressed terms, then, we might propose that divine beauty be conceived as the form of love of the Son for the Father and the Father for the Son,[19] a dynamic self-surrender that implies not merger or homogeneity but the "distance" of love. Insofar as the Spirit is the personal unity of the mutual outgoingness of Father and Son, the impulse toward self-sharing in God's life, and the one who establishes particularity, we might describe the Spirit as the "beautifier" in God.[20] The integrity and proportion of God's beauty are the ceaseless self-donation of Father to Son and Son to Father in the ecstatic energy of the Spirit. Further, if Christ is the measure of God's beauty, so also of creaturely beauty. Here — in the one conceived and empowered by the Spirit, born in a stable, dragged to a shameful death, vindicated by God on the third day, and exalted as a "spiritual body," the stuff of the earth made new — creation's beauty is brought to its culmination. Further still, it makes

17. Karl Barth, *Church Dogmatics*, II/1, ed. Thomas F. Torrance and Geoffrey W. Bromiley (Edinburgh: T&T Clark, 1970), pp. 650-66.

18. "[W]e must be careful not to start from any preconceived ideas, especially in this case a preconceived idea of the beautiful. . . . God is not beautiful in the sense that he shares in an idea of beauty superior to him, so that to know it is to know him as God. On the contrary, it is as he is God that he is also beautiful, so that he is the basis and standard of everything that is beautiful and of all ideas of the beautiful." Barth, *Church Dogmatics*, II/1, p. 656.

19. Undoubtedly, the Reformed luminary Jonathan Edwards (1703-1758) has a considerable amount to offer when accounting for beauty in trinitarian terms, whatever hesitations we may have about a Platonic seam in his thought. He writes of "primary beauty," whose chief instance is God's own triune benevolence, the mutual generosity and "infinite consent" that constitutes the life of God. Roland André Delattre, *Beauty and Sensibility in the Thought of Jonathan Edwards: An Essay in Aesthetics and Theological Ethics* (New Haven, CT: Yale University Press, 1968), chs. 7 and 8; Amy Plantinga Pauw, *The Supreme Harmony of All: The Trinitarian Theology of Jonathan Edwards* (Grand Rapids: Eerdmans, 2002), pp. 80-85 et passim; Farley, *Faith and Beauty*, ch. 4.

20. For an exposition of the Spirit in relation to beauty, see Sherry, *Spirit and Beauty*.

good sense to see the Spirit as related directly to the axis of attraction and longing, allure and desire that seems integral to our perception of the radiance of both divine and created beauty.

What, then, of beauty and the arts? Even if we reject a *necessary* mutual entanglement of the two, this does not mean rejecting the category of beauty (carefully qualified) as naming a *desideratum* in the arts. On this, I limit myself to three comments, with the Reformed tradition especially in view.[21] First, a vision of beauty re-formed along the lines suggested above will celebrate the ability of the arts *to voice creation's praise,* and thus its beauty, *in its very createdness.* This was another key concern of Barth, exemplified in his (doubtless inflated) adulation of Mozart. For Barth, Mozart's music embodies the ability of creation to praise its Creator, *as created.* This composer, Barth writes, "simply offered himself as the agent by which little bits of horn, metal and catgut could serve as the voices of creation."[22] In another place he says of Mozart: "The sun shines but does not blind, does not burn or consume. Heaven arches over the earth, but it does not weigh it down, it does not crush or devour it. Hence *earth remains earth,* with no need to maintain itself in a titanic revolt against heaven."[23] This is not a demeaning of creatureliness in the name of divine transcendence, as is so often thought.[24] The point is that creation fulfills its character precisely insofar as it *is* limited, not-divine (yet fully real); its distinctive beauty and goodness are inseparable from its createdness.[25]

21. I have said rather more in "Beauty, Sentimentality and the Arts," in Treier et al., eds., *The Beauty of God,* pp. 45-69; and in "Created Beauty: The Witness of J. S. Bach," in *Resonant Witness: Conversations between Music and Theology,* ed. Jeremy S. Begbie and Steven R. Guthrie (Grand Rapids: Eerdmans, 2011), pp. 83-108.

22. Karl Barth, *Church Dogmatics,* III/3, ed. Geoffrey W. Bromiley and Thomas F. Torrance (Edinburgh: T&T Clark, 1960), p. 298.

23. Karl Barth, *Wolfgang Amadeus Mozart,* trans. Clarence K. Pott (Grand Rapids: Eerdmans, 1986), p. 53. My italics.

24. Novelist John Updike remarks that Barth's insistence on God's Otherness "seemed to free him to be exceptionally (for a theologian) appreciative and indulgent of this world, the world at hand." John Updike, "Foreword," in Barth, *Wolfgang Amadeus Mozart,* p. 7.

25. In a number of places I have attempted to outline a view of creativity that takes full account both of God's trinitarian agency and of humans' full participation in that agency, and in such a way that created order is neither ignored nor abrogated but enabled to articulate fresh praise. See, e.g., *Voicing Creation's Praise: Towards a Theology of the Arts* (Edinburgh: T&T Clark, 1991), part III; "Christ and the Cultures: Christianity and the Arts," in *The Cambridge Companion to Christian Doctrine,* ed. Colin E. Gunton

Another dimension of this is worth highlighting. For Barth, Mozart enables creation's praise while still conceding that its beauty has been marred and corrupted. Some writers and artists broadly in the Reformed tradition have thus spoken of a "broken beauty,"[26] where the artistic evocation of beauty bears the marks of the world's tragedy that Christ has penetrated and healed at Golgotha. John Walford has shown how some seventeenth-century Dutch landscape painters portray the natural world in anything but idealized terms; here is a beauty that takes account of the marks of distortion (transience, decay, storm damage).[27] Ultimately such beauty can be discerned and interpreted aright only through the lens of the crucifixion. And this takes us to our second main comment about a re-formed vision of beauty for the arts: insofar as it refuses to marginalize the cross and all that is implicated there, it *spurns sentimentality.*[28] God's self-presentation in Christ intrudes starkly on all sanitized beauties. Divine love speaks its most exalted word just as it plunges into unspeakable degradation. In God's humiliation and ex-

---

(Cambridge: Cambridge University Press, 1997), pp. 101-18; *Resounding Truth: Christian Wisdom in the World of Music* (Grand Rapids: Baker, 2007), ch. 8.

26. E. John Walford, "The Case for a Broken Beauty: An Art Historical Viewpoint," in Treier et al., eds., *The Beauty of God*, pp. 87-109. See also Theodore L. Prescott, *A Broken Beauty* (Grand Rapids: Eerdmans, 2005).

27. E. John Walford, *Jacob van Ruisdael and the Perception of Landscape* (New Haven, CT: Yale University Press, 1991), ch. 4, esp. pp. 99-100. In the course of a wide-ranging book, written from what he describes as a "Reformed" perspective, William Dyrness asks what "Reformed Protestantism" can bring to a "poetic theology." William A. Dyrness, *Poetic Theology: God and the Poetics of Everyday Life* (Grand Rapids: Eerdmans, 2011), ch. 6; see also p. 9. Following up his belief that "a critical aesthetic category of a Protestant aesthetic is dramatic action," Dyrness writes that Protestants have "inherited a particular aesthetic framework that is different from . . . that of the Catholic and Orthodox traditions" (p. 153). He speaks of three categories illuminating this framework: "brokenness, hidden character, and the prophetic." The element of "brokenness" (pp. 166-73) is congruent with what I have been developing here. I am unclear as to the central meaning of "hiddenness," since Dyrness includes such diverse things under this umbrella — e.g., Calvin Seerveld's "allusiveness," Wolterstorff's "fittingness," and the way in which art's beauty is often concealed. At times the main point seems to be about simplicity, the way in which art hides its artifice. In any case, the third category, the "prophetic," alludes to a protest against the world's brokenness, and to the way in which art should "encourage viewers and hearers to reconstrue the pattern of their lives, to re-interpret or *re-read* that pattern in accordance with the biblical truth, and, more importantly, to discern their lives in accordance with what is seen and heard" (pp. 177-80). There is clearly an eschatological dimension to this.

28. Begbie, "Beauty, Sentimentality and the Arts."

ecution we witness God's supreme self-revealing, the ultimate triumph over sin and death. God enacts beauty *this* way.

Of course, Reformed thinkers are not the only ones to argue in this manner, and they have often failed to do so, despite the fact that many of their theological distinctives strongly resist a sentimental ethos. From a Roman Catholic perspective, for instance, Richard Viladesau has written along these lines;[29] Balthasar has insisted that a theology of beauty can do no other than proceed by way of the cross;[30] and distinguished composer James MacMillan has consistently sought to defy the seduction of sentimentality through resolute attention to the crucifixion.[31]

A third comment: a re-formed vision of beauty will *be charged with promise.* If the risen and exalted Christ prefigures the final re-creation of all things, then earthly beauty at its richest will share in that prefigurement. Reformed theologian Eberhard Jüngel writes: "the beautiful . . . carries within itself the *promise* of truth to come, a future *direct* encounter with the truth . . . the beautiful is a *pre-appearance directed to a goal.*"[32] The agent of this pre-appearance is the Spirit, the evidence and

---

29. Viladesau, *The Beauty of the Cross; The Triumph of the Cross: The Passion of Christ in Theology and the Arts from the Renaissance to the Counter-Reformation* (Oxford: Oxford University Press, 2008); "The Beauty of the Cross," in *Theological Aesthetics after Von Balthasar,* ed. Oleg V. Bychkov and James Fodor (Aldershot: Ashgate, 2008), pp. 135-51; "Theosis and Beauty," *Theology Today* 65 (2008): 180-90. Viladesau writes: "In Christ our understanding of the transcendental quality of beauty is raised to a deeper and more inclusive level, one that embraces even what appears (from a merely inner-worldly perspective) to be irrational, disordered, lacking in attractiveness and goodness." He explains: "though the other may not be beautiful, generous self-giving love for the needy other is perceived by the eyes of faith as a (morally, spiritually) beautiful act in the 'theo-drama' in which we are involved, a drama created by God's artistry." Viladesau, "Theosis and Beauty," p. 188. (I am not entirely convinced, however, that the metaphysics Viladesau espouses in this and other writings is adequately focused and grounded to support this vision.)

30. Balthasar asks: "How could we . . . understand the 'beauty' of the Cross without the abysmal darkness into which the Crucified plunges?" Balthasar, *The Glory of the Lord,* vol. 1, p. 117. David Luy highlights the affirmation — "never dimmed" in Balthasar's work from the outset of his theological aesthetics — "that the horrific event of the crucifixion, the agony of Jesus through his passion and death, represents at once the paradigmatic expression of the divine, and the apex of God's glory shining in the world." David Luy, "The Aesthetic Collision: Hans Urs von Balthasar on the Trinity and the Cross," *International Journal of Systematic Theology* 13, no. 2 (2011): 154-69, at 154.

31. See Begbie, *Resounding Truth,* pp. 176-82.

32. Eberhard Jüngel, "'Even the Beautiful Must Die' — Beauty in the Light of

guarantee of the glory yet to come. For a contemporary example of this in action, a recent sculpture from Mozambique comes to mind. It bears the title "The Tree of Life," and for a short time it stood in the atrium of the British Museum in London. A tree grew in the Garden of Eden but access was forbidden. In Revelation 22 the tree reappears, standing on each side of the river of the water of life that flows from God's throne, its leaves for the healing of the nations. This sculpted tree is constructed entirely from weapons reclaimed after Mozambique's civil war. We recall Isaiah's vision of peace: "They shall beat their swords into plowshares, and their spears into pruning hooks" (Isa. 2:4).[33]

The Power of Sacrament

The appeal to "sacrament," the "sacramental," and "sacramentality" abounds in the current theology and arts arena, especially in connection with the visual arts.[34] To conceive the arts as in some sense sacramental appears to be a relatively recent move in intellectual history — something rarely acknowledged by those who like to make the same move today.[35] In any case, today it has become extraordinarily popular, and especially among the artistically inclined who have been reared

---

Truth," in *Theological Essays*, vol. 2, ed. J. B. Webster (Edinburgh: T&T Clark, 1989), pp. 59-81, at 76.

33. "Tree of Life," on the British Museum website (accessed 2005): http://www.britishmuseum.org/explore/highlights/highlight_objects/aoa/t/tree_of_life.aspx.

34. Among numerous examples, see David Brown and Ann Loades, eds., *The Sense of the Sacramental: Movement and Measure in Art and Music, Place and Time* (London: SPCK, 1995); David Brown and David Fuller, *Signs of Grace: Sacraments in Poetry and Prose* (Ridgefield, CT: Morehouse, 1996); David Brown, *God and Enchantment of Place: Reclaiming Human Experience* (Oxford: Oxford University Press, 2004), ch. 1; David Brown, *God and Grace of Body: Sacrament in Ordinary* (Oxford: Oxford University Press, 2007), pp. 3-4, 246-47, 371; Albert L. Blackwell, *The Sacred in Music* (Cambridge: Lutterworth, 1999), pp. 16, 28, et passim; Scott Cairns, "Elemental Metonymy: Poems, Icons, Holy Mysteries" (unpublished paper delivered at the Calvin College Interdisciplinary Conference in Christian Scholarship, Grand Rapids, MI, 27-29 September 2001).

35. See the remarks of Roger Lundin, *Believing Again: Doubt and Faith in a Secular Age* (Grand Rapids: Eerdmans, 2009), pp. 24-29. Wolterstorff's "unsupported hunch" is that the link first appears in John Keble (1792-1866), though he underlines the caution with which Keble makes the connection. Nicholas Wolterstorff, "Evangelicalism and the Arts," *Christian Scholar's Review* 17, no. 4 (June 1988): 449-73, at 460-62. See John Keble, *On the Mysticism Attributed to the Early Fathers of the Church* (London: J. G. F. & J. Revington, 1841).

in "low" Protestant churches and who suddenly find themselves awakened to pre-Reformation, Roman Catholic, and Orthodox sacramental sensibilities.

What motivates this enthusiasm to speak of the arts as "sacramental"? One factor seems to be an eagerness to recover a sense of the physicality of the arts — in particular, to validate the worth and integrity of the physical and its capacity to mediate the non-physical, against quasi-Gnostic tendencies in some theology to undervalue or even denigrate materiality. Another is that the supposed sacramentality of the arts gives us a way of conceiving God's presence in culture at large: if art by its very nature is sacramental, it can act as a conduit of divine presence far beyond ecclesiastical boundaries.[36]

Metaphysical concerns can also be at work. Behind much talk of art and sacrament, modernity's much-discussed "disenchantment" of the cosmos is presumed, the modern drive to reduce the world to a bare, godless mechanism. Today, as Roger Lundin remarks, "Question the wisdom of calling poetry a sacrament, and you will be accused of denying mystery and disenchanting the world."[37] The movement known as "Radical Orthodoxy" comes to mind in this connection, with its commitment to a rehabilitated Christianized Platonism and to narrating modernity and postmodernity as a tale of poignant decline. In the late medieval period, Europe is said to have abandoned a "participatory" worldview such that created reality comes to be treated as an autonomous zone of inert, flat materiality. This de-sacralization (or "desacramentalizing") of the cosmos inevitably leads by virtue of its own destructive logic to various manifestations of nihilism. A counter-ontology is proposed in which the material world is seen as "suspended" in the uncreated immaterial, "engraced" *ab initio.*[38] These proposals owe

---

36. This is a characteristic stress of the voluminous writing of David Brown, an ardent advocate of the "sacramental" potential of the arts. See note 34 above. According to Brown, music, for example, through its combination of the "ethereal and material," is a finite reality through which "God's presence in our midst [can] once more be made known." Brown, *God and Grace of Body*, pp. 220-22, at 247.

37. Lundin, *Believing Again*, p. 25. Whether the arts can in some sense "re-enchant" the world is a theme much discussed in recent literature: see, e.g., David Morgan, "The Enchantment of Art: Abstraction and Empathy from German Romanticism to Expressionism," *Journal of the History of Ideas* 57, no. 2 (1996): 317-41; Gordon Graham, *The Re-Enchantment of the World: Art versus Religion* (Oxford: Oxford University Press, 2007).

38. John Milbank, Catherine Pickstock, and Graham Ward, eds., *Radical Ortho-*

a hefty debt to the French Jesuit Henri de Lubac (1896-1991), with his call for a renaissance of a conception of the "supernatural" as always already present with and within "ordinary" creation.[39] De Lubac has recently received fervent support from Hans Boersma, who pleads that evangelicals, among others, embrace a "sacramental ontology" for the sake of an effective Christian witness in late modern/postmodern society.[40]

For our purposes, we should note the way the arts are drawn into these sweeping theological brushstrokes, to counter our culture's drift into a nihilist void. One of Radical Orthodoxy's original group, Philip Blond, maintains that the painter Kazimir Malevich (1878-1935) offers a highly evocative sense of the form(s) inherent to the visible, physical world. Citing two of his works of the late 1920s and early 1930s, Blond tells us:

> Even where the face of a human figure is left blank, the colors surrounding it edge around and mark out in the absence of a face the shape of what might fulfill such a request. . . . In this sense, all of Malevich's work was indeed *iconic*, a visible testament to *the presence of the ideal in the real*, and a belief that the artist could depict such a fact.[41]

Blond insists that recognizing such presence calls for nothing less than a theological construal: "it is *worldly form* as God-given (as culminated and expressed in the union of word and flesh in Christ) that is revelatory, and nothing else . . . the world shows and exhibits its participation in universal theological forms that can and must be seen."[42]

Something of the same outlook characterizes the forthright and impassioned studio director, curator, art historian, and theorist Daniel

---

doxy: *A New Theology* (London: Routledge, 1999); James K. A. Smith, *Introducing Radical Orthodoxy: Mapping a Post-Secular Theology* (Grand Rapids: Baker, 2004).

39. Substantial writing on de Lubac has appeared in recent years: see, e.g., John Milbank, *The Suspended Middle: Henri de Lubac and the Debate concerning the Supernatural* (Grand Rapids: Eerdmans, 2005); Rudolf Voderholzer and Michael J. Miller, *Meet Henri de Lubac* (San Francisco: Ignatius, 2008); Bryan C. Hollon, *Everything Is Sacred: Spiritual Exegesis in the Political Theology of Henri de Lubac* (Eugene, OR: Cascade, 2009).

40. Hans Boersma, *Nouvelle Théologie and Sacramental Ontology: A Return to Mystery* (Oxford: Oxford University Press, 2009); *Heavenly Participation: The Weaving of a Sacramental Tapestry* (Grand Rapids: Eerdmans, 2010).

41. Philip Blond, "Perception: From Modern Painting to the Vision in Christ," in Milbank et al., eds., *Radical Orthodoxy*, pp. 220-42, at 231. My italics.

42. Blond, "Perception," p. 235. My italics.

Siedell. Irritated especially by Protestantism's proneness to retreat into like-minded ghettoes, he pleads that his readers join him in the contemporary art gallery and discern God's presence there. Drawing an analogy between the "logic of the icon" in Eastern Orthodoxy and the way in which modern and contemporary art might be read theologically, he contends that because material objects can become bearers of sacramental presence, contemporary art can offer an "embodied transcendence," a "material spirituality," of a type consistent with the ancient Nicene traditions of the early church.[43]

With regard to music, Albert Blackwell has drawn on a broad range of sources to demonstrate its "sacramental potential" — where "sacramental" applies to *"any finite reality through which the divine is perceived to be disclosed and communicated, and through which our human response to the divine assumes some measure of shape, form, and structure."*[44] Blackwell delineates two broad traditions of sacramental encounter that have been applied to music: the "Pythagorean" and the "incarnational," the former focusing on the intellectual apprehension of the world's mathematical constitution through music, the latter on the sensual, bodily experience music affords.[45]

I find myself deeply sympathetic to the concerns that make the notion of sacramentality so appealing to many at work in the theology and arts world. At the same time, awkward questions are bound to arise, and they are not eased by the fact that I have not yet found a sufficiently robust and theologically compelling case for extending the language of sacramentality to the practices and products of the arts. That is not to say a case could not be made, only that to my knowledge a good one has not yet appeared, especially with respect to non-visual and non-literary art.

If the Reformed tradition has a particular contribution here, it is its repeated concern to orient (or re-orient) our thinking about sacrament/

---

43. Daniel A. Siedell, *God in the Gallery: A Christian Embrace of Modern Art* (Grand Rapids: Baker Academic, 2008), esp. ch. 4. See Jeremy S. Begbie, "On the Strange Place of Contemporary Art, article review of *On the Strange Place of Religion in Contemporary Art*, James Elkins, New York: Routledge, 2004 and *God in the Gallery: A Christian Embrace of Modern Art*, Daniel Siedell, Grand Rapids, Michigan: Baker Academic," *Image* 64 (December 2009): 105-13.

44. Blackwell, *The Sacred in Music*, p. 28; Blackwell is here quoting Richard McBrien; Richard P. McBrien, *Catholicism*, vol. 2 (London: G. Chapman, 1980), p. 732. Italics original.

45. Blackwell, *The Sacred in Music*, ch. 1, et passim.

sacramentality in rather more obviously scriptural directions than we find in much of the "art and sacrament" discourse presently in vogue. Specifically, we are pressed in the direction of what some call a "covenant ontology," where created reality is resolutely interpreted as grounded in the Father's love for the Son in the Spirit, which is to say in a manner made possible by, and consistent with, what has been disclosed and accomplished in Jesus Christ. Many Reformed theologians have expounded this kind of perspective (with different accents) but with little evident impact so far in the theology and arts world.[46] Much depends here on hold-

46. See, e.g., Michael S. Horton, *Covenant and Salvation: Union with Christ* (Louisville: Westminster John Knox, 2007); Alan J. Torrance, "Creatio Ex Nihilo and the Spatio-Temporal Dimensions, with Special Reference to Jürgen Moltmann and D. C. Williams," in *The Doctrine of Creation: Essays in Dogmatics, History and Philosophy*, ed. Colin E. Gunton (Edinburgh: T&T Clark, 1997), pp. 83-104; Thomas F. Torrance, *Divine and Contingent Order* (Oxford: Oxford University Press, 1981); Colin E. Gunton, *The Triune Creator: A Historical and Systematic Study* (Edinburgh: Edinburgh University Press, 1998); Kevin J. Vanhoozer, *Remythologizing Theology: Divine Action, Passion, and Authorship* (Cambridge: Cambridge University Press, 2010). Rowan Williams tellingly writes: "Sacramentality is not a general principle that the world is full of 'sacredness': it is the very specific conviction that the world is full of the life of a God whose nature is made known in Christ and the Spirit." Rowan Williams, "Foreword," in *The Gestures of God: Explorations in Sacramentality*, ed. Geoffrey Rowell and Christine Hall (London: Continuum, 2004), pp. xiii-xiv, at xiii. The same conviction appears in a more recent article. Williams says: "Sacramentality has been too often understood as a rather static manifestation of the sacred (the familiar language about sacramental understanding of the world can mean simply that the world affords glimpses of the holy); but if divine presence is always necessarily divine action, what is sacramental about the Church is its transparency to the divine act of mutual self-gift." Rowan Williams, "Divine Presence and Divine Action: Reflections in the Wake of Nicholas Lash," on the Archbishop of Canterbury website, 30 June 2011, http://www.archbishopofcanterbury.org/articles .php/2131/divine-presence-and-divine-action-reflections-in-the-wake-of-nicholas -lash.

It is intriguing to find Pope Benedict XVI speaking of the integration of covenant and creation in his Easter Homily of 2011 in ways that draw directly on the language of Karl Barth: "communion between God and man does not appear as something extra, something added later to a world already fully created. The Covenant, communion between God and man, is inbuilt at the deepest level of creation. Yes, the Covenant is the inner ground of creation, just as creation is the external presupposition of the Covenant. God made the world so that there could be a space where he might communicate his love, and from which the response of love might come back to him." Homily of Pope Benedict XVI, The Easter Vigil, St. Peter's Basilica, 23 April 2011, as quoted in Rocco Palmo, "In the Resurrection, 'Creation Has Been Fulfilled,'" blog entry (2011), http://whispersintheloggia.blogspot.com/2011/04/in-resurrection-creation

ing to what has been uniquely *enacted and achieved* in Christ — himself the culmination of God's covenant with Israel and the foretaste of the new creation to come — and on reading the created world and God's commitment to this world resolutely through this prism.[47]

I confine myself to just three comments that issue from this, again with a particular eye to Reformed perspectives. The first concerns that heavily laden word (a seemingly close friend of "sacrament") — *presence*. If we have in view the covenanting God of Israel, dedicated unconditionally to the redemption of all things in and through his Son in the Spirit, then the concept of divine "presence" must be rescued from anything that suggests an inert "thereness," or a deity of bland infinitude, a nameless "Other." Ironically, there are potent resources within the arts for helping us to recover a fuller vision of presence — as I have tried to show elsewhere with respect to music.[48] For the moment I point to two recent reflections on presence by Rowan Williams, who, although not writing from a self-consciously Reformed angle, gives pointed expression to sentiments of the sort I am recommending. In a journal on Christianity and the arts, he reflects on the conundrum that "the change associated with Jesus is incapable of representation," yet "for the change to be communicable it must in some way be representable."[49] The key challenge here is: "how do you show transcendent difference in the representation of earthly events?"[50] This comes to a head if we consider how we

----

-has-been.html. Cf. Karl Barth, *Church Dogmatics*, III/1, ed. Geoffrey W. Bromiley and Thomas F. Torrance (Edinburgh: T&T Clark, 1958), §41. I am grateful to Tanner Capps for directing me to these sources.

47. Merely describing Christ as the "primordial sacrament," while doubtless defendable, is hardly enough if we are to prevent Jesus from being seen merely as the supreme instance of a preconceived "sacramentality," ontologically prior to and epistemically accessible (by a simple act of perception) independently of him. This is why much of what I am saying about "sacramental" could also apply to the term "incarnational." "At times, Protestant advocates of the arts in particular have promoted the incarnation as a general concept of divine blessing of the world rather than as a doctrine of the specific redemptive activity that God has accomplished through the person and work of Jesus Christ." Daniel J. Treier, Mark Husbands, and Roger Lundin, "Introduction," in Treier et al., eds., *The Beauty of God*, p. 10.

48. Jeremy S. Begbie, "Music, Mystery and Sacrament," in *The Gestures of God: Explorations in Sacramentality*, ed. Geoffrey Rowell and Christine Hall (London: Continuum, 2004), pp. 173-91; and, more widely, *Theology, Music and Time* (Cambridge: Cambridge University Press, 2000).

49. Rowan Williams, "Presence," *Art and Christianity* 43 (2005): 1-4, at 2.

50. Williams, "Presence," p. 3.

portray Jesus Christ. We cannot represent divinity as something simply added to humanity ("the human with inspirational extras"),[51] nor merely by picturing humanity taken to some extreme. Somehow the artist needs to show how the world is "enlarged" through the coming of Christ without creatureliness being distorted or overridden. "How does presence *alter* things? That is what the artist tackling this most impossible of tasks is after."[52] And this can be achieved very subtly. Through irony, for example, we can show the sheer oddity of the gospel at work in the world. Williams alludes to a painting by Roger Wagner, *Menorah* (1993), in which Holocaust victims "are wandering in the neighborhood of a distantly seen, conventionally depicted crucifixion, the background dominated by . . . immense towers exuding gas, arranged in the pattern of [a] ceremonial [Jewish] candlestick." Our world becomes strange, different, "as a result of having this particular stranger, Jesus, introduced into it."[53] Presence, in other words, is presence for *change*: God makes things different, and our perception of things different, as part of his judgment and renewal of the world.[54]

In another article Williams warns against imagining that presence can be discerned without a transformation on the part of the discerner.[55] He finds himself critical of what he calls "the aestheticizing of the notion of divine presence" — where the problem of God's absence is seen

> as being that we cannot discern God and need to be educated in the skills that will allow us to perceive or experience the divine or the sacred. This is not by any means a waste of time . . . but to the extent that it sees the issue as something to do with the latent capacities of

51. Williams, "Presence," p. 3.
52. Williams, "Presence," p. 4. My italics.
53. Williams, "Presence," pp. 3, 4.
54. For something of the background to this, see Williams's essay, "Sacraments of a New Society," in *On Christian Theology* (Oxford: Blackwell, 2000), pp. 209-21. In this connection, Wolterstorff is, I believe, fully justified in questioning the drift of David Jones's well-known essay on art and sacrament. Wolterstorff, "Evangelicalism and the Arts," pp. 455-59. Note also the observations of theologians John Inge and Alistair McFadyen about the tendency of the concept of sacrament to become "static," as they reflect on working with a sculptor on a piece installed at Ely Cathedral. Alistair I. McFadyen and John Inge, "Art in a Cathedral," in *Sounding the Depths: Theology through the Arts*, ed. Jeremy S. Begbie (London: SCM, 2002), pp. 119-58, esp. 153-57.
55. Williams, "Divine Presence and Divine Action," cited in note 46 above (no page numbers — subsequent quotations will be referred to by paragraph [¶] number).

the ego and how they are to be fully activated, it carries some difficulties.[56]

The crucial problem is that all too easily an independent, self-directing
ego stands at the center of the story, needing to be taught to search for
truth. In turn this suggests a passive deity: "the hiddenness of God becomes a sort of accident which could be prevented or surmounted if better conditions prevailed."[57]

Williams insists that "divine presence . . . does not stand still to be
'discovered.'" Divine presence is the redemptive God at work: it is "the
action that constitutes the human self as a responding self, as already
'implicated.'"[58] This action is irreducibly threefold, shaped as it is by
God's own triunity. Williams outlines a subtle account of this momentum: apprehending God's presence involves being caught up in the eternal responsiveness within God, through the Spirit, sharing in the Son's
self-giving response to the Father's self-bestowal.[59] This brings with it
disruption, a disturbance of the self.

> Divine presence . . . is . . . the recognition of a prior [divine] related-
> ness, a relatedness that has already established the very conditions
> for awareness and is acknowledged only in being appropriated in
> some way, *through the disorientation or displacement of the individual
> ego.*[60]

Williams is perhaps at his most Reformed when he comments on
the intellectual transformation this entails; there is a danger, he says, of

56. Williams, "Divine Presence and Divine Action," ¶2.
57. Williams, "Divine Presence and Divine Action," ¶2.
58. Williams, "Divine Presence and Divine Action," ¶3.
59. "The Christian narrative and grammar of God is of an inseparably continuous
agency, 'bestowing' itself in such a way that it makes itself other to itself; that otherness
in turn answers the act of bestowal by returning itself wholly to its source, holding on
to nothing but making its identity a gift; and in this reciprocal flow of life, a third level
of agency is generated as the act performed by the first two together, not identical with
either, nor with the bare fact of their juxtaposition. . . . The central moment, if we can so
speak of it, is one in which the unconditioned response to the movement of life into the
other becomes generative of a further difference — in which, to use at last the familiar
dramatic idioms of doctrine, the Son's self-giving to the will of the Father releases the
gift of the Spirit." Williams, "Divine Presence and Divine Action," ¶4.
60. Williams, "Divine Presence and Divine Action," ¶7. My italics.

not thinking through "what it means to believe — as classical Christian theology has maintained — not only that God is by definition active in every imaginable circumstance but also that God is more particularly active in the life of the mind."[61]

None of this discounts claims to discern divine presence in the world at large. But, Williams cautions:

> Where we recognize — as we undoubtedly have to — certain human experiences as moments of openness to the sacred or the holy, to a dimension in reality that is not exhausted by even the fullest accounts of working and function, we have to be wary of turning this into an encounter with something that is essentially just there to be looked at. . . . The holy is what we, knowingly or not, *inhabit:* more exactly, it is what actively inhabits us as a form or shape of life, the unceasing exchange of life from self to other and back again.[62]

61. Williams, "Divine Presence and Divine Action," ¶3.

62. Williams, "Divine Presence and Divine Action," ¶9. Italics original. Williams concludes that "The role of the Church, then, is neither to go in eager search of experiences of the divine, hoping to produce some kind of evidence for its convictions about God, nor to deny any true awareness of God outside its own practice and discipline. It is to try and keep alive the connection between the disorienting moment of perceiving the holy and the comprehensive narrative and (we may as well use the word) metaphysic of trinitarian activity." Williams, "Divine Presence and Divine Action," ¶10.

One way of interpreting Williams here is to see him as wanting to distinguish between two types of *contemplation* — one that presumes a posture of intellectual distance between self and other such that the self's mind remains sovereign and firmly in control (even if the language of "disinterestedness" is employed liberally); and another that presumes a radically dispossessive attitude on the part of the knower, resulting in a relation sustained not by the self but by what is known, an affective relation entailing ongoing transformation. Williams is deeply sympathetic to and supportive of the latter (as he has shown in many writings) but eschews the former. In this respect he parallels those who have questioned the assumption of a certain kind of "disinterested" contemplation as the *sine qua non* of a proper posture toward art (e.g., Wolterstorff, *Art in Action,* part 2).

William Dyrness has recently argued (and with good reason) that the Protestant Reformed tradition has been severely marred by *over*-reacting to the notion of contemplation. Dyrness, *Poetic Theology,* ch. 7. I am not convinced, however, that a contemporary recovery of affective pre-Reformation contemplative practices of the sort that Dyrness urges (healthy and culture-sensitive as this might be) can be sustained without being intertwined much more closely with the kind of Christological and trinitarian perspectives that he so keenly endorses earlier in the book, and that Williams is recommending (see Dyrness, *Poetic Theology,* pp. 146-52).

A second comment on art and sacrament: much of the relevant writing is marked by a heavy *reliance on certain binaries*, especially that of visible and invisible (or material and immaterial, real and ideal, finite and infinite) in ways that frame the supposed pathology of the human condition and our conception of created reality as a whole. (This is especially noticeable, for example, in the Philip Blond essay mentioned above.) Sometimes the dichotomy is located within the creaturely realm, sometimes between creature and Creator (and the two senses are often confused). To be oriented more scripturally, however, and more resolutely toward the Christological and covenantal means that the critical ontological distinction is seen to be that between Creator and creation, God and all that is not God, a distinction that is logically prior to any fall or corruption. Concomitantly, the pivotal crisis is not about visibility, materiality, reality vs. ideality, or even finitude, but the moral rupture of God and creature, to which the arts are prone as much as any other human endeavor. The climax of the divine response is not merely an epiphany of perceptible (though veiled) divine presence but a materialized drama of reconciliation: the Son assumes human flesh, identifying with us in the depths of our calamity, journeying through crucifixion to resurrection on the third day. In *this* way the breach is healed and the covenant renewed. A little while ago, Reformed philosopher Adrienne Chaplin offered a pointed critique of Radical Orthodoxy along these lines, centering on the arts. It repays careful reading.[63]

From this perspective, a multitude of possibilities open up for the arts. To cite just one example, we will be far better equipped to address the positive potential of the arts in contexts of injustice — less inclined

---

63. Adrienne D. Chaplin, "The Invisible and the Sublime: From Participation to Reconciliation," in *Radical Orthodoxy and the Reformed Tradition: Creation, Covenant and Participation*, ed. James K. A. Smith and James H. Olthuis (Grand Rapids: Baker, 2005), pp. 89-106. I have made similar comments about Siedell's *God in the Gallery* in relation to Nicene theology in Begbie, "On the Strange Place of Contemporary Art." Hans Boersma observes that many evangelicals wish to construe the God-world relation as having "covenantal shape," but his caricature of this view as "an agreed-on (covenantal) relationship between two completely separate beings" is unfortunate, to put it mildly. Boersma, *Heavenly Participation*, p. 24. Boersma appears to be confusing covenant and contract, as well as supposing that advocates of a covenant ontology are (generally?) guilty of some sort of deism and of assuming a univocity of being with regard to Creator and creature. Construing the God-world relation in terms of covenant need not in any way weaken a robust vision of creation as being upheld, suffused with, and charged with God's active presence.

to seek divine presence in and of itself, and more likely to be open to the irruptive, novel, and transformative possibilities of divine agency, as explored, for example, by Reformed South African John de Gruchy.[64]

My third comment: if we do wish to employ the conceptuality that surrounds "sacramentality" as a way of speaking of the potential theological efficacy of the arts, we could do a lot worse than turn to *Calvin's eucharistic theology* for assistance.[65] It may have its limitations, but Calvin does at least have the considerable advantage of refusing to presume that the critical theological axis of the Lord's Supper is about the mediation of the invisible in the visible (though of course this is included), or the inherent capacity of material things to convey divine presence, still less the addition of causal powers to material elements. Rather, it turns on the ascended and human Christ's transformative action among us, by way of and through our actions with material things.[66] In this account, the Holy Spirit plays a leading role, so that the entire eucharistic action becomes a means through which the church encounters and shares in the ascended reality of Jesus Christ, as a foretaste of the fullness of eschatological life to come. This is not a denigration of materiality — of the elements or of our bodies — but it does open up a way of setting this materiality within the context of an essentially dynamic, Christological, and Spirit-driven frame of reference.[67]

---

64. John W. de Gruchy, *Christianity, Art, and Transformation: Theological Aesthetics in the Struggle for Justice* (Cambridge: Cambridge University Press, 2001).

65. For sensitive treatments, see Julie Canlis, *Calvin's Ladder: A Spiritual Theology of Ascent and Ascension* (Grand Rapids: Eerdmans, 2010), ch. 4; B. A. Gerrish, *Grace and Gratitude: The Eucharistic Theology of John Calvin* (Minneapolis: Fortress, 1993); George Hunsinger, *The Eucharist and Ecumenism: Let Us Keep the Feast* (Cambridge: Cambridge University Press, 2008), pp. 34-39; Thomas J. Davis, *This Is My Body: The Presence of Christ in Reformation Thought* (Grand Rapids: Baker Academic, 2008), esp. chs. 3-8. Laura Smit has written a fascinating essay on Calvin's eucharistic theology, arguing that, along with "[his] understanding of God's overflowing goodness," it can provide "the ground for a Neoplatonic metaphysic and aesthetic that is similar to, but also importantly different from, Radical Orthodoxy's conclusions." Laura Smit, " 'The Depth Behind Things': Towards a Calvinist Sacramental Theology," in Smith and Olthuis, eds., *Radical Orthodoxy and the Reformed Tradition*, pp. 205-27, at 206. While sympathetic to an application of Calvin's insights on the Eucharist to other fields, I am not convinced that it can lend support to the distinctive theology of creation that Smit is keen to approve.

66. See Nicholas Wolterstorff, "Afterword," in Begbie, ed., *Sounding the Depths*, pp. 221-32, at 231.

67. In this context, the notion of agency will require careful handling. I have found

Pausing for a moment to look back over our discussion of beauty and sacrament, it is notable that issues revolving around the doctrine of creation appear more than any others. It is here, I believe, that the Reformed tradition can make probably its most telling contributions to the theology and arts conversation today. Needless to say, there is diversity within the tradition here; I am obviously being selective.[68] The key matter, I suggest, is the extent to which we are prepared to pursue a Christological and pneumatological reading of the created world at large. The Reformed tradition has been zealous in upholding and guarding the Creator-creature differentiation, the absolute ontological distinction between Creator and created. When sensitively articulated, this has nothing to do with imagining a gulf between the two, even less with a diminution of the creature. Nor does it entail denying the possibility of communion between the creature and Creator: paradoxically, it is only by upholding the distinction that true fellowship is possible.

The Christological orientation of the New Testament should be our guide here: God's covenant purposes for creation have been instantiated in this person, in a historically achieved hypostatic union of Creator and creature, empowered and enabled by the Spirit. God's act in Jesus Christ

---

that many discussions of art as sacramental center around the question: "can music, painting (or whatever) mediate divine presence?" This too easily shifts the focus of attention away from personal agency, divine and human, to the inherent causal powers of a physical object, which comes to be thought of as a quasi-agent. With regard to sacramental theology, Wolterstorff helpfully distinguishes "sign-agent" conceptuality in which new and fresh causal powers are thought to be imparted to the material sign, and "God-agency" conceptuality in which God is the agent of change — in the case of the Eucharist, sealing or assuring us of his promises. Nicholas Wolterstorff, "Sacrament as Action, Not Presence," in *Christ: The Sacramental Word*, ed. David Brown and Ann Loades (London: SPCK, 1995), pp. 103-22. The latter need not render the causal powers of the material object irrelevant or "empty," but it does shift the center of agency to God and God's transformative purposes.

68. In my own view, the most fruitful and compelling vision for the doctrine of creation for late modernity along Reformed lines was offered by the late Colin Gunton in various writings. See, e.g., Colin E. Gunton, *Christ and Creation* (Exeter: Paternoster, 1993); Colin E. Gunton, ed., *The Doctrine of Creation: Essays in Dogmatics, History and Philosophy* (Edinburgh: T&T Clark, 1997); Gunton, *The Triune Creator*. Gunton has been criticized on many counts, probably most of all for his highly negative reading of Augustine. But whatever his weaknesses, he had an uncanny and unerring eye for the theological issues at stake in any field, and never more so, in my own view, than with regard to the doctrine of creation. His work in this area has yet to receive the attention it deserves.

is the outworking of God's eternal "decision" to reconcile humanity to himself, and as such is the ground of God's act of creation. Creation out of nothing is therefore not a neutral "let there be" but the outworking of love, rooted in the eternal commitment of the Father to the Son and of the Son to the Father in the Spirit. Divine transcendence is accordingly to be conceived in gracious and positive terms; God's free otherness makes his covenant dedication to the world *as other* possible. Insofar as God is free *from* the world, God is free *for* it. Likewise, God's engagement with creation is for the sake of the flourishing of the creature as created and finite, not its debasement, still less its absorption into divinity. And from this perspective, the world's tragedy is shown to be at root a moral dislocation that requires a restoration of fellowship or communion.[69] I am suggesting that it is within a theological environment of this sort that the notions of beauty and sacrament are most fruitfully set, and especially if we want to relate them effectively to the arts.

It needs to be conceded that the history of Reformed theology shows it is by no means uniformly strong on these matters. Karl Barth's determination stands out above all, whatever questions may be asked of him. Keith Johnson's acute summary of a key difference between Balthasar (writing in 1951)[70] and Barth is telling:

> Von Balthasar failed to see the full implication of what Eberhard Jüngel calls Barth's "decisive innovation" in his doctrine of creation: Barth's decision to make the human Jesus of Nazareth the condition for the possibility of knowledge of human being as such. What von

---

69. There may well be appropriate ways of speaking of "participation" of humans in God, through Christ in the Spirit, and perhaps in a strongly qualified sense of creation as a whole "participating" through the Mediator in the life of God. Radical Orthodoxy is committed to the notion of participation as applying not only to a saving participation of the believer in Christ but also to a general metaphysics. It is not clear to me, however, that Radical Orthodoxy's notion of the "suspension" of the material in the divine can do justice to a biblical, dynamic ontology of grace that upholds the irreducible Creator-creature distinction, or to an appropriate distinction between creation and redemption. For discussion, see Smith, *Introducing Radical Orthodoxy*, pp. 74-77 and ch. 6; Horton, *Covenant and Salvation*, chs. 8 and 9; Vanhoozer, *Remythologizing Theology*, pp. 280-83.

70. Hans Urs von Balthasar, *Karl Barth: Darstellung und Deutung Seiner Theologie* (Köln: Verlag Jacob Hegner, 1952); translated as Hans Urs von Balthasar, *The Theology of Karl Barth: Exposition and Interpretation*, trans. Edward T. Oakes (San Francisco: Communio, Ignatius, 1992).

Balthasar failed to realize is that this innovation enables Barth to posit that God's eternal decision to reconcile humanity in the person of Jesus Christ is the presupposition *of creation*. . . . For von Balthasar, the relationship between humanity and God is an intrinsic feature of humanity as such by virtue of God's act of creation viewed in distinction from God's act in Jesus Christ. . . . Although Barth also believes that creation signifies that the human exists in relationship with God, it does so solely because creation as such cannot be defined in distinction from the covenant of grace.

And for Barth, Johnson continues, "the covenant is not a programme but a *person*: Jesus Christ."[71]

The Infirmities of Language

"Where words fail, music speaks."[72] The aphorism attributed to Hans Christian Andersen gives voice to a recurring sentiment in modern and late modern culture, that the non-verbal arts blossom where words fall short — or, in its stronger forms, that these arts afford access to a realm that lies beyond the reach of any verbal claims to truth or falsity, a realm language may gesture toward but can never directly mediate. For some this

71. Keith L. Johnson, *Karl Barth and the Analogia Entis* (London: T&T Clark, 2010), pp. 202, 205, 206. Italics original. After I delivered the lecture from which this essay emerged, sensing in me a certain sympathy with Karl Barth, a member of the audience asked: "Do you believe Barth would be the man to give a novice Christian artist the theology he or she needs?" I didn't answer well at the time. Now I think I would reply as follows. No one theologian can give any artist the theology he or she requires, and many questions can and should be asked of Barth's (limited) account of the arts. Barth's inestimable contribution comes not principally from the specifics of what he says about any particular facet of culture, but from the way he repeatedly orients his readers to the energizing center of the Christian gospel, namely Jesus the Messiah as attested in Scripture, and the way he repeatedly makes us sense the wonder and limitless ramifications of all that has been opened up in Christ. No theologian of the last hundred years has done this more consistently, resolutely, and joyfully. Insofar as every artist requires this constant life-giving orientation (and it is hardly an option), it is difficult to think of a modern theologian who would prove a more inspiring and fruitful companion.

72. The original wording, "Where words fail, sounds can often speak" (popularly abridged to "Where words fail, music speaks") is from "What the Moon Saw," in Hans C. Andersen, *What the Moon Saw: And Other Tales*, trans. H. W. Dulcken (London, 1866), p. 38.

opens up a distinctly theological role for the arts. They are richly meaning-ful yet stubbornly resist being reduced to language: this surely suggests a prime place for them among those who sense both the reality of God and God's sheer inexpressibility. Where words fail God, the arts speak.

Undoubtedly, very often the backdrop to this intuition is an aware-ness of modernity's inflated confidence in the powers of language, in our capacity to seize and order the world through speech and writing. In theology this has all too regularly led to what Nicholas Lash calls a "cataphatic cockiness,"[73] a breezy assurance that our speech and writ-ing can name and grasp the things of God with relative ease. Religious fundamentalisms typically expand their control base through imply-ing that God is in some manner linguistically seizable. "Thus says the Lord. . . ." The tendency is symbolized by the hyper-Protestant pastor, ensconced in his book-lined office, crafting glittering orations for the pulpit, deeply grateful that most of his congregation have not reached his level of linguistic competence; or by the theologian, graced with the dazzling verbal dexterity to ensure a senior appointment but whom even her colleagues struggle to understand. The Reformed Churches are hardly innocent here, as Edwin Muir reminds us:

> The word made flesh here is made word again
> A word made word in flourish and arrogant crook.
> See there King Calvin with his iron pen,
> And God three angry letters in a book,
> And there the logical hook
> On which the Mystery is impaled and bent
> Into an ideological instrument.[74]

Straining against this hubristic attempt at control-through-words lies another current moving in the opposite direction, acutely sensitive to the limits of language, not least when it comes to the "Mystery" of Muir's lament. Words are marred not only by finitude but also by cor-ruption — "bent," as Muir puts it. All God-talk, it is said, is a kind of forced entry, a desecration of transcendence, a raid on sacred infinity,

73. Nicholas Lash, *The Beginning and the End of "Religion"* (Cambridge: Cambridge University Press, 1996), p. 170.

74. "The Incarnate One," in Edwin Muir, *One Foot in Eden* (London: Faber & Faber, 1956), p. 47. Reprinted by permission of Faber & Faber Ltd.

and to that extent will almost inevitably lead to some kind of violation of others in the name of the "God" we have supposedly attained and in whose name we too effortlessly utter. The widespread appeal today of various brands of "negative theology" is perhaps hardly surprising.

It is just here that some call in the arts to assuage the anxiety. I have lost count of the number of times I have been told at conferences that the church has been hidebound for too long by its fixation with language and conceptual abstractions, entwined with corrupting power ploys; that it is time to renounce the iconoclastic drive of (Reformed) Protestantism and recover a sense of the infinitely "unsayable" through a rehabilitation of the (non-verbal) arts. Although the visual arts are often appealed to here, the art that is probably favored most in modernity in the face of a widely felt embarrassment with language is music. This appeal finds its most sophisticated and potent expression in the early German Romantics of the late eighteenth and early nineteenth centuries. Wordless music, long regarded by their forebears as inferior to music set to texts (because of language's capacity for representative precision), now becomes exalted not just as the highest form of music but as the highest form of art. J. N. Forkel claimed in 1778 that music "begins . . . where other languages can no longer reach,"[75] and Willhelm Heinse declared, "Instrumental music . . . expresses such a particular spiritual life in man that it is untranslatable for every other language."[76] Music grants immediate access to that dimension of being-in-the-world that underlies and makes possible all linguistic, conceptual, cognitive, and representational activity; indeed, music can mediate the infinite, surging, sacred spirit that courses through all things. The quasi-divine power of music is famously celebrated in a review of Beethoven's Fifth Symphony by E. T. A. Hoffmann in 1810, probably the most influential piece of music criticism ever written:

> Music discloses to man an unknown realm, a world that has nothing in common with the external sensual world that surrounds him, a world in which he leaves behind him all *definite* feelings to surrender himself to an inexpressible longing [*unaussprechlichen Sehnsucht*].[77]

75. As quoted in Andrew Bowie, *Music, Philosophy, and Modernity* (Cambridge: Cambridge University Press, 2007), p. 54.

76. As quoted in Bowie, *Music, Philosophy, and Modernity*, p. 54.

77. As translated in W. Oliver Strunk, *Source Readings in Music History: The Romantic Era*, 5 vols., vol. 5 (London: Faber & Faber, 1981), pp. 35-36. My italics. Andrew Bowie

In these circles, typically the ineffable spirit of the "unknown realm" is seen as coming to its most concentrated expression in the inner struggles and strivings of the heart, supremely the heart of the composer, a sanctuary we are honored to enter through his music. Carl Friedrich Zelter wrote to the composer Joseph Haydn in 1804: "Your spirit has penetrated into the sanctity of divine wisdom; you have brought fire from heaven, and with it you warm and illuminate mortal hearts and lead them to the infinite."[78]

We might be tempted to dismiss all this as the quirky hyperbole of a historically remote corner of European modernity struggling with the challenges of disenchantment. But these ideas were to have massive influence in the nineteenth century, and it is not hard to find them today — not least in the church. There are, for example, "contemporary worship" streams I have worked with that show an extraordinary confidence in music's power to mediate God's saving power directly, without words, and where the singer/song-writer/worship leader is revered in ways that bear more than a passing resemblance to Romantic depictions of the priest-like artist — photographed on CD covers against the background of some vast sublimity of the natural world, or else lost in the silent contemplation of the heart (the haven to which we are invited to travel). As Roger Lundin has often pointed out (though with relatively little recognition), many evangelicals amid the arts seem deeply attracted to sentiments that owe rather more to Romanticism than to the New Testament.[79]

A full response to these currents is impossible here, and I certainly have no wish to decry them wholesale. Again I offer only some brief comments. The first reiterates a commonplace of classical Christianity, namely, that *human language has been incorporated directly into the momentum of God's self-communication* in such a way that it is irreplaceably *intrinsic to* that momentum. This finds its climactic focus in the incarnation — the Word becomes flesh, and our fallen language is in-

---

paraphrases Hoffmann thus: "What music expresses is the essence of Romanticism . . . precisely *because* it cannot be said in words." Andrew Bowie, "Romanticism and Music," in *The Cambridge Companion to German Romanticism*, ed. Nicholas Saul (Cambridge: Cambridge University Press, 2006), pp. 243-55, at 245. My italics.

78. As quoted in Mark Evan Bonds, *Music as Thought: Listening to the Symphony in the Age of Beethoven* (Princeton, NJ: Princeton University Press, 2006), p. 16.

79. See, e.g., Lundin, *Believing Again*, pp. 24-39.

tegral to that flesh so assumed.[80] Our speech — no less than any other dimension of our humanity — has, in this speaking person, the Word-made-Word-user, been purged and renewed, re-forged and re-shaped. As a result, through the Spirit, a fresh form of communally embedded speech has been generated and, in due course, inscribed as authoritative text. Christians are those baptized into a new community of speaking, a speaking that, through the Holy Spirit, shares by grace in the language-renewing event of Jesus Christ.

Obviously, all this would take far more space than I have to develop and defend adequately. But in a sense I do not need to, for a steady stream of highly sophisticated Reformed writing along these lines has appeared in recent decades: for example, from T. F. Torrance,[81] Alan Torrance,[82] James Smith,[83] Nicholas Wolterstorff,[84] and Kevin Vanhoozer.[85] There are important differences between these writers, but their common commitment to the "intrinsicity" of human language to God's redemptive ways with the world is never in doubt, nor is their acute awareness of the baleful effects of modernity's overconfidence

80. It is telling that those at work at the theology-arts interface who advocate a recovery of "the sacramental" seem reluctant to talk about the sacramental role of Christian proclamation. Commenting on David Jones, Wolterstorff remarks: "It is characteristic of someone working within the medieval concept [of sacrament], as Jones does, to ignore the sacramental quality of proclamation entirely." Wolterstorff, "Evangelicalism and the Arts," p. 460. Or again, it is significant that those who speak most fervently about recovering a eucharistic sensibility rarely acknowledge that among the Eucharist's physical elements and actions are words. "*Contra* Marion . . . the 'real presence' of the Eucharist depends not only on iconic items and gestures but also on the words of institution ('This is my body. Do this in remembrance of me.') . . . The personalizing of the divine self-giving does not mean its de-verbalizing." Vanhoozer, *Remythologizing Theology*, p. 103.

81. Thomas F. Torrance, *Theological Science* (Oxford: Oxford University Press, 1969); *The Ground and Grammar of Theology* (Charlottesville: University Press of Virginia, 1980); *Transformation and Convergence in the Frame of Knowledge: Explorations in the Interrelations of Scientific and Theological Enterprise* (Belfast: Christian Journals, 1984).

82. Alan J. Torrance, "*Auditus Fidei*: Where and How Does God Speak? Faith, Reason, and the Question of Criteria," in *Reason and the Reasons of Faith*, ed. Paul J. Griffiths and Reinhard Hütter (London: T&T Clark, 2005), pp. 27-52; *Persons in Communion: An Essay on Trinitarian Description and Human Participation* (Edinburgh: T&T Clark, 1996).

83. James K. A. Smith, *Speech and Theology: Language and the Logic of Incarnation* (London: Routledge, 2002).

84. Nicholas Wolterstorff, *Divine Discourse: Philosophical Reflections on the Claim That God Speaks* (Cambridge: Cambridge University Press, 1995).

85. Vanhoozer, *Remythologizing Theology*.

in humankind's linguistic powers. What is disappointing is that none of this material seems to have found its way into the Christianity and arts discussions. There, all too often, theological language is treated as if it could be entirely abstracted from, and was only *extrinsically* related to, God's reconciling engagement with humanity in Jesus Christ (as if it were merely a humanly originated commentary on or witness to this engagement), whereupon the (non-verbal) arts are appealed to as alternative communicative media — perhaps even superior media, with the power to generate fresh norms of theological truth.

A second comment: just *because* language has been assumed into the reconciling purposes of *this* God, *it can never be thought capable of encompassing, circumscribing, or in any manner controlling God*. A concern for divine freedom vis-à-vis language is, I think, a large part of what drives the suspicion or even fear of language among many Christians at work in the arts, perhaps most of all among evangelicals (and "post-evangelicals"), some of whom have been reared on what is undoubtedly a highly constrictive view of theological language, in which a certain kind of declarative proposition and a certain kind of representative view of language is assumed to be definitive of "meaningfulness." In the midst of what feels like an over-secure, over-systematized, word-imprisoned Protestantism, it is not surprising that many will run to the arts for refuge, for they appear to promise a much-needed semantic freedom, an allusiveness and openness that the discourses of doctrinal orthodoxy seem to disallow.

Part of the response to this will be along the lines of the comment I have just made, about language being intrinsic to the momentum of divine grace. But that left on its own will likely land in the place so many want to escape. We also need a recognition that the God who appropriates human language directly into his purposes is the God of gracious freedom, who exceeds anything that can be spoken or thought, all that can be said or conceived. Today, a stress on the linguistic "uncontainability" of God is usually associated with the post-structuralists and the pre-modern theological traditions on which they regularly draw. But that the finite cannot contain the infinite has always been near to or at the heart of the Reformed tradition. It is especially distinctive of its Christology (enshrined in the so-called *extra Calvinisticum* — the Son of God becomes human without abandoning heaven),[86] and to a signifi-

---

86. See Myk Habets, "Putting the 'Extra' Back into Calvinism," *Scottish Journal of Theology* 62, no. 4 (November 2009): 441-56.

cant extent drives its suspicion of constructing visual images of God.[87] Divine self-*dis*closure prohibits divine self-*en*closure. And this applies to any language appropriated in the process. To be sure, Reformed theology has not always articulated divine freedom in ways that head off the danger of reducing God to an arbitrary will, a deity of abstract, absolute power *(potentia absoluta)*. At its strongest, however, the tradition, in taking its bearing from God's positive engagement *with* language, can celebrate God's uncontainability *in* language, which is to say, the free, uncontainability of God's covenant commitment.[88]

Third, it is a commonplace of language theory that by its very nature language is embedded in and relies upon a host of non-verbal means of interaction with the world (bodily movement and gestures, symbol-making, and so forth), and that these things cannot be dismissed as meaningless simply because they are not reducible to verbal articulation. It is in this context that the non-verbal arts' relation to language, and theological language in particular, needs to be set. The struggle is to hold at one and the same time that the church is called to a faithfulness to the discourse God has graciously appropriated *and* that *other communicative media such as the non-verbal arts will possess their own distinctive capacities to mediate dimensions of the very realities of which this discourse speaks and in which this discourse is caught up.* The arts are able to do their own kind of work in their own kind of way, articulating depths of the Word of the gospel and our experience of it that are otherwise unheard or unfelt, while nonetheless being responsible and faithful to the normative texts of the faith. (This, we might interject, is what Calvin came to believe with regard to music in worship.)[89] A major research agen-

---

87. See VanDrunen, "Iconoclasm, Incarnation and Eschatology," p. 133, and n. 10.

88. From a very different (Roman Catholic) perspective, Nicholas Lash deftly writes: "Why is it so difficult to speak sensibly of God? From the deist standpoint that defines and dominates the modern imagination, it seems obvious that the reason is that God is *so far away* from us. . . . But suppose we come at it from a different angle, from a Christian angle; from, that is to say, a standpoint shaped by recognition of God's uttered Word and outpoured Spirit. When some Romeo starts stammering, unable to find words that will do justice to his love, it is not because the beloved is *unknown* to him . . . it is because she has become too *well* known for glib description to be possible. . . . God is not far from us. God's self-giving constitutes our very being, intimates each element and movement of our heart. *It is not those who know not God who find God difficult to talk about, but those who know God well.*" Lash, *The Beginning and the End of "Religion,"* pp. 170-71. The italics of the last sentence are mine.

89. See Jeremy S. Begbie, "Music, Word and Theology Today: Learning from

da opens up here, as well as a major practical challenge to all who care about the arts in the church. The New Testament scholar N. T. Wright has written: "If all theology, all sermons, had to be set to music, our teaching and preaching would not only be more mellifluous; it might also approximate more closely to God's truth, the truth revealed in and as the Word made flesh, crucified and risen."[90]

In my teaching in the United States and the United Kingdom over many years, I have often met students who long to find the one theologian who will provide all the answers to their struggles and quandaries, or the one tradition into which they can sink and be released from the frantic but paralyzing sense that they need to read everything. It would be foolish in the extreme to claim this of the Reformed tradition or of any Reformed theologian, as of course it would be of any movement or figure in theology. My claim in this essay is more modest, namely, that as the theology and arts conversation continues to unfold apace, resources from the Reformed world — so often buried beneath an understandable but exaggerated shame — have considerably more to offer than is often supposed, especially if we are seeking to delve more deeply into the plotlines and harmonies of a scripturally rooted and vibrant trinitarian faith.

John Calvin," in *Theology in Dialogue: The Impact of the Arts, Humanities and Science on Contemporary Religious Thought,* ed. Lyn Holness and Ralf Wüstenberg (Grand Rapids: Eerdmans, 2002), pp. 3-27.

90. N. T. Wright, "Resurrection: From Theology to Music and Back Again," in Begbie, ed., *Sounding the Depths,* pp. 193-212, at 210-11.

CHAPTER 8

Emerging Conversations:
Race and Redemption in the Age of Obama

KATHERINE CLAY BASSARD

If the title of my essay looks familiar, it is because it is a not-so-subtle revision of the title of Roger Lundin's important book, *Invisible Conversations: Religion in the Literature of America*.[1] The shift from "invisible" to "emerging" redirects the image from a conversation that is heard but not seen to the possibility of a conversation that is emerging from the shadows. I was privileged to be a part of Lundin's "American Literature and Religion" group that met periodically to discuss the intersection of religion, literature, and academic discourse. Indeed, it is the work of Christian scholars that has moved the conversation of religion and literature from being voiced but not heard, to being heard and somewhat visible.

What I want to do here is to map the progress of this emerging discourse about faith in the academy and public square onto the rapidly changing (we might borrow the term "emerging" here as well) discourse about race. That the conversation about race has changed significantly is nowhere more evident than in the candidacy, election, and presidency of Barack Obama, himself a figure at the crossroads of racial, ethnic, and religious identities. What I have to say here is not about politics but about language. In other words, I am not so much interested in Obama as a political figure or policy maker, but as a symbolic representation of the hopes and fears in America around the nexus of race and religion, a collective anxiety formed in the history of American chattel

---

1. Roger Lundin, ed., *Invisible Conversations: Religion in the Literature of America* (Waco, TX: Baylor University Press, 2009).

slavery. In thinking about what types of discourse are emerging at this complicated time through this complicated history, I will point to three African American novels that are situated at this intersection of shifting languages: Edward P. Jones's *The Known World* (2003); James McBride's *Song Yet Sung* (2008); and Toni Morrison's latest novel, *A Mercy* (2008).

First, a story.

Teachable Moments

In the fall of 2009, my husband and I took our children on a bus trip to Washington, D.C., with Virginia Commonwealth University's Office of Multicultural Affairs to attend the National Museum of American History's exhibit for Hispanic Heritage month. What we did not know is that the Tea Party Express, at that time just beginning to form and forge its identity in American cultural politics, had planned a demonstration on the Washington Mall that same day. They had occupied the end of the Mall toward the Capitol, not a large crowd by any means; they were, in many ways, a stark contrast to the images of the Washington Mall seared into my mind — and the nation's cultural unconscious — of the sea of humanity that had filled every nook and cranny of the space and overflowed into the streets of D.C. at Barack Obama's historic inauguration.

On that same day, along with the Hispanic Heritage exhibit that was our original destination, a large gathering of African Americans was attending the annual Black Family Reunion at the other end of the Mall near the Washington Monument. This event was sponsored by the National Council of Negro Women and celebrates the strength and values of African American families. The festival was arrayed in a series of tents that included free concerts, arts and crafts, an international marketplace, health screenings, food, and activities for kids. In the years since, I have often returned to that odd convergence of gatherings in the nation's capitol as I have thought about the clash of discourses of race and religion in academia and in the public square.

What I took away, initially, was the tremendous multicultural and international presence in Washington as tourists from every corner of the globe filed into and out of museums and monuments. At the Museum of Natural History, for example, just in walking the halls I heard every imaginable language, saw every imaginable ethnic group. Seeing tourists from Japan, India, France, and dozens of other places that I lacked the discernment to name globalized the visit for me. As we sat for a break (visiting the museums in D.C. is exhausting!) I was approached by a young man with a thick French accent who asked me what the protests were about (indicating the disturbance toward the Capitol). I told him I didn't know exactly but that I guessed some people were protesting the President's economic policies.

In contrast to this multicultural, global context, the Tea Party was starkly homogenous. Responding to my fourteen-year-old daughter's anger at the protests and my nine-year-old son's bewilderment, I said that President Obama was elected and is hard at work protecting the protestors' rights to demonstrate.

WE SPENT MOST of our time at the Black Family Reunion. The groups mingled during lunch as the Tea Partiers drifted toward the tents that were offering scrumptious ethnic cuisine. I noticed that there were no incidents of violence, anger, argument, not even political banter as people interacted. Tea Party protestors, laying their signs aside momentarily to eat, were graciously welcomed by a community that, I think, was beginning to grasp a symbolic moment.

At the National Archives, we stood in the long line that leads to the hushed, vaulted hall that houses the founding documents of the nation: the Constitution and the Declaration of Independence. As viewers filed past, solemnly, there was no chatter, no glib remarks. The heavily guarded documents were treated with reverence.

In another hall in the Archives, I lost time as I stood and gazed at the original copy of the Emancipation Proclamation, a text that forever changed the fate of my people. With one stroke of a pen, one was changed from slave to free, from subhuman to human. A verse of Scripture floated up to my consciousness in the rarified hall: "He canceled the record of the charges against us and took it away by nailing it to the cross" (Col. 2:14, New Living Translation).

I marveled at the power of texts, words, and language to shape, bend, and construct our worlds and our selves. I thought about why what I do as a literary scholar, a Christian, an African American is so important.

WE FOUND OURSELVES among Tea Party–goers at the end of the trip as we waited for our respective buses outside the Air and Space Museum.

My daughter's anger was at low ember but still smoldering. "Why do they have to drag Jesus into this?" she said, indicating a sign that had some religious reference on it. I pulled her aside gently and asked, "How should we react when we have disagreements with others? How would Jesus want us to act?" So we chose to smile and greet people.

How are you?

Have a nice day.

God bless you.

One man who looked tired and weary had laid down his huge sign and sat on the steps. After learning that this was his first trip to the nation's capital, I asked how he had enjoyed Washington, D.C. He answered, missing the irony, "I haven't really seen much of it."

When we got home, cable news had all cameras on the most inflamed elements of the protest, including angry faces, angry slogans, signs with Obama in Joker-face and witch doctor garb. No mention of the Black Family Reunion. No mention of Hispanic Heritage Month. My daughter asked, "Were they in the same place we were?" I answered, "Apparently not."

I have taken the time to tell this story because it offers a glimpse into the difficulty we face when we broach topics of race and religion, a discussion that is becoming increasingly frustrating to those of us who have dedicated our professional lives to studying literatures of oppressed minorities. I have noticed a shift in the classroom. At the beginning of my African American literature class, I fill the board with names that have historically been used to describe African Americans — black, negro, colored (with and without a u), Afro-American, African American (with and without a hyphen) — and we discuss the positives and negatives of each term. What in years past generated a largely historical discussion followed by a general consensus of the superiority of the politically correct terms (African American, without the hyphen) has more recently ended with students expressing a dislike for *all* of the terms, regardless of historical context. When I ask what words they would like to use to replace the current terms, no one has an alternative, though someone usually speaks up for Black (with a capital B à la the Black Arts movement of the 1960s), and someone invariably says, "Why can't we just use American?" To my suggestion, Americans of African descent, a few raised brows and wrinkled noses are the nonverbal replies. This is anecdotal, but it is obvious to me that something has shifted dramatically in the way we discuss race, although what will emerge as the "correct" language is yet to be determined. How can we, as Christian scholars, position ourselves at the forefront of these emerging conversations? How can we do our part to restore balance, civility, even sanity to national discourse? I believe that as Christian scholars we should, indeed must, lead in developing a discourse of reconciliation and redemption. Jesus himself is our example: "For Christ himself has brought peace to us. He united Jews and Gentiles into one people when, in his own body on the cross, he broke down the wall of hostility that separated us" (Eph. 2:14, NLT).

Redeeming Race?

My subtitle is "Race and Redemption" rather than "Race and Religion" for a reason. The distinguishing feature of Christianity is the redemptive power of the Cross — the "old redemption story" and "let the redeemed of the Lord say so." The question I pose here is a complex one: Can or should race be redeemed as a category of identity or scholarly analysis?

It is obvious that past ways of discussing race are inadequate to the current moment. The Afrocentrism of the 1960s and 1970s gave way to hyphenated identities, multiculturalism, and vernacular theories of the 1980s and 1990s. Keith Byerman has noted, correctly, that late-twentieth-century American discourse vacillates between a dialectic of "race and racelessness when discussing matters of difference."[2] In an article in the *Chronicle of Higher Education*, John Hartigan Jr. notes that we have been "advancing and regressing in matters of race as a nation." He concludes:

> Conversations depend on codes of etiquette and decorum that shape our expectations of who can say what and which kinds of topics are appropriate. The conventions informing those codes are powerful and deeply naturalized. Unless we can begin to think about them consciously . . . we will make little progress in talking about race.[3]

---

2. Keith Byerman, *Remembering the Past in Contemporary African American Fiction* (Chapel Hill: University of North Carolina Press, 2005).

3. John Hartigan Jr., "What Does Race Have to Do with It? Making Sense of Our 'National Conversation,'" *The Chronicle of Higher Education*, 15 August 2010.

Hartigan suggests little in the way of a solution but does call for academics to intervene in the media's appropriation of racial discourse.

What I propose is not a solution, but I do want to offer redemption (understood as redemptive reading) as a category of analysis for Christian literary scholarship in particular. Christian scholars have long made use of biblical and theological concepts, such as incarnation and resurrection, in a variety of disciplines. A good example is Hans Frei's *sensus literalis* — founded on the narrative of Christ's birth, death, burial, and resurrection — as a ground of biblical interpretation.[4] While all of these terms are appropriately Christ-centered, the way believers appropriate Christ's sacrifice within our own individual lives is through the narrative of personal redemption. "Redeem" in the Old Testament is from the Hebrew *ga'al* and involves the idea of "doing something on behalf of others because they are unable to do it for themselves." Its most common use is in the reconciliation of a debt, but it is sometimes used "to refer to rescue or deliverance in general. In this vein, God is the ultimate redeemer." In the New Testament, the Greek verb is *apolutromai*, and it is most often characterized as ransom. Beyond a mere business transaction, however, "Christ redeems by his death in that he gives humanity the forgiveness that humanity could not give itself."[5]

By way of definition as a critical rubric, I want to distinguish redemption from other current vernaculars in racial discourse and in historical and literary scholarship. "Reconciliation" and "reparations" are two terms often employed in the effort to move conversations on race forward. In Richmond, Virginia, in an area known as Shockoe Bottom, which once housed the old slave markets and the notorious Lumpkin's Jail or holding pens for slaves to be sold in what was the largest internal slave-trading market in the nation before the Civil War, there stands the Richmond Slavery Reconciliation statue. Two identical statues are located in Liverpool, England, and Benin, West Africa, marking the triangular route of the transatlantic slave trade. The statue depicts two abstract but recognizably human figures in an embrace and symbolizes all three nations' apologies for participation in the slave trade. While such gestures are significant and offer hope of healing, words such as "recon-

---

4. Hans W. Frei, *The Eclipse of Biblical Narrative: A Study of Eighteenth and Nineteenth Century Hermeneutics* (New Haven: Yale University Press, 1974).

5. Bruce Manning Metzger, ed., *Oxford Companion to the Bible* (New York: Oxford University Press, 1993), p. 644.

ciliation" and the more economically based "reparations" focus on human acts. By contrast, redemption is a God act. Moreover, redemption gives us a language that allows us to view history within a field of hope and radical change.

To distinguish further, redemption is not historical revisionism that presupposes not singular "truth" but different points of view and thus revises the past according to alternative or counter narratives. Rather, redemption is a *reinvestment* of history to account for change, even radical change, in the present and future. It does not seek to rewrite the "facts" or "truth" of history but to reinvest those truths with new meanings and significance.

The biblical figure associated most with the idea of redemption is Paul, converted from Saul in Acts 9. "If anyone is in Christ," Paul writes, "there is a new creation: everything old has passed away; see, everything has become new!" (2 Cor. 5:17). A more pertinent passage, perhaps, is found in Philippians 3, where Paul outlines the "one thing I do": "forgetting what lies behind and straining forward to what lies ahead, I press on toward the goal for the prize of the heavenly call of God in Christ Jesus" (Phil. 3:13-14). Even here, however, Paul begins by reciting the very past he exhorts us to forget:

> If anyone else has reason to be confident in the flesh, I have more: circumcised on the eighth day, a member of the people of Israel, of the tribe of Benjamin, a Hebrew born of Hebrews; as to the law, a Pharisee; as to zeal, a persecutor of the church; as to righteousness under the law, blameless. (vv. 4b-6)

It is clear that Paul has not forgotten the past, but that his past has been redeemed, given new valuation. What has changed are not the facts of his personal history but his evaluation of it:

> Yet whatever gains I had, these I have come to regard as loss because of Christ. More than that, I regard everything as loss because of the surpassing value of knowing Christ Jesus my Lord. For his sake I have suffered the loss of all things, and I regard them as rubbish, in order that I may gain Christ and be found in him. (vv. 7-9a)

A redemptive view of race, for example, would not seek to erase race as a category of identity or slavery as historical fact. Instead, it would reinvest race and slavery with significance within a larger narrative of freedom and future (present) hope and possibility. It would be, in other words, both intellectually honest and ethically responsible. The "never forget" mantra of liberation and civil rights movements comes from a legitimate fear of the repeatability of structures of oppression that could result from collective amnesia. Redemption allows us to hold two narratives in view simultaneously, privileging the one (and the One) that offers us "hope and a future" (Jer. 29:11, New International Version).

Redemptive Conversations: Three African American Novels

I want now to turn to three novels — Edward P. Jones's 2003 *The Known World*, James McBride's 2008 *Song Yet Sung*, and Toni Morrison's novel of the same year, *A Mercy* — to see how these contemporary writers anticipate the complications surrounding race in the millennium and enact what I call redemptive readings. Significantly, all three are within the subgenre of what Blyden Jackson calls "neo-slave narratives" — contemporary novels that, as Asraf Rushdy puts it, "assume the form, adopt the conventions and [or] take on the first person voice of the antebellum slave narrative."[6]

Henry Louis Gates Jr. has counted over 6,000 extant slave narratives from the antebellum or pre-Emancipation period. Defined as the written or oral testimony of ex-slaves, slave narratives typically recount the slave's transition from slave to free, South to North, chattel to human. Neo-slave narratives have been described by Asraf Rushdy (in his book studying the "social logic" of this literary form) as "belated participants in an earlier cultural conversation." Neo-slave narratives perform a peculiar type of intertextuality. Rushdy places neo-slave narratives within the larger generic context of the historical novel, which he describes as "the product of several interrelated impulses: the historiography of the subject it purports to represent, the social and cultural conditions from which it emerges, the literary form it adopts and the literary 'tradition' into which it is potentially subscribed."[7]

---

6. Ashraf Rushdy, *Neo-Slave Narratives: Studies in the Social Logic of a Literary Form* (New York: Oxford University Press, 1999), p. 3.

7. Rushdy, *Neo-Slave Narratives*, p. 17.

In other words, there is an interplay between four different "narratives": the historical period of the setting (slavery/antebellum), the social and cultural makeup of the historical setting (place of race and religion within the system of American slavery), the literary form being adopted/adapted (slave narrative), and the contemporary literary form (postmodern novel). It is this complex interplay of overlapping narratives within the neo-slave narrative as historical fiction that holds the potential for redemptive reading strategies within and outside the world of the novel. My fascination with these three novels is that, at a time when slavery has all but disappeared from the public discourse, Jones, McBride, and Morrison choose to write novels set during the time of slavery. Indeed, *A Mercy* is Morrison's second novel of slavery following *Beloved* in 1987 and her Nobel Prize in 1993. Why are African American writers continuing to return to the slave past? What are they seeing in connecting past with present in these novels? What are they trying to say to us now? As Rushdy points out, neo-slave narratives are not only nostalgic about the past and revisionist in the future; they are also definitive in that the writers frame the discussion of the past in order to define future debates about race, culture, and academic politics. They are, in other words, using the past to say something about contemporary times and to impact current and future debate.

Keith Byerman notes that postmodern black writers are "the first generation to make [historical narrative] the dominant mode" in African American literature. He regards these writings primarily as "trauma stories" that tell of "tremendous loss and survival; they describe the psychological and social effects of suffering. More importantly, perhaps, they tell of the erasure of such history and, as a consequence, its continued power to shape black life." For Byerman, neo-slave narratives have "a dialectical sensibility that problematizes as it affirms historical narrative." He concludes: "The very choice of history as subject is determined by authors' experiences of the recent past and the present. But the connection is primarily indirect and metaphoric."[8] Clearly the neo-slave narrative has potential for redemptive readings even of traumatic events such as racialized slavery.

---

8. Byerman, *Remembering the Past*, pp. 1-3, 22.

Edward P. Jones, *The Known World*

In an interview with *Publisher's Weekly*, award-winning novelist Edward P. Jones stated that the idea for a novel featuring black slave owners as the protagonists came to him while reading "a small book about a Jew who had joined the Nazis during World War II." In *The Known World*, Jones tells the story of a slave named Augustus who purchases himself, his wife Mildred, and his son Henry out of slavery, only to have his son become a slaveholder himself. Henry's purchase of Moses upsets all coordinates of black/white and slave/free within the novel:

> Moses was the first slave Henry Townsend had bought: $325 and a handshake from William Robbins, a white man. It took Moses more than two weeks to come to understand that someone wasn't fiddling with him and that indeed a black man, two shades darker than himself, owned him and any shadow he made. Sleeping in a cabin beside Henry in the first weeks after the sale, Moses had thought that it was already a strange world that made him a slave to a white man, but God had indeed set it twirling and twisting every which way when he put black people to owning their own kind. Was God even up there attending to business anymore?[9]

Later in this passage, we are introduced to another of Henry's slaves, Elias:

> Elias had never believed in a sane God and so had never questioned a world where colored people could be owners of slaves, and if at that moment, in the near dark, he had sprouted wings, he would not have questioned that either. (p. 9)

Taking on the taboo subject of free black slave owners in fictional Manchester County, Virginia, Jones approaches slavery from an entirely different angle of vision, one not so easily mapped onto coordinates of black/white, slave/free, or even female/male. To this end, he uses the figure of a white male character, Sheriff Skiffington, to illuminate the contradictions behind the Bible defense of slavery that emerged in the nineteenth

---

9. Edward P. Jones, *The Known World* (New York: Amistad, 2003), pp. 8-9. Hereafter, page references will be given parenthetically in the text.

century. Skiffington is privately opposed to slavery but publicly charged with upholding the institution because of his position in law enforcement; he is determined to stay in power by representing to the slaveholding community "the good face of the law" (p. 147).

Throughout the novel, Skiffington is associated with two texts that represent the problem of slavery in antebellum America: a map entitled "The Known World" hanging on his office wall, and a Bible that is his constant companion at home. What Jones does with these emblems of authority in Skiffington's world is to blur the boundaries — between private and public, between the home and the office, between individual experience and social experience — that Skiffington tries to construct to justify his passivity in opposing slavery (indeed, his active engagement in maintaining slavery). For Jones, this dichotomy between individual private conscience and collective public ill will allowed whites to remain anti-slavery in the private sphere (home, faith, conscience) while continuing to support it publicly (marketplace, law, social structures). Moreover, Jones maintains that the Bible was the primary text used to support this: "Despite vowing to never own a slave Skiffington had no trouble doing his job to keep the institution of slavery going, an institution even God himself had sanctioned throughout the Bible" (p. 43). Skiffington's prior commitment to the Bible defense of slavery even outweighed what the third-person narrator suggests was a series of prophetic dreams: "Wash your hands of all that slavery business, God had said in his dreams" (p. 33).

At home, particularly at his bedside, Skiffington is constantly shown reading his Bible, yet he lacks any hermeneutic other than the Bible defense of slavery to give the text meaning:

> He went back to the parlor and picked up the Bible where he had left off. But that chapter was not what he felt he needed right then so he flipped through the book and settled on Job. . . . (p. 154)

> Skiffington flipped through the pages of the Bible, wanting something to companion his mood. He came to the place in Genesis where two angels disguised as strangers are guests in Lot's house. . . . It was one of the more disturbing passages in the Bible for Skiffington and he was tempted to pass on, to find his way to Psalms and Revelation or to Matthew, but he knew that Lot and the daughters and the angels

posing as strangers were all part of God's plan. . . . So he read through the passage, and not for the second time, and not for the third, and not for the fourth. Then he moved on to Psalms. . . . (p. 162)

The Bible is reduced to a book Skiffington "flip[s] through," looking for meaning, guidance, and consolation that will not come because the text remains at least partially closed to him. The failure to interpret the plight of African American slaves through the lens of Job the innocent sufferer and the unwillingness to wrestle with difficult passages like Genesis 19 in favor of favorite proof texts renders the Bible mute. Skiffington's worldview depends on being guided by a book that he cannot, in the final analysis, either hear or understand. In this sense, he fulfills the prophetic injunction spelled out in the book of Isaiah: "Hear ye indeed, but understand not; and see ye indeed, but perceive not" (Isa. 6:9, King James Version).

The inability to read the Bible outside of the defense of slavery renders Skiffington unable to make a clear moral choice with respect to slavery. At the end, when he is shot attempting to apprehend Moses, who had run away, the moment of his death is described as a metaphorical transition to a different afterlife than the one he had imagined:

Skiffington was entering the house he had taken his bride to. He ran up the stairs because he felt there was something important he had to do. He found himself in a very long hall and he ran down the hall, looking in all the open rooms and wanting to stop but knowing he did not have time. . . . At the very end of the hall there was a Bible, tilting forward, a Bible some three feet taller than he was. He got to it in time to keep it from falling over, his hands reaching to prop it up, his open left hand on the O in *Holy* and his open right on the second B in *Bible*. (p. 369)

Skiffington is crushed by the text he "upholds," a text that, in his view, upholds the institution of slavery.

Similarly, Henry Townsend, the main character of *The Known World*, is a free black man who owns slaves of his own. The Bible for Henry is not a religious text as much as it is part of the Western literary tradition from which he forms his identity as a slave owner. Henry is "mentored" as a slave owner by his former master William Robbins, even as he draws his identity from the canonical texts of Western culture: Shakespeare's plays, the poems of Thomas Gray, John Milton's *Paradise Lost,* and the King James Bible. Henry is (mis)educated by Fern Elston, a free black woman (who refuses to pass as white though light enough to do so) who teaches him to worship the superiority of Western culture. Fern says of Henry, who admired the Devil's speech from Milton's *Paradise Lost:*

> He thought only a man who knew himself well could say such a thing, could turn his back on God with just finality. I tried to make him see what a horrible choice that was, but Henry had made up his mind about that and I could not turn him back. He loved Milton and he loved Thomas Gray. (pp. 134-35)

Thomas Gray is recalled at the moment of Henry's death, when he has an after-life experience similar to that of Skiffington:

> His wife and Fern were discussing a Thomas Gray poem. He thought he knew the one they were talking about but as he formed some words to join the conversation, death stepped into the room and came to him: Henry walked up the steps and into the tiniest of houses, knowing with each step that he did not own it, that he was only renting. He was ever so disappointed. . . . Whoever was renting the house to him had promised a thousand rooms, but as he traveled through the house he found less than four rooms, and all the rooms were identical and his head touched their ceilings. "This will not do," Henry kept saying to himself, and he turned to share that thought with his wife, to say, "Wife, wife, look what they have done," and God told him right then, "Not a wife, Henry, but a widow." (pp. 10-11)

In contrast to Henry and Skiffington, Alice Night, a slave woman thought to be insane from being kicked in the head by a mule, turns out to be the character who embodies transcendental knowledge and artistic vision. At the novel's end, despite overwhelming odds, Alice leads several of the characters to freedom, and they converge in, of all places, Washington, D.C. The multi-media installation she creates becomes a sort of Bible that restores the community's vision and hope:

> an enormous wall hanging, a grand piece of art that is part tapestry, part painting, and part clay structure — all in one exquisite Creation, hanging silent and yet songful on the Eastern wall. It is . . . a kind of

map of life of the County of Manchester, Virginia, but a "map" is such a poor word for such a wondrous thing. . . . It is what God sees when He looks down on Manchester. (p. 384)

This God's-eye view in Alice's very human creation represents the eruption of the vision of another world into the text of the novel, the promise of another way of seeing that is not confined to a "map" or "narrative" but is at once immanent and transcendent. Not only does Alice survive and escape from slavery, but her art survives as well as a new text that overwrites the social, legal, and literary discourse that upheld slavery. The power of Alice's narrative as a redemptive text is evidenced in the reaction of Calvin (another black slave owner) at the end of the novel:

There are matters in my memory that I did not know were there until I saw them on that wall. . . . What I feared most at that moment is what I still fear: that they would remember my history, that I, no matter what I had always said to the contrary, owned people of our Race. (p. 386)

The redemptive text, then, provokes a confrontation with the past in the present that offers the possibility of a different future. For us as readers, Alice's art is to be seen as having redeemed the narrative of slavery that rendered black women in particular powerless and voiceless.

James McBride, *Song Yet Sung*

Like *The Known World*, James McBride's *Song Yet Sung* inverts power relations by rendering strong female characters: Liz Spocott, an escaped slave, and Patty Cannon, a notorious slave trader of the Delmarva Peninsula in real life. The novel is set on the eastern shore of Maryland in 1850 and is a clear revisioning of Frederick Douglass's 1845 *Narrative of the Life of Frederick Douglass: An American Slave* and the story of Harriet Tubman. The story centers on Liz Spocott, a fugitive slave who escaped from captivity after suffering a devastating head injury (as did Alice Night and Harriet Tubman). Liz is plagued by a series of visions from the future, precipitating in the reader a shock of recognition:

She dreamed of Negroes driving horseless carriages on shiny rubber wheels with music booming throughout, and fat black children who smoked odd-smelling cigars and walked around with pistols in their pockets and murder in their eyes. She dreamed of Negro women appearing as flickering images in powerfully lighted boxes that could be seen in sitting rooms far distant, and colored men dressed in garish costumes like children, playing odd sporting games and bragging like drunkards — every bit of pride, decency, and morality squeezed clean out of them.[10]

As we recognize that Liz's future is our present, the novel takes on a multilayered significance, particularly as McBride invests these characters with moral authority to indict the shallowness and superficiality of our own times.

Liz, with her bold defiance and prophetic dreams, is the disruptive character within the novel who threatens to destabilize the social order. Within the novel, Liz's story takes on a life of its own, becomes a legend within the narrative frame: "this glorious news spread from lips to lips like a wild virus, growing by leaps and bounds as it went. Jokes were formed. Poems created. Songs were sung" (p. 20). Dubbed the "two-headed woman," "the Dreamer," even "witch" and "conjurer," Liz as protagonist of the communal lore emboldens the efforts of the very active underground railroad operated through its mysterious code. In person, however, Liz is not only ambivalent about the code but threatens to derail the entire freedom enterprise through her startling revelations of the future. To the blacksmith, who is the very hub of the whole freedom train enterprise spiriting fugitives North, she says:

You love the North. . . . You love a place. There aint nothing there to love. Not today. Not tomorrow. I seen it already, seen the colored up there, in their tomorrows. You know what's up there? Colored men walking round free as birds. They don't love their women. They don't love their children. They love horseless carriages. And money. And boxes of candy. Clothing. Long cigarettes. And chains. Chains of gold. They cry for their chains. They even kill for them. Aint nothing they won't do for them. (pp. 160-61)

---

10. James McBride, *Song Yet Sung* (New York: Riverhead, 2008), p. 1. Hereafter, page references will be given parenthetically in the text.

What Liz's dreams force us to confront is how the currency of freedom has been spent by succeeding generations. It is an indictment not only of the black community but of the larger society consumed with materialism and entertainment. As the blacksmith tells Liz, the problems she is envisioning are not just in the black community but are a sign of a general moral lapse in the nation as a whole: "they aint no different than the folks around here," he says. "Some is up to the job of being decent, and some aint. Color aint got a thing to do with it" (p. 162).

Everyone with whom Liz shares the dreams becomes bewildered at their implications. Amber, who belongs to Kathleen Sullivan, a widow on a farm that is, in a sense, a picture of "benign" slavery but slavery nonetheless, remains puzzled by Liz's visions:

He had never heard anything like them before: Fat colored children who sang songs of murder and sat in front of glowing boxes with moving pictures — he had never seen a fat colored child his entire life! Young colored men who yelled at white people while riding in giant horseless chariots. Coloreds and whites riding in the same car? With coloreds yelling at whites? Impossible! Colored boys shooting rifles out the windows of horseless chariots at other colored boys? Colored women with fake blue eyes; white children who ran from books like they were poison. These ideas sounded ridiculous. . . . The coloreds claimed the North was all pancakes and syrup. The whites claimed it was hell on earth, a place where coloreds were starved to death and turned out to the cold and ice. . . . That was the problem with the Dream's vision: Trouble in his own time he could handle. Trouble in tomorrow, however, he could not. She had said the North wasn't worth running to. (p. 127)

In problematizing the geographical coordinates of North and South, Liz undermines the very ground of the antebellum slave narrative and its ready equation of the North with freedom. Not only that, but with this geographical shift, white/black, male/female, freedom/slavery, past/present (future) are blurred as well. Yet it is within Liz's prophetic visions, as in Alice Night's artwork, that the possibility of a redemptive narrative might occur:

They were small people, and what she dreamed of was big, another world beyond imagination that reached far, far beyond the world they all knew, or even dreamed of. . . . And all of it held in a song she had not yet heard and might never hear.

Seeing tomorrow, she said thinly, grasping Amber's hand tightly, is more than a soul can bear. (p. 216)

Toni Morrison, *A Mercy*

It is hard to think of neo-slave narratives and not think of Toni Morrison's *Beloved*. In her latest novel, *A Mercy*, Morrison depicts an Edenic, nascent America where categories of race and gender had not yet solidified and were subject to a degree of negotiation. Jacob Vaark becomes the unwitting master to a community made up of a slave girl, Florens, whom he acquires in settlement of a debt, a Native American woman whose entire village had been destroyed by "the Europes," two white male indentured servants, and a severely traumatized white female who had washed up on shore after a shipwreck. The collective maintains a certain order until two events destabilize their fragile social hierarchy: the arrival of a free black male blacksmith, hired by Vaark to create the ironwork for his huge house; and Vaark's death. The undercurrent in the novel is the difficulty of forming any meaningful sense of community, as "a love-broken girl,"[11] Florens, misreads her mother's sacrificial action. Florens operates under the assumption of maternal abandonment and falls in love with the blacksmith. Driven by a desire she does not understand and fueled by her presumed undesirability, Florens's psyche consistently misreads what she sees as a preference for black boys (first her brother and then Malaik) with disastrous consequences. The tension in the novel stems from Florens having been sent on a mission of mercy to save her dying mistress by finding and bringing back the one person who has the cure: the blacksmith. The projection of her own rejection causes her to kill, rendering her as (narratively) deaf to her mother's voice as Skiffington is to his Bible. When Florens returns blood-soaked to the house, not only does she fail to redeem the community, but any semblance of community is foreclosed forever. As it is put in the thoughts of Scully, one of the white indentured servants:

11. Toni Morrison, *A Mercy* (New York: Knopf, 2008), p. 58. Hereafter, page references will be given parenthetically in the text.

They once thought they were a kind of family because together they had carved companionship out of isolation. But the family they imagined they had become was false. Whatever each one loved, sought or escaped, their futures were separate and anyone's guess. One thing was certain, courage alone would not be enough. Minus bloodlines, he saw nothing yet on the horizon to unite them. (p. 156)

The hope, however, is in the word "yet," which hovers in this passage like the mother's discourse at the novel's end: "It was not a miracle. Bestowed by God. It was a mercy. Offered by a human heart" (pp. 166-67).

Like Alice Night's art and Liz Spocott's dreams, the mother's discourse at the end of *A Mercy* occurs too late to redeem the characters in the novel, but not too late for us.

CHAPTER 9

"The History and Future of the World":
Christian Scholars and Race, Culture, and Nation

SUJIT SIVASUNDARAM

In an age when it is increasingly apparent that the next Christendom lies away from Europe and America, what should be the goal of scholars working within a Christian tradition? In order to answer this question, I propose in this essay to study the history of Christian scholarship about the world and its peoples, in the long nineteenth century, a period that witnessed the unprecedented expansion of European empires, and with them the dispersal of Christian missionaries to all corners of the globe. In particular, I wish to pay attention to three intellectual concepts that arguably arose in part out of this wave of Christian evangelism and study: namely, race, culture, and nation. For an argument can be made that these primary concepts in thinking of the world have a Christian inheritance. It is important to qualify this statement: I do not wish to claim that Christianity is the sole point of origin of these terms, but rather that it played a critical part in their dispersal across the world. It is striking that this history of global understanding has been largely forgotten in the popular memory of the church. Whereas Christianity's role in the civilizing mission is better known, the intellectual ramifications of that program are sometimes missed.

Standard questions of historical definition might be posed in response to the use of these terms, "race," "nation," and "culture." What is a race? What is a culture? What is a nation? In contemporary parlance these terms have rather ambiguous reference, and this bears out the fact that they have been historically mutable and changeable. Indeed, a case might be made that the original interpretation and meaning accorded to these terms by Christians is quite removed from the sense that we attach to these terms. Today, race can be taken to indicate biology, and at times it is seen to traverse the ground of culture as well. Culture can indicate everything from language to habits, and sometimes it is still used in its old sense as an alternative to civilization and as an indicator of progress of civilizational norms. Nations might be pointed to in the boundaries of the world map — but here too there is ambiguity about how much the idea of the nation can be approached in abstract terms to denote a historical reality.

The argument of this essay is that Christian interpretations of race, culture, and nation in the nineteenth century stretched over unity and diversity. There was an attempt among believers to use these categories to indicate the oneness of humanity, even as they were concepts that charted differences in appearance, language, heritage, political tradition, etc. This balance between the sense of the terms as indicators of commonality and of difference has been lost over time. What might it mean for scholars working within Christian institutions to return to the study of the world, equipped with a better sense of the need to emphasize both global symmetries and local circumstances in keeping with a critical engagement with this history?

As entry points into my deliberations into the history of race, culture, and nation, I present three individuals whose lives spanned continents and the two ends of the long nineteenth century, and who are yet strangely interrelated. Each of the three Christian individuals I will focus on struggled with the intellectual history of global understanding, trying to work out exactly how to make sense of the world without falling into the trap of essentialisms, social conservatisms, and manifold forms of oppression. They were certainly imperfect individuals, who, despite their interest in standing against racism, imperialism, or hardened nationalism, were sometimes drawn to these very evils. Yet the struggle of their lives — to understand the world and to chart its future — serves as an intriguing way of thinking about our own intellectual agenda. So let me begin with race.

James Cowles Prichard: Race

One critical ingredient in the history of the understanding of race is the work of a rather quiet and bookish Quaker turned Anglican evangelical, who was heavily influenced by Scottish common-sense philosophy during his time as a student in the University of Edinburgh from 1805 to 1808.[1] This was James Cowles Prichard (1786-1848), who is credited with the founding of the science of ethnology, the study of peoples around the world, which later became anthropology. In mid-life, he was described by a visitor from America in these words: "a short, compact, close-made man, with bluish gray eyes, large and prominent features and expression uncommonly mild, open and benevolent."[2] Prichard, like so many intellectuals of his day, found time for his scholarship alongside a career as a medical doctor in Bristol, working with the insane and the poor. He published a series of important books, the most important of which was his *Researches into the Physical History of Man,* which came out first in 1813; in later editions, the work expanded to include second and third volumes. The third volume was a sort of anthology of the characteristics of the people of the world. Prichard's work arose partly out of his concern about the onset of scientific secularism, emblemized for instance in the French Revolution. His life-work had one central aim: to prove the unity of humankind as set out in Scripture and to dispute the growing interest in polygenism, the idea that humans had multiple and separate places of origin.

Perhaps the best evidence for Prichard's role in influencing how we see the world lies in a series of six "ethnographic maps" published in 1843 that accompanied his book *Researches* and that plot the people of Asia, Europe, Africa, North America, South America, and the Great Ocean.[3] In these maps, the people of the world were divided into separate categories according to language and the form of their skull and pelvis. So, for instance, the map of North America has a range of colors; going down the eastern seaboard, we have "Eskimaux" in off-white, "Algonkin Lenape" in green, "Iroquois" in purple, "Catawhas" in orange, "Cherokees" in gray, and "Muskogees or Creeks" in beige. A recitation of these names alone raises the specter of racism and racial differentiation.

---

1. The remarks in this section on Prichard draw on two main sources: H. F. Augstein, *James Cowles Prichard's Anthropology: Remaking the Science of Man in Early Nineteenth-Century Britain* (Atlanta: Rodopi, 1999); and George W. Stocking Jr., "From Chronology to Ethnology: James Cowles Prichard and British Anthropology, 1800-1850," in James Cowles Prichard, *Researches into the Physical History of Man,* ed. George W. Stocking Jr. (Chicago: University of Chicago Press, 1973), pp. ix-cx.

2. Augstein, *Prichard's Anthropology,* p. 12.

3. James Cowles Prichard, *Six Ethnographic Maps with a Sheet of Letterpress* (London, 1843).

How could a map like this then sit with Prichard's ardent wish to prove the unity of humankind? As H. F. Augstein notes, Prichard's "principal starting point had a touch of paradox about it: how could one believe in the unity of species given that human beings looked so different from each other?"[4]

These maps were not to be interpreted as unchanging descriptions of people over the centuries; rather, they demonstrated the earliest information available about which people occupied which lands. People had migrated across the world from an original source and after the Flood, and these maps were an attempt to trace their migration and subsequent diversification. In the map of Asia printed in Prichard's book, for example, we find the earliest depiction I have seen indicating the location of racial groups on Sri Lanka, with "Tamuls" in the north and "Singalais" in the south — a bone of contention in the island's ethnic politics until today. Farther to the west, however, lies a key to Prichard's thesis of the single origin of humanity, in the gray-colored territory labeled "Iranian Race," which he later relabeled "Arian," a term that had none of today's associations. It was here, in a stretch of territory linking northern Africa to India, that Prichard rather controversially believed humans had first emerged. Prichard urged in his work that Europeans had an Eastern origin, going against the popular view that humanity had originated with Caucasians, and he also held, at first, that the original color of humankind was not white but black.

In the first edition of his book Prichard argued that the diversity of humanity had emerged when accidental varieties arose suddenly among groups and were then passed on to offspring, rather than as the result of climate, which many of his peers privileged as the source of diversity. Prichard's was a pre-destined vision, which hoped to show how skin colors had been changed as people migrated across the world.[5] Later, this thesis, with its attendant developmental philosophy, was taken as a precursor of evolution. As one of his closest readers argues: "Just as man had progressed in culture from savagery to civilization, so he had 'progressed' in physical type from the black African to the white European."[6]

One relationship brought an element of doubt into Prichard's the-

---

4. Augstein, *Prichard's Anthropology,* p. 105.
5. Augstein, *Prichard's Anthropology,* p. 110.
6. Stocking, "From Chronology to Ethnology," p. lv.

ory. It was his encounter with Rammohan Roy, the Indian reformer and liberal writer, who is sometimes called the "father of the Indian nation."[7] Roy, as I have written elsewhere, had a close and contested relationship with evangelical missionaries in Bengal, and he arrived in Britain with a commitment to the modernization of Hinduism as a rational faith.[8] Yet the key point of importance for Prichard was Roy's color: in the ethnologist's eyes, the nobleman was too black for such an intelligent high caste Brahmin. The third edition of his *Researches* provided an image of Roy and added this description as a footnote: "Ram-Mohun Roy was much darker than many Africans."[9] For Prichard, Roy became another example of the importance of individual variations that could spring up at any point. While Prichard traveled very little out of his native land, the way in which he was open to learning from contact with non-Europeans in Britain is clear from this account. As a Christian intellectual, and as demonstrated by his theory of accidental variations, Prichard was continually flexible, seeking not to generalize but to accommodate divergences. Despite the vicissitudes of his thought, in particular on the role of climate in determining difference, throughout he was attached to the biblical account of the common origin of humanity and sought to defend this as his central idea against his opponents.

In hoping to encompass the increasing empirical information arriving from the intrusion of European colonists and travelers in far-off lands, and in particular the three influential voyages of Captain James Cook, Prichard hoped to guard the sciences as theological treasure. So this was an attempt to combat secularization among scholars by responding to new ideas within a Christian framework. Yet the irony was that in doing this he took a place in the unfolding history of the modern idea of race, so much so that some have labeled him a "scientific racist."[10] Despite his pleas for the intelligence of the "Negro," those who followed in his tracks utilized his work to distinguish peoples rather than to unify humanity as one. As for the term "race" itself, Prichard was clear that it was impossible to prescribe exact boundaries between racial types, and

7. This relation is studied in Augstein, *Prichard's Anthropology,* pp. 135-38.

8. Sujit Sivasundaram, "'A Christian Benares': Orientalism, Science and the Serampore Mission of Bengal," *Indian Economic and Social History Review* 44 (2007): 111-45.

9. James Cowles Prichard, *Researches into the Physical History of Man,* 3rd ed. (London, 1836-47), vol. 4, p. 237.

10. Stocking, "From Chronology to Ethnology," p. lvi.

that there could be differences within any racial group that was named by him; but the discipline he founded, ethnology, became a ground for the articulation of racist views in the mid-nineteenth century. In particular, ethnology turned from the study of language and external marks of difference to innate and internal biological difference as constitutive of race. This fell in line with polygenist theology. By the last quarter of the nineteenth century, however, intellectual currents shifted course again with the impact of Darwinian theory. For Darwinians took on Prichard's views in arguing for the unity of humankind and its improvability, even if humanity had a primate ancestor.[11]

It was in the period just sketched, which came after the European Enlightenment, that race took its modern reference as a descriptor of human difference. The modern category of race has been seen as the product of secularization; as it emerged it moved away from the biblical narrative to the new sciences of comparative anatomy, biology, zoology, and botany — and, later, evolutionary science.[12] Yet Prichard's story shows that the concept of race emerged partly in Christianity's quest to respond to new information from far-off lands and to fit such information into the biblical narrative. In taking this position, it is important to present the qualification that, in its original sense, race was not about inferiority or exact difference, but about variability from common descent. All races were one for Prichard. Yet such a meaning of race with its delicate balance between the unity and diversity of humankind was difficult to hold for long. Though the concept of race emerged from a humanitarian and Christian concern for the defense of the capacity and standing of other peoples — Prichard, for example, was linked with the movement for the abolition of slavery — it was adopted by others who stressed diversity over unity and employed the concept to justify colonization and exploitation. So Prichard's intellectual struggle to formulate a theory to describe and categorize the world leaves us, too, with a quandary: Is it possible for the Christian scholar to engage with the globe, while respecting its internal differentiation? How is it possible for the oneness of humanity and its ethnic diversity to be held together?

11. See also Sujit Sivasundaram, "Race, Empire and Biology before Darwinism," in *Biology and Ideology,* ed. Denis Alexander and Ron Numbers (Chicago: University of Chicago Press, 2010), pp. 114-28.

12. For a recent study of the status of theology in the history of race, see Colin Kidd, *The Forging of Races: Race and Scripture in the Protestant Atlantic World, 1600-2000* (Cambridge: Cambridge University Press, 2006).

Let me use Prichard's story, which took place at a critical juncture in the history of the concept of race, to urge us, who also stand at a critical juncture in the understanding and fear of peoples far away, to embrace both the unity of humankind and its diversity. It is important that our researches are trans-racial. By this I mean that it is critical that Christians have a curiosity about peoples far away and from very different backgrounds, combined with an understanding of their own starting point. There needs to be a greater amount of work in all disciplines across the boundaries of language, ethnicity, and religion. It is rather striking that the number of Christian scholars who study the world outside the traditional heartlands of Western Christianity is rather low in relation to other fields. Prichard did not travel far from home, despite theorizing about the world. But his informants were travelers and missionaries spread far and wide. In forging trans-racial scholarship, it will be critical, then, to form alliances and to work collaboratively; but it will also be important to learn and work alongside people from the world outside Europe and America, as Prichard did. Trans-racial scholarship should be so, not simply in terms of method, but also in terms of the composition of those who undertake it.

Following Prichard, I also take trans-racial scholarship to be motivated by a desire to show the superficiality of tokens of difference such as skin color, forms of speech, or even political systems. In all of this, an eschatological vision is critical: for it is important to sketch not only how humans have been one and are one, but how they will live in unity in the future. I do not mean here to write in hagiographic terms about Prichard. His writings, despite his intentions, are stained by what we now can easily class as offensive ideas. From his story we see that even those who seek after a universal vision of unity can themselves end up being racist. So those who undertake trans-racial forms of inquiry should be wary of falling themselves into racial typifications and essentialisms. Of course there is undeniable human diversity, but such diversity should not be classified or categorized into immutable forms in our thinking. This means that, paradoxically, while understanding other peoples and human diversity is critical for trans-racial scholarship, it is also important to hold any theory of human differentiation rather lightly. For when one theory of human difference becomes hegemonic, racial consequences can follow quite easily. Finally, the Christian trans-racial scholarship I am calling for must include a particular agenda as its defining feature: at the end of the day, such scholarship is Christian writing, like Prichard's, that watches and actively works against the on-set of racism in the world around it.

John Williams: Culture

It is time to escape from the bourgeois setting of Bristol, England, to the far-flung islands of the South Pacific to meet someone who was at the other end of the network of ethnology. Though now strangely for-gotten, he became Britain's first missionary hero, when he was alleg-edly eaten by cannibals in today's Vanuatu in 1839. Unlike Prichard, this man, like so many missionaries of the early nineteenth century, was self-made. He started life as an apprentice in metalwork in Tottenham, north London. His mother had come under the influence of Congrega-tional preaching. In 1816, two years after he was converted, he was sent without further training to the South Pacific as a missionary. His name was John Williams (1796-1839).[13]

In the frontispiece to a volume of memoirs of Williams's life (pub-lished after his death), a print shows him pointing to the sea.[14] The cap-tion, which is Williams's most famous sentence, reads: "For my own part I cannot content myself within the narrow limits of a single reef."[15] With these words Williams positioned himself somewhere quite differ-ent from Prichard in the methods of cultural theorizing. For Williams was a restless explorer and a roving evangelist who roamed the vastness of the ocean; he wasn't satisfied with one station, like Prichard. As he traveled, he sought to discover new lands, describe their people, plot their positions on a map, and spread the message of Christianity. Re-turning to the frontispiece, the portrait shows him gesturing to those he has left behind, making the point that this missionary wasn't work-ing in isolation. In fact, theorists like Prichard depended on the ac-

13. For biographical accounts of Williams, see Sujit Sivasundaram, "John Wil-liams," in *Biographical Dictionary of Evangelicals*, ed. Timothy Larsen (Leicester: Inter-Varsity, 2003), pp. 737-39; and Niel Gunson, "John Williams and His Ship: The Bour-geois Aspirations of a Missionary Family," in *Questioning the Past: A Selection of Papers in History and Government*, ed. D. P. Crook (St. Lucia: University of Queensland Press, 1972), pp. 73-95.

14. E. Prout, *Memoirs of the Life of John Williams* (London, 1843), frontispiece.

15. This became the title of a biography of Williams by J. Gutch, *Beyond the Reefs: The Life of John Williams* (London: Macdonald and Jane's, 1974).

counts of missionaries to form new scientific knowledge. In this image, the island with conspicuous mountains in the background is the new reef that Williams wants to explore and Christianize. As it comes above the horizon, it symbolizes land to be reached with the gospel. The scroll in his hand is crucial in this project. For the words of that gospel are preserved in such scrolls. Not to be missed because of its prominence is the ship that Williams stands on. One claim to Williams's fame was the account, which took on a life of its own, of how this missionary had built a ship, *The Messenger of Peace,* with simple tools and raw materials in a three-month period when stranded on the island of Rarotonga. John Campbell, who wrote a philosophical work on missions at the time of Williams's death, noted of Williams's mechanical feats: "Mechanical ingenuity was a striking feature in the character of Mr. Williams. . . . His exhibitions in this way spoke to the senses of the savages, who stood in dumb amazement and confessed the white man's superiority."[16]

Before this line of argument is misunderstood, I should caution against a simplistic separation of Prichard and Williams, as theorist versus field worker or thinker versus mechanic. In my recent work, I have sought to restore Williams and his compatriot missionaries as intellectuals in their own right. Perhaps the best evidence for this is Williams's best-selling work *A Narrative of Missionary Enterprises* (1834), which had a large readership. The difficulties of his vocation as a missionary formed a central organizing theme of the book. As Williams related his journeys abroad — the loss of his children, the perilous voyages to discover new islands, the plots on his life, and the near loss of life at sea — he kept the reader riveted. Yet the book was not simply a popular work but was addressed as well to men of science, the nobility, and other explorers. The compiler of his memoirs tells us that Williams held the "conviction that if he could induce men of rank and science, with the merchants and ship owners of Britain to ponder over its pages, they would no longer occupy neutral ground in the great contest with heathenism."[17] He was able to reach this audience by presenting his claims in bold language that asserted his own authority as a theoretician, with long experience of the islands of the South Pacific. In writing about the formation of the islands in geological time, he noted: "Here

16. J. Campbell, *The Martyr of Erromanga or the Philosophy of Missions* (London, 1842), p. 215.

17. Prout, *Memoirs*, p. 454.

I may assert that in all the range of my travels in the South Seas, I have perceived no animal agency at work adequate to the formation of a reef or island of any extent within a period of many thousands of years."[18] In his — and other missionaries' — use of natural theological language, I argue that they devised an alternative science, of a godly kind, which encompassed exploration, evangelicalism, and everyday experience to account for natural phenomena.[19] Like Prichard, Williams was motivated then by an attempt to keep new knowledge within the realm of the religion of the spirit.

Yet I wish to take up another way in which Williams is critical in the history of the intellectual encounters of globalization. For one recent commentator has pointed to Williams, and others who served alongside him — including his compatriot William Ellis, author of an ethnographic encyclopedia entitled *Polynesian Researches* (1829) — as early agents in the production of the concept of culture. In this argument culture is posited as a system, with constitutive elements held organically together. The role of interpreters and cultural observers is to immerse themselves in such cultural forms through fieldwork and bring to light their rules.[20] For Williams and Ellis and other South Pacific missionaries, theology was critical to their cultural observation; for South Pacific island cultures were taken as epitomes of heathenism. The missionary maps that were produced by evangelicals of this period are rather interesting in this context, ranging as they do from black to denote "heathen" to the pure whiteness of (Protestant) Christianity, with Muslims and Roman Catholics in the shades in between. Christian culture was thus an identifiable unit, which could be territorialized and marked off from "heathen" culture. Nineteenth-century missions such as the South Pacific one also necessitated a dramatic cultural transformation, as every element of the pre-Christian way of life was changed into a new form. In taking this view, missionaries equated religion with culture, and so the missionaries were driven by a civilizing mission. Yet there was a contradiction here: for even as they sought to change the culture of the Pacific, and to see it as distinct and other, they were drawn deeper into it, so much so that they recorded it in detail. Meanwhile, quite a

---

18. John Williams, *A Narrative of Missionary Enterprises* (London, 1834), pp. 25-26.

19. Sujit Sivasundaram, *Nature and the Godly Empire: Science and Evangelical Mission in the Pacific, 1795-1850* (Cambridge: Cambridge University Press, 2005).

20. This is the claim of Christopher Herbert, *Culture and Anomie: Ethnographic Imagination in the Nineteenth Century* (Chicago: University of Chicago Press, 1991), ch. 3.

few missionaries ended up "going native" in the Pacific. In summary, evangelicals charted culture while crossing culture; they were rather supremacist about their own culture, but were open to learning from others. At the heart of this contradiction was the nature of culture: for while missionaries divided the peoples of the world into types, they still believed in the unity of humankind, for otherwise there was no need to seek for the salvation of their charges. Unity and diversity were therefore held together in tension in the evangelical missionaries' concept of culture.

These points may be demonstrated by closer attention to Williams's book. In the preface, Williams describes the book as a "simple and unadorned narrative of facts." He notes that he kept a minute record of all the interviews he had undertaken and that he sought to preserve the phraseology of the islanders in his translations, aided by his familiarity with their language and habits. All of this bears out the sense that missionaries were at the forefront in the emergence of what might now be termed participant-observation. Yet the aim of such observation comes through in the forceful language that Williams uses to describe the missionary project in the preface: "an apparatus for overthrowing puerile, debasing, and cruel superstitions; for raising a large portion of our species in the scale of being; and for introducing amongst them the laws, the order, the usages, the arts and comforts of civilized life."[21]

One island that lay close to Williams's heart was Rarotonga, which he claimed, erroneously, to have discovered. Williams's descriptions of Rarotonga provide evidence of the attention paid by these missionaries to recording the culture of the South Pacific. Williams himself learned the Rarotongan dialect rather quickly; he recorded information about the extent of the population, the different districts and political divisions of the island, the relations between chiefs, and how food was procured.[22] Since the mission had to devise a code of law for Rarotonga, Williams detailed how punishments had been enacted in the past; for instance, a thief could be "murdered on the spot," while the chief, Makea, could order that "the body should be cut in pieces."[23] On Rarotonga, according to Williams's book, there were elaborate practices of succession. "As soon as a man reached manhood he would fight and wrestle

21. Williams, *A Narrative*, preface, p. ix.
22. Williams, *A Narrative*, p. 123.
23. Williams, *A Narrative*, p. 127.

with his father for the mastery, and if he obtained it, would take forcible possession of the *kainga* or farm previously belonging to his parent."[24] It was through these kinds of early commentaries on the islands that the missionaries established the "culture" of these islands.

One remarkable fact about Rarotonga was its quick conversion, within twelve months of Williams's first arrival. Williams quoted another missionary: "In Tahiti, European Missionaries laboured for fifteen years before the least fruit appeared. But two years ago Rarotonga was hardly known to exist . . . and now I scruple not to say, that their attention to the means of grace, their regard to family and private prayer, equal whatever has been witnessed at Tahiti and the neighboring islands."[25] Such dramatic conversion was related to the changing of every aspect of the culture of the island. Williams described the polygamous social relations of the island, and then noted what conversion had meant for Chief Makea's relations to his wives. The missionaries asked the men who had converted to publicly choose one of their wives and then to be united with that wife in a marriage ceremony; the other wives would need to be set apart, but provided for in financial terms. In Makea's case, he chose his younger wife, and his older wife Pivai had to take her mat, her children, and some other possessions and leave Makea's house. This event caused great distress, for she was a popular and respected woman. But she reportedly told the missionaries that "she had made up her mind to the painful event . . . [for] if she remained she should become the occasion of his living in sin."[26] The reorganization of sexual relations took place alongside the general civilizing mission: women started wearing bonnets and other European clothes so as to "raise the character and promote the comfort of the female sex." Both men and women attended classes in the "useful arts," so as to learn how to be industrious and how to build European houses. Williams built a sugar mill for the islanders and taught them how to boil sugar; he also taught them how to make rope and urged them to grow tobacco.[27] Conversion and wholesale cultural change were linked; but that link was possible through the program of ethnography and cultural observation that the missionaries undertook on their first arrival.

24. Williams, *A Narrative*, p. 137.
25. Williams, *A Narrative*, p. 111.
26. Williams, *A Narrative*, p. 136.
27. Williams, *A Narrative*, p. 166.

Even as this cultural transformation was under way, the cultural norms of the island did not disappear into a vacuum. They had an impact on Williams: he became the authority on the pre-Christian history of this island. His status as a writer and theorizer was dependent not simply on the narrative that he wrote but also on the objects that he procured. The South Pacific missionaries were ardent collectors of artifacts, which were displayed in the burgeoning museums in London, including one run by the London Missionary Society. These objects became the physical relics of disappearing cultures.[28] The events on Rarotonga are typical here. On his second visit to the island, Williams was honored by a procession that dropped at his feet "fourteen immense idols, the smallest of which was about five yards in length." He describes these as composed of iron wood, and intricately carved with the "human head at one end, and with an obscene figure at the other."[29] They were adorned with red feathers and pearl shells. Some of these artifacts were torn to pieces to signify conversion; but, curiously, others were preserved so that they could be displayed in the Christian chapel erected in the island, to denote their subjugation. One was sent to London to the museum run by the missionaries, where it towered as a central piece of the collection. In fact, when he returned to London, Williams was known to enjoy bringing out objects while with friends and pretending to be a chief.[30] All of this leads to the claim that the making and changing of culture was not simply an activity that involved words and texts; it depended on visual and material exchanges, which transformed life in the Pacific as well as in London.

Just as Prichard relied on friendships with people from other lands, it is critical to describe how Williams relied on friendships with islanders to become a successful missionary. Take his alleged discovery of the island of Rarotonga. Williams was rather exasperated to have drawn a blank in his search for the island; he then adopted a new strategy. He gave up using the map and compass as his only guides and adopted the Polynesian pattern of navigation. Anthropologists have now revealed how this system allowed islanders to traverse vast distances across the Pacific Ocean, by use of the stars and winds, and by calculating distances from a fixed point of origin. Williams was one of the first Europeans to

28. Sivasundaram, *Nature and the Godly Empire*, ch. 6.
29. Williams, *A Narrative*, pp. 116-17.
30. Sivasundaram, *Nature and the Godly Empire*, p. 186.

rely on this knowledge. He writes: "The natives, in making their voyages, do not leave from any part of an island, as we do, but invariably, have what may be called starting points. . . . They have certain landmarks, by which they steer, until the stars become visible." Upon using the islander system of computing location, Williams found Rarotonga, and a man atop the mast shouted, *"Teie, teie, taua fenua nei!"* — "Here, here is the land we are seeking!"[31] The conversion of Rarotonga was also accomplished by islander agency; after his first visit, Williams left two "native teachers," who got the process of evangelism under way. On the island, Williams developed a close friendship with Chief Makea, "a handsome man, in the prime of life . . . his body is most beautifully tattooed."[32] After witnessing the building of the *Messenger of Peace* on Rarotonga, Makea expressed a desire to become an explorer, despite never having left the island. While on board Makea followed Williams everywhere and, according to the missionary, felt "safe only at [his] side."[33] Having made one voyage, Makea eagerly made another with Williams. Makea was not the only chief who established a close friendship with Williams, for Williams describes similar relationships that developed during his time in Tahiti. The missionary's project of civilization and conversion depended on collaboration and patronage in the islands; and mimicry proved to be a key component of these relations, as chiefs sought to become like missionaries and missionaries worked to become like chiefs. Cultural transformation was not unidirectional but went in multiple directions for those on either side of the cultural encounter.

There is much that is troubling about Williams's views of culture, and elsewhere I have termed this category of missionaries "godly colonists" to denote the violence and territoriality of the missionary project in the South Pacific, and its contested but open relationship with the imperial project. In thinking about how we engage with the world, it is clear that we need a more subtle understanding of how religion and culture should be related. The easy equation of religion and culture that evangelical missionaries of the early nineteenth century espoused is certainly not a viable option. For in their own work and biographies alone, it is clear that it is impossible to move from one religion and culture to another religion and culture, as if these two sets come in neat

31. Williams, *A Narrative*, p. 98.
32. Williams, *A Narrative*, p. 100.
33. Williams, *A Narrative*, p. 153.

packages and the prior pairings are easily separable from their successors. So if this is the case, should we disavow Christianity's role in creating the concept of culture in our own practice of cultural investigation? I would not go this far, for the presence of cultural diversity is manifest to anyone, as is the need for projects of observation and study. At the same time, the necessity of cultural critique — for instance, in relation to practices that infringe human rights in particular cultural settings — is an important principle for Christians to uphold. Here it is important not to deny the validity of missionary critiques of culture in the nineteenth century, ranging from sati, the practice of widow burning, to infanticide. While the history of evangelical mission shows that religion and culture cannot be equated, it is right to acknowledge that religious change will inevitably necessitate cultural change and that cultural change may set the context for religious change.

Instead of denouncing the idea of culture, I am calling for forms of scholarship that take the religious history of culture seriously, while engaging in what might be termed trans-cultural work. Trans-cultural work will not seek to reify the cultures of the world, or indeed Christian culture, as identifiable units. Rather, trans-cultural work will seek to take seriously the fact that evangelicals have been at the forefront of the emergence of cultural observation, while seeking to avoid the premise that was sometimes seen in early evangelical work that cultures are systems. For the idea that cultures are systems denies the fact of human unity. Trans-cultural work should take account of cultures as dynamic and changeable in space and time and should consider the long legacy and impact of past cultures on our own cultures and on those of people elsewhere in the world. There is a spectrum of cultures rather than a systematic classification of them. Trans-cultural work should in this sense break down the boundaries between cultural stereotypes and descriptions. Trans-cultural work, following the evangelical missionaries, should also in this context seek to live by the possibility and importance of working and studying quite different cultural settings from those in which the scholar and student has grown up. If total immersion was a missionary idea, it is one that we can applaud. Yet in this program of study, it is vital somehow to keep a critical distance from culture, so that we can critique the cultural settings that we study. In this way, too, it makes sense to call what I am advocating "trans-cultural studies." And, taking a page from Williams, trans-cultural work should not be textual alone, but should engage with the range of forms of expression, visual and material. While it should not steal the objects of other cultures, it should give and take in processes of exchange that are full of mutual understanding. The idea of culture has a great deal of use, yet it should not be exalted to create orders or scales of difference.

Pandita Ramabai Saraswati: Nation

As we move to our third biography, we make a jump from Prichard and Williams, who were contemporaries, to a person from the late nineteenth century and from the generation that followed the one I have just been describing. Yet the individuals who were caught up in the global intellectual history of later nineteenth-century Christianity were responding to the writings of figures such as Prichard and Williams, with their categorization of races and cultures. In many ways, though with rather limited success, they were seeking to fulfill the visions of these earlier thinkers. The figure I move to next is Pandita Ramabai Saraswati, who campaigned for the rights of oppressed women in India and was one of the earliest Christian women scholars of the subcontinent. Rather to my surprise, I discovered that she is already commemorated at Wheaton College in the Rotunda of the Billy Graham Center. Throughout her life, Ramabai became increasingly reliant on a personal relationship with Jesus Christ. Ramabai's connection to the world of Prichard and Williams lies in her appreciation for Rammohan Roy, the Brahmin whose skin color intrigued Prichard. Ramabai wrote that if not for Roy's campaign against sati, the practice of widow burning, the British government of India would not have banned it in 1829.[34] She took the view that the British had paid little heed to the needs of India's women, and in this light her campaign for women's rights was an attempt to take further the thought of Rammohan Roy.

Roy was a rather eclectic figure in his intellectual orientations, for he drew from evangelicalism and Unitarianism in order to reform and modernize Hindu thought. He died in Bristol, England, just when he was thinking of traveling to the United States to take up the invitation

---

34. Leslie A. Fleming, "Between Two Worlds: Self-Construction and Self-Identity in the Writings of Three Nineteenth-Century Indian Christian Women," in *Women as Subjects: South Asian Histories*, ed. N. Kumar (Charlottesville: University Press of Virginia, 1994), p. 101.

of some Unitarians from Boston. Ramabai was equally eclectic in the inspiration of her thought. She has been described as follows: "Clearly standing at the intersections of several communities, Ramabai was an extremely complex personality, who consciously selected the values and norms of several different and at least partially competing Indian and European communities."[35] Her life was led at the intersection of Hinduism and Christianity and in the very different settings of Britain, America, and India. Unlike Roy, she was able to travel widely in the United States over the course of two and a half years.

Ramabai was born in 1858 as a high caste Brahmin; but, rather unusually, she married a man who was not of high caste.[36] Long before her marriage, her father had been determined to give her an education in classical Sanskrit texts and to delay her marriage, and both of these decisions made her think beyond the traditional limitations set by gender in India at this time. Before she married, she lost all of her family in a series of tragic circumstances. Her family had taken up an incessant life of travel as pilgrims to holy places in India, and in 1874, in the midst of a severe famine, both her parents died. It was after her two remaining siblings died of cholera that she married Bipin Behari Das Medhavi. But after two years together, her new husband also died of cholera in 1882. By this time Ramabai was already gaining fame as a scholar; for she had been drawn into the circle of the Brahmo Samaj, a reforming Hindu body that arose out of the reform activities of Rammohan Roy. She had also received accolades for her proficiency with Sanskrit learning.

Ramabai's views on the uplift of women were increasingly controversial and unpopular among the conservative Hindu social reformers of the period who held the ascendancy. For these men, matters of reform had to be initiated by men, and the status of women as mothers and wives rather than independent thinkers was paramount. A widow such as Ramabai did not have the right to harbor reforming views. Accompanied by her daughter, Ramabai traveled to England in 1882 in order to study medicine, and while there she came under the influence of the Sisters of the Anglican Community of St. Mary the Virgin at Wantage, where she taught Marathi to the nuns, and she later stud-

35. Fleming, "Between Two Worlds," p. 101.

36. The biographical account that follows draws heavily on the introduction to Meera Kosambi, ed., *Pandita Ramabai through Her Own Words: Selected Works* (New York: Oxford University Press, 2000), pp. 4-6.

ied at Cheltenham Ladies College. Here she converted to Christianity and was baptized in an Anglican church in 1883. But in the years that followed, Ramabai was insistent on making up her own mind about a number of theological issues. She rejected the doctrine of the incarnation and would not believe in the Trinity, claiming that it was unscriptural; nor did she embrace the Thirty-Nine Articles. Initially, she sought to accept Christianity from her point of view, rather than from a Western or colonial one, and she was attached to the idea of Christianity as a philosophy, rather like Hindu thought, which could be abstracted from its moorings in church tradition. The sisters feared that she would become a Unitarian.[37] She got into a dispute with Sister Geraldine, her mentor in the community, about the style of cross that should be displayed in the Pune branch of the mission connected to the community. She insisted that it should not be one inscribed in Latin, but in Sanskrit: "I stick fast to Sanskrit, not because I think it to be sacred or the language of the gods, but because it is the most beautiful and the oldest language of my dear native land."[38] Later she composed Marathi and Hindi psalms and translated the Bible into Marathi.[39]

When she returned to India after traveling in the United States, she broke through this period of wrestling with traditions and authorities. She wrote of her response to the denominational traditions of the West:

> No one can have any idea of what my feelings were at finding such a Babel of religions in Christian countries. I recognized the Nastikas of India in the Theosophists, the Polygamous Hindus in the Mormons, the worshippers of ghosts and demons in the Scripturalists, the Old Vedantists in the Christian Scientists.[40]

She also described how her search for Christianity was molded by her Hindu upbringing: "I came to know after eight years from the time of

---

37. For a reading of Ramabai's time in England and her dispute with the sisters, see Antoinette Burton, "Colonial Encounters in Late-Victorian England: Pandita Ramabai at Cheltenham and Wantage, 1883-6," *Feminist Review* 49 (1995): 29-49, at 35.

38. Cited in Burton, "Colonial Encounters," p. 34.

39. M. Kosambi, "Multiple Contestations: Pandita Ramabai's Education and Missionary Activities in Late Nineteenth-Century India and Abroad," *Women's History Review* 7 (1998): 202.

40. Kosambi, ed., *Pandita Rambai through Her Own Words*, p. 308.

my baptism that I had found the Christian *religion*, which was good enough for me; *but I had not found Christ, Who is the Life of the religion*, and 'the Light of every man that cometh into the world.' "[41] In a narrative typical of evangelical conversion accounts, she then documented how she turned to Christ "and unconditionally surrendered [herself] to the Savior and asked Him to be merciful to [her] and asked Him to become [her] Righteousness and Redemption, and to take away all [her] sin."[42] She then experienced joy and acceptance. "The only thing that must be done by me is to tell people of Him and of His love for sinners and His great power to save them."[43]

Ramabai's views on gender and the moving accounts that she wrote documenting the plight of orphaned girls and widowed women have been studied by others; but I wish here to pick up another legacy in her writings, which might be seen as a product of the intersection of Hindu and Christian ideas in this period. The central location of Ramabai's work was the city of Pune, which was also the base of the activities of one of the most critical nationalists and Hindu reformers of India in this period, who was of the same caste as Ramabai. This was B. G. Tilak, who sought to create a public and resurgent Hinduism in this period, through elaborate street processions in honor of gods and Hindu heroes, and to radicalize the newly founded Indian National Congress Party. In Pune, just prior to leaving for England, Ramabai set up the Arya Mahila Samaj, an association to raise consciousness about women. After returning to western India, with money in part from the United States, she founded a home for widows, the Sarada Sadan. During the great famines in the later nineteenth century, her work was much expanded, with further homes being opened. But her rival Hindu reforming nationalists boycotted her work, alleging that she was merely seeking to covert women to Christianity. Tilak wrote of "widows caught in Ramabai's net during the unique opportunity of the famine years."[44] Yet Ramabai's social reform activities were molded in the context of the revival of Hinduism and the emergence of the first indications of formal nationalism in India in this period. Ramabai was defining an idea of the Indian nation from a Christian point of view in her writ-

41. Kosambi, ed., *Pandita Rambai through Her Own Words*, p. 309.
42. Kosambi, ed., *Pandita Rambai through Her Own Words*, p. 310.
43. Kosambi, ed., *Pandita Rambai through Her Own Words*, p. 314.
44. Kosambi, "Multiple Contestations," p. 199.

ings. Indeed, directly on returning to India in 1889, she made a point of attending the annual meeting of the Indian National Congress, one of few women to do so. The *Kesari* newspaper, run by Tilak, noted in that year: "It is to her credit that she did not discard her patriotism with her religion."[45] The idea of Ramabai as a nationalist has generally been discredited for two reasons: on the one hand, it has seemed impossible that there could be a nationalist who had converted to Christianity; on the other hand, the defining quality of the increasingly popular and socially engaged nationalism of this period has been seen to be conservative Hinduism.

A close reading of her travel journal in the United States — which was written in Marathi and published under the title *United Stateschi Lokasthiti ani Pravasavritta* (The peoples of the United States) — bears out Ramabai's nationalism. This text has been published in English, and the book's editor describes the aim of Ramabai's work as being a "nationalistic and anti-British attempt, significantly mediated by Christianity, to install the USA as an acceptable Western model for India's independence and many-sided progress."[46] Ramabai's American sojourn was not anomalous: the Chicago World Parliament of Religion of 1893, which followed her visit, included the presence of Swami Vivekananda, an important Hindu thinker from India, as well as Anagarika Dharmapala, the Buddhist nationalist of Sri Lanka. At the same time, American theosophists such as Henry Steel Olcott played a critical role in the consolidation of nationalism in South Asia. America became a new conduit for defining the relationship between religion, modernity, and the idea of the nation. In the USA, Ramabai met a wide range of individuals, including Harriet Tubman, the activist for African Americans, teachers, and leaders of the temperance movement.[47] A Ramabai Association was formed in Boston in 1888, and sixty-three circles in support of Ramabai's efforts were established across the country.[48] Throughout her

45. M. Kosambi, ed., *Pandita Ramabai's American Encounter: The Peoples of the United States (1889)* (Bloomington: Indiana University Press, 2003), p. 31.

46. Kosambi, ed., *Pandita Ramabai's American Encounter*, p. 6.

47. For an excellent study of the reception of Ramabai in America, see Edith Blumhofer, "From India's Coral Sand: Pandita Ramabai and U.S. Support for Foreign Missions," in *Foreign Missionary Enterprise at Home: Explorations in North American Cultural History*, ed. Daniel H. Bays and Grant Wacker (Tuscaloosa: University of Alabama Press, 2003), pp. 152-70.

48. Kosambi, *Pandita Ramabai's American Encounter*, p. 23.

travel journal, Ramabai presents the examples of Britain and the USA as opposites, and seeks to urge India to follow the course of the USA rather than Britain.

She deeply admired the liberal freedoms of America:

> The most distinctive aspect of American society is the public-spirit-edness (concern for the good of all) of the people's thinking, government, and everything else of importance. In India, England, or other old nations, all facilities and conveniences are intended for a chosen class, and not available to the general mass of people.

Central to this opposition between Britain and the USA was the contrast between different styles of government. Ramabai argued that Americans were free from the lordship of kings, because Americans were themselves the rulers of their domain. She referred to America as a "nation 'of the people, by the people, for the people,' all the people are consulted, and whatever is approved by the majority is accepted."[49] These observations dovetailed with her insistence that the women of India had rights; the kind of nation that she hoped for in the subcontinent would take the rights of its citizens into account. Other lessons for nation building followed. One was the need for a common language for all — for the America that Ramabai had experienced was one where the French, Scandinavians, Spanish, Dutch, Italians, Welsh, Bohemians, Poles, and Portuguese had adopted English. "Only English is taught in public schools, the administration is conducted in English, and all the things like trade and commerce, accounts etc. have to be carried on with the help of the English language."[50] Keeping this description in view, Ramabai critiqued the divisiveness of the use of English in the Indian subcontinent, arguing that it separated the classes. Writing of the dominance in the Indian National Congress by elites, she noted:

> When our National Congress meets in Calcutta, Madras, Bombay, or the Punjab, the words of the speakers from one part of India cannot be understood by the people from another. Then they deliver long orations in English; but what use are they to common people? Erasing all the existing languages of our country and putting English in

49. Kosambi, *Pandita Ramabai's American Encounter*, p. 95.
50. Kosambi, *Pandita Ramabai's American Encounter*, p. 149.

their place is like drowning India in the sea and installing the British Isles in that spot.[51]

The anti-British rhetoric of this travel journal echoes some of the wider arguments presented by the early nationalists of India against British rule. For instance, Ramabai asserted that Britain had impoverished the subcontinent by depleting its resources to bolster its own wealth. She made an explicit comparison between the status of native Americans and Indians in her writing: "Like the Indians of North America, we have succumbed to the lure of shiny, colored glass beads; and we have sold our precious gem-studded land to foreigners in return for glass beads and glass bottles filled with wine." In contrast, Ramabai found Americans to have harnessed the land to their purposes and improved themselves. She reported that the speed with which America was building railways meant that it would soon have more tracks laid than the whole of the rest of the world. The spread of the telegraph and the telephone was also detailed. In these comments, Ramabai demonstrated an appreciation of modern technology; thus, she did not believe, as did some other nationalist thinkers of India, that mechanization was a threat to traditional industries in India. She wrote of America: "These waterways and railroads are like arteries in the body of the nation. Through them incessantly courses the lifeblood of the nation in the form of commerce."[52]

But her text also includes criticisms indicative of Indian eyes observing modern America. For instance, late-nineteenth-century India had seen a wide proliferation of activities connected with the protection of cows, which were taken to embody motherhood, fertility, and the sacred. Cow-protection societies and campaigns to rescue cows on the way to the slaughterhouse were a means of rejuvenating national pride and combating the vices of Western habits of excessive consumption, and this movement cemented national sentiment in India prior to the rise of Gandhi. This context is important in understanding Ramabai's comments on practices of animal slaughter in America and her praise of the activities of the Society for the Prevention of Cruelty to Animals. She wrote of America: "An excessive number of animals are killed in this country because of the general practice of eating meat." She criticized

---

51. Kosambi, *Pandita Ramabai's American Encounter*, p. 149.
52. Kosambi, *Pandita Ramabai's American Encounter*, p. 226.

the "heartless butchers" who were simply filling their purses without due attention to animal welfare. "Hundreds of thousands of cattle on the Great Plains are scorched by the sun, drenched by the rain, frozen in the snow; and die in agony. They are not even provided with shelters under which to stand or lie down."[53] She said that she "shuddered at the very memory" of the "distress" she witnessed when touring cattle farms in Iowa and Nebraska. She described in detail the conditions in which animals were bred and the extent of the human appetite for meat in America.

In a few decades, the events arising from this historical moment would help produce a mass movement of anti-colonial protest in India, which would become a model for independence movements across the world. Where do the origins of Indian nationalism lie? This has been a heavily contested question. I do not mean here to claim that Christianity is the whole answer, or even a major answer, to this question. Yet it is undeniable that Christianity did play a role in birthing the idea of the nation on the world stage. This holds not only for Pandita Ramabai. More broadly, education of local people by Christian missionaries played a critical role in the early origins of nationalism in India, as in other parts of the world. In Africa, by the early twentieth century, the biblical narrative of a small tribe seeking its home had served as a text for a variety of nationalist movements, and Africans educated by missionaries quickly became the representative voices of the people. If there were multiple sources and forms of nationalism, one distinctive aspect of the Christian contribution was its internationalism. Even as Ramabai spoke of the Indian nation, she drew from her experiences in the West. There was no contradiction between being an admirer of America while still being attached to Indian traditions, such as cow-protection. The global linkages of benefaction, print, and travel, underpinned by her enthusiasm for the West and her growing attachment to biblical Christianity, sat alongside her firm commitment to reforming India as a place where women were liberated.

Just as I have used the two other biographical sketches above to comment on Christian understandings of race and culture, I would like to use Ramabai's story to reflect on Christian understandings both in the past and in our own times of the idea of the nation. If late-nineteenth- and early-twentieth-century global Christianity was at

53. Kosambi, *Pandita Ramabai's American Encounter*, p. 132.

once national and international, it was witness to an increasing narrowing of the idea of nation as the twentieth century unfolded. For there were tragic attempts in the century that has just passed to link nationality more exclusively to ethnicity, tribe, and religion. For scholars today, particularly within the context of a Christian tradition, it is important to be trans-national: not in the sense of throwing out the idea of the nation, but in the sense of decontextualizing it within a conversation that is more mutually respectful, open, and global. For this was the way in which Christians sought to help define the nation on the world stage in the period I have just outlined.

Christian and trans-national scholarship can embrace the biblical idea of the nation in the Old Testament, as a concept open to outsiders and migrants, and yet characterized by an enthusiasm for history, genealogies, and tradition. It is important not to define nations too exclusively in relation to Christianity, for the Christian's primary citizenship is in another kingdom. A Christian understanding of the nation that is historically inflected should also have room for respect for other ways of life and cultural traditions, and Indian respect for animals is just one example of this. The nation should be the terrain where everyone has rights and where Christians stand up to elitism, patriarchy, tyranny, racism, and imperialism. As an advocate of such a view of the nation, Ramabai with her engagement with internationalism is instructive. For Christianity has been at the forefront of the globalization of the idea of the nation, even if the seeding of the notion in particular contexts drew on existent philosophies, religions, and cultural norms. In response to this, scholars working in a Christian tradition should not restrict their analyses to national units. Rather, Christian scholarship should map the impact of trans-national linkages both in the past and in the present. This will raise the question: How can globalization be made more Christian? For if Ramabai's age was one of global travel and contact, ours is certainly equally so. If hers witnessed a proliferation of humanitarian associations and bodies spread globally, what is the Christian response to our digital age of globalization?

Conclusion

Each of us utilizes certain modes of thinking in engaging with the world and with places far away. My aim has been to show how some of the key concepts at work in this respect — namely, race, culture, and nation — have been influenced and shaped by the globalization of Christianity in the past. It is important to clarify the nature of this contribution. Christian definitions of these terms straddled the local and the global, the specific and the general, unity and diversity. Yet even within these early articulations in Christian thought, the balance between these dichotomous pairings was difficult to hold, as imperialism, political agendas, and the need to justify the achievements of Christianity exalted the racial, cultural, and national characteristics of one group over another. Yet a further tragedy was that the creative tension in the Christian definition of these terms was lost as time passed and as other thinkers and advocates beyond the church took a greater hold over them. And these categories started to imprison people within stereotypes of the mind and programs of war, discrimination, and injustice.

Placed as we now are at a point where Christians have largely forgotten their historical contribution to the emergence of global understanding, it is important to retrieve this history — but not in a hagiographic and triumphal fashion. Rather, the endeavor should be an attempt to reengage the status of the globe, while attempting to regain the difficult balance between an attachment to our own starting point as people with a unique ethnic, cultural, and national heritage and the responsibility to think beyond these and to critique more limited definitions of global categories. Such a project of what I have called trans-racial, trans-cultural, and trans-national scholarship is especially important even as the center of gravity of Christianity shifts away from the West. If scholars find this balance between respect for difference and a fundamental attachment to unity, global Christianity may continue to be cohesive.

Then we might remember the vision in Revelation 7:9: "After this I looked, and there was a great multitude that no one could count, from all tribes and peoples and languages, standing before the throne and before the Lamb." The unity of humankind seen in Genesis is redeemed. Yet Revelation does not suggest that differences are obliterated. These are still worshipers from different nations, tribes, peoples, and languages, now united in adoration.

Index